■ The New Hampshire State Constitution

**The Oxford Commentaries on the State Constitutions of the United States**
*G. Alan Tarr, Series Editor*

*Professor G. Alan Tarr,* Director of the Center on State Constitutional Studies at Rutgers University, serves as General Editor for this important new series which in its entirety will cover each of the 50 states. Each volume of The Oxford Commentaries on the State Constitutions of the United States contains a historical overview of the state's constitutional development, plus a section-by-section analysis of the state's current constitution. Other features included in the volumes are the text of the state's constitution, a bibliographic essay, table of cases, and index. This series provides essential reference tools for those investigating state constitutional development and constitutional law.

# The New Hampshire State Constitution

## Second Edition

Lawrence Friedman

*Foreword by John T. Broderick, Jr.*

THE OXFORD COMMENTARIES ON THE STATE CONSTITUTIONS OF THE UNITED STATES
*G. Alan Tarr, Series Editor*

OXFORD
UNIVERSITY PRESS

OXFORD
UNIVERSITY PRESS

*Oxford University Press is a department of the University of Oxford. It furthers the University's objective of excellence in research, scholarship, and education by publishing worldwide.*

Oxford New York
Auckland Cape Town Dar es Salaam Hong Kong Karachi Kuala Lumpur Madrid
Melbourne Mexico City Nairobi New Delhi Shanghai Taipei Toronto

With offices in
Argentina Austria Brazil Chile Czech Republic France Greece Guatemala Hungary
Italy Japan Poland Portugal Singapore South Korea Switzerland Thailand
Turkey Ukraine Vietnam



Published in the United States of America by
Oxford University Press
198 Madison Avenue, New York, NY 10016



Library of Congress Cataloging-in-Publication Data

Friedman, Lawrence, 1967-author.
The New Hampshire state constitution/Lawrence Friedman.—Second Edition.
pages cm.—(The Oxford commentaries on the state constitutions of the United States)
Includes bibliographical references and index.
ISBN 978-0-19-996502-1 (hardback)
1. Constitutions—New Hampshire. 2. Constitutional law—New Hampshire. 3. Constitutional history—New Hampshire. I. New Hampshire. Constitution (1784) II. Title.
KFN16011784.A6 F75 2015
342.74202—dc23

2014038675

**Note to Readers**

This publication is designed to provide accurate and authoritative information in regard to the subject matter covered. It is based upon sources believed to be accurate and reliable and is intended to be current as of the time it was written. It is sold with the understanding that the publisher is not engaged in rendering legal, accounting, or other professional services. If legal advice or other expert assistance is required, the services of a competent professional person should be sought. Also, to confirm that the information has not been affected or changed by recent developments, traditional legal research techniques should be used, including checking primary sources where appropriate.

*(Based on the Declaration of Principles jointly adopted by a Committee of the American Bar Association and a Committee of Publishers and Associations.)*

# CONTENTS

# SERIES FOREWORD

In 1776, following the declaration of independence from England, the former colonies began to draft their own constitutions. Their handiwork attracted widespread interest, and draft constitutions circulated up and down the Atlantic seaboard, as constitution-makers sought to benefit from the insights of their counterparts in sister states. In Europe, the new constitutions found a ready audience seeking enlightenment from the American experiments in self-government. Even the delegates to the Constitutional Convention of 1787, despite their reservations about the course of political developments in the states during the decade after independence, found much that was useful in the newly adopted constitutions. And when James Madison, fulfilling a pledge given during the ratification debates, drafted the federal Bill of Rights, he found his model in the famous Declaration of Rights of the Virginia Constitution.

By the 1900s, however, few people would have looked to state constitutions for enlightenment. Instead, a familiar litany of complaints was heard whenever state constitutions were mentioned. State constitutions were too long and too detailed, combining basic principles with policy prescriptions and prohibitions that had no place in the fundamental law of a state. By including such provisions, it was argued, state constitutions deprived state governments of the flexibility they needed to respond effectively in changing circumstances. This—among other factors—encouraged political reformers to look to the federal government, which was not plagued by such constitutional constraints, thereby shifting the locus of political initiative away from the states. Meanwhile, civil libertarians concluded that state bills of rights, at least as interpreted by state courts, did not adequately protect rights and therefore looked to the federal courts and the federal Bill of Rights for redress. As power and responsibility shifted from the states to Washington, so too did the attention of scholars, the legal community, and the general public.

During the early 1970s, however, state constitutions were "rediscovered." The immediate impetus for this rediscovery was former President Richard Nixon's appointment of Warren Burger to succeed Earl Warren as Chief Justice of the U.S. Supreme Court. To civil libertarians, this appointment seemed to signal a decisive shift in the Supreme Court's jurisprudence, because Burger was expected to lead the Court away from the liberal activism that had characterized the Warren Court. They therefore sought ways to safeguard the gains they had achieved for defendants, racial minorities, and the poor during Warren's tenure from erosion by the Burger Court. In particular, they began to look to state bills of rights to secure the rights of defendants and to support other civil-liberties claims that they advanced in state courts.

The "new judicial federalism," as it came to be called, quite quickly advanced beyond its initial concern to evade the mandates of the Burger Court. Indeed, less than two decades after it originated, it became a nationwide phenomenon. For when judges and scholars turned their attention to state constitutions, they discovered an unsuspected richness. They found not only provisions that paralleled the federal Bill of Rights but also constitutional guarantees of the right to privacy and of gender equality, for example, that had no analogue in the U.S. Constitution. Careful examination of the text and history of state guarantees revealed important differences between even those provisions that most resembled federal guarantees and their federal counterparts. Looking beyond state declarations of rights, jurists and scholars discovered affirmative constitutional mandates to state governments to address such important policy concerns as education and housing. Taken altogether, these discoveries underlined the importance for the legal community of developing a better understanding of state constitutions.

Yet the renewed interest in state constitutions has not been limited to judges and lawyers. State constitutional reformers have renewed their efforts with notable success: since 1960, ten states have adopted new constitutions and several others have undertaken major constitutional revisions. These changes have usually resulted in more streamlined constitutions and more effective state governments. Also, in recent years political activists on both the left and the right have pursued their goals through state constitutional amendments, often enacted through the initiative process, under which policy proposals can be placed directly on the ballot for voters to endorse or reject. Scholars too have begun to rediscover how state constitutional history can illuminate changes in political thought and practice, providing a basis for theories about the dynamics of political change in America.

In this second edition, Lawrence Friedman updates the original study of the New Hampshire Constitution by Susan E. Marshall as part of *The Oxford Commentaries on the State Constitutions of the United States*, a series which reflects the renewed interest in state constitutions and will contribute to our knowledge about them. Because the constitutional tradition of each state is distinctive, the volume begins with the history and development of constitutionalism in New Hampshire. It then provides the complete text of the state's current constitution, with each section accompanied with commentary that explains the provision and traces its origins and its interpretation by the courts and by other governmental bodies. Finally, the book concludes with a bibliography, a table of cases cited in the volume, and a topical index.

*G. Alan Tarr*

# FOREWORD TO THE SECOND EDITION

I have more than a passing interest in the New Hampshire Constitution. Indeed, it was my workshop on many days in cases large and small, civil and criminal, during my fifteen years on the New Hampshire Supreme Court. New Hampshire's constitution was the first permanent constitution adopted by the original colonies, has five years seniority on the U.S. Constitution, and is the second shortest of all state constitutions. Only Vermont can claim greater brevity. The New Hampshire Constitution is direct in its simplicity and ambitious in its reach. It has governed well.

On some occasions during my judicial service our court was called upon to bring the state constitution to bear on the challenge of a criminal defendant standing alone against the state, while on others we were asked to draw lines to resolve conflicts between the other branches of government, and sometimes those boundary disputes involved the judicial branch itself. From time to time we were called upon to interpret our state constitution in circumstances affecting the rights and welfare of virtually all our citizens. The number and types of disputes and the issues and challenges they represented implicating the New Hampshire Constitution during my time on the court seemed endless in their variety, but our founding document was always up to the task of addressing interesting and sometimes novel arguments that were the product of the ingenuity and appellate skills of able lawyers.

On one occasion an interpretation of a provision of the New Hampshire Constitution by a substitute supreme court abruptly interrupted my statutory tenure as chief justice in 2004. Fortuitously, I was later nominated as chief justice by the governor and began my second term in that office. I learned quickly that constitutional service is more stable than the unconstitutional alternative. On a less personal level, other New Hampshire constitutional provisions relating to the state's obligations to cherish public schools and levy only equal and proportionate taxes helped define what some believed was my most important and controversial service as a justice in the numerous decisions of our supreme court involving school funding issued over more than a decade.

During my years of service I came to revere our state constitution as a result of the unusual privilege and responsibility I was bestowed to interpret it, and from a growing and increasingly informed respect for the genius and courage of those who crafted it and those who developed it through amendments generated by constitutional conventions for more than two hundred years. The New Hampshire Constitution has been an integral part of my professional life, so I was honored when Professor Friedman asked me to pen this brief foreword to his exceptional volume.

What is often underappreciated is that, when the New Hampshire Supreme Court grounds a decision on a state constitutional provision—something it does frequently—that provides protection equal to or greater than that provided by the U.S. Constitution, its decisions are final. On those occasions the New Hampshire Supreme Court is the highest court in the land, and the need to "get it right" is never more imperative. But despite the importance and on occasion the primacy of state constitutional law decisions under our system of judicial federalism, there has been far too little attention paid to state constitutions themselves and the jurisprudence they have spawned.

On many days during my judicial service I longed for a concise and direct resource providing—or at least marking the paths—where the history and nuanced meanings of our state constitution could be found. Whatever one's judicial philosophy on constitutional interpretation, original meaning and intent are critical. Historical context is key. Professor Friedman's meticulous and exhaustive work on the New Hampshire Constitution in this volume, following the foundational work of Susan Marshall in 2004, with its detailed attention to our constitution's history, its enactments, its constitutional conventions, its numerous amendments, and the contextual meanings of its numerous articles, will add immeasurably to available legal scholarship and prove an invaluable resource to jurists and practitioners alike.

John T. Broderick, Jr.
Chief Justice, New Hampshire Supreme Court, 2004–2010
Associate Justice, New Hampshire Supreme Court, 1995–2004

# PREFACE

In the annals of American constitutional history, New Hampshire enjoys the distinction of having enacted the first written constitution in what would become the United States—indeed, the state's original constitution predated the U.S. Declaration of Independence by six months.[1] New Hampshire's fifth provincial congress quickly drafted the 1776 constitution to give the people a "Form of Government" designed to create a governmental structure that would carry New Hampshire through the Revolutionary War. That constitution gained general acceptance despite the lack of submission to the people for ratification.[2]

As the war neared its end, the need for a more stable governmental structure presented itself, and in 1778 the world's first modern constitution convention was held in Concord. The voters rejected the initial drafts produced by that convention,[3] but they ratified the third draft in 1783, and it took effect in 1784, five years before the framers of the U.S. Constitution met in Philadelphia to consider revisions to the Articles of Confederation.[4] Based in large part upon the Massachusetts Constitution of 1780, the New Hampshire Constitution of 1784 underwent reshaping and improvement when the voters ratified some fifty-six amendments just eight years later, in 1792.

The constitution of 1784, as amended in 1792, remained essentially unchanged for the next eighty-four years, save a single amendment ratified in 1852. The eleven amendments adopted as a result of the 1876 convention made significant changes which modernized New Hampshire government. Between 1889 and 1950, voters ratified twenty amendments; in the last half of the twentieth century and the early years of the twenty-first, they ratified another fifty-eight. These amendments continued the trend toward modernization

---

[1] Richard Francis Upton, *Revolutionary New Hampshire: An Account of the Social and Political Forces Underlying the Transition from Royal Province to American Commonwealth* (New York: Octagon Books, 1971), 68, 176.

[2] Jere R. Daniell, *Colonial New Hampshire: A History* (Millwood, NY: KTO Press, 1981), 248.

[3] Only Massachusetts and New Hampshire of the original colonies submitted their constitutions to popular vote for approval. Walter Farleigh Dodd, *The Revision and Amendment of State Constitutions* (Baltimore: The Johns Hopkins University Press, 1910), 24–25.

[4] With the vote to adopt the U.S. Constitution on June 21, 1788, New Hampshire became the ninth state to ratify, resulting in the Constitution's adoption. See Jere R. Daniell, "Ideology and Hardball, Ratification of the Federal Constitution in New Hampshire," in William M. Gardner, Frank C. Meyers, & Richard F. Upton, eds., *New Hampshire, the State That Made Us a Nation: A Celebration of the Bicentennial of the United States Constitution* (Portsmouth, NH: Peter E. Randall, 1989), 1.

and reflected contemporary fiscal concerns as well as an interest in harmonizing the state and federal constitutions. Despite more than two hundred years of tinkering, the structure created by the constitution of 1784 endures in its basic form—the second oldest permanent constitution in the United States, after the Massachusetts Constitution of 1780;[5] and the second shortest, after Vermont's.[6]

Part 1 of the constitution contains the bill of rights, which closely resembles its Massachusetts counterpart. The New Hampshire Constitution protects such individual rights and liberties as equality and privacy, while later additions protect the freedom of expression, the right to bear arms, access to counsel for indigent defendants, and the public's right to know. Part 2 of the constitution sets forth the form of government; it establishes the three branches—legislative, executive, and judicial—as well as certain state and county officers, including the secretary of state and county treasurers.

The legislative branch consists of a house of representatives and senate, collectively known (as they are in Massachusetts) as the "general court"—and herein the terms "legislature" and "general court" shall be used interchangeably. The house has from the start been a large body; over the years, the voters have considered numerous amendments and proposed amendments relating to its size, the basis of representation, and the compensation of members. A 1942 amendment set the maximum size of the house at four hundred; the number of senators was set in 1877 at twenty-four, and all subsequent attempts to increase the size of the senate have met with failure.

The governor heads the executive branch. The powers of the New Hampshire governor are more limited than under other state constitutions. The governor shares executive power with a five-member executive council elected from councilor districts. Among other responsibilities, the council must approve gubernatorial appointments. The governor has a general veto power over acts of the legislature, but no line item veto power. Along with members of both houses of the General Court, the governor must run for reelection every two years.

Since the temporary constitution of 1776 New Hampshire has maintained a strong tradition of checks on executive power. Indeed, that constitution did not even provide for a chief executive, and the 1784 constitution did not create a fully independent executive branch. Amidst the amendments that constituted the 1792 revision, the people elected to strengthen the chief executive's authority by granting the governor veto power over acts of the legislature; they also elected to establish a process of gubernatorial succession.

---

[5] James Duane Squires, *The Granite State of the United States, A History of New Hampshire from 1623 to the Present* (New York: The American Historical Company, 1956), I, 153.

[6] Robert L. Maddex, *State Constitutions of the United States* (Washington, D.C.: CQ Press, 1998), 251.

The judicial branch, though independent today, began its history closely aligned with the general court. The 1776 constitution allowed the legislature to appoint judges and to remove them at will. Indeed, the legislature often appointed judges from among its own members, who continued to serve in both capacities. The 1784 constitution established an independent judicial branch and prohibited plural office holding, specifying that judges would serve "so long as they behave well" and guaranteeing they should receive "honorable salaries, ascertained and established by standing laws." A 1792 amendment imposed age limits on judges.

Because the 1784 constitution did not provide for specific courts with general trial and appellate jurisdiction, the legislative and executive branches continued for many years after its adoption to exercise a great deal of control over the judiciary. During the nineteenth century, and coinciding with changes in political power, the general court abolished and reconstituted the courts no fewer than six times, each time removing sitting judges and replacing them with new appointees. Though the legislature established the modern court system by statute in 1901, the superior and supreme courts did not receive constitutional status—and protection from restructuring at the whim of the legislature—until 1966. A 1978 amendment granted the supreme court supervisory and rulemaking authority over the court system.

The penultimate article of Part 2 describes the methods by which the constitution may be amended. Until 1964, amendments to the constitution could be proposed only by the duly elected members of a constitutional convention—not always the most straightforward path toward constitutional revision. Today, amendments may be proposed by convention or by the legislature; in the latter case, a proposal must be approved by a 60 percent majority. Next, the constitution requires that an amendment be ratified by a supermajority of two-thirds of the persons voting on the question, as opposed to the simple majority required by some state constitutions.

What follows is an annotated exploration of the many provisions of the current version of the New Hampshire Constitution. This text is based upon Susan E. Marshall's initial effort, published in 2004. The text has been substantially revised and references many new cases and developments. The annotations that accompany the text provide information about the history of each provision and discuss the major interpretive issues that have arisen. Please note, however, that the text does not cover every issue that may have arisen or that potentially could arise, and that these annotations should not be considered as current after this volume's publication date. The text should not be relied upon as legal advice or as a substitute for specific research on an issue.

Throughout, this book relies upon the decisions of New Hampshire's highest court, the supreme court, as the main source of interpretive authority in respect to the New Hampshire Constitution. Other sources are cited for the light they may shed on the meaning of the constitutional text. Included in this category are "advisory opinions" of the justices of the supreme court. As their citation form suggests (for example, "Opinion of the Justices"), these opinions represent judicial responses to abstract legal questions posed by the legislative or executive branches. As such, the court views these opinions as technically not binding in cases that may later be brought before it, when it must resolve a constitutional issue based upon the actual facts and circumstances of the controversy. Nonetheless, the frequent citation to these opinions in later decisions and practical realities make them a reasonable guide as to how the court might rule in future cases.

# ■ ACKNOWLEDGMENTS

I am grateful to Oxford University Press for offering me the opportunity to revise the volume on the New Hampshire State Constitution in its series on state constitutions, and to G. Alan Tarr, the series editor, for his guidance and support. My research assistants Lisa Baker, Beth Nicoll, Nadine Petsuck, and Abbi Shirk all did yeoman's work in helping me to prepare the manuscript for publication; they should not be held responsible for any errors that remain.

I could not have completed this work without the support of the law school and its dean, John O'Brien, as well as the help supplied by law school's librarians and those at the Boston Athenæum.

Thanks as well to Dean Broderick for taking the time to write a new foreword for this revision, and for his many years of friendship.

Finally, thanks to my constant, Elizabeth Sullivan: for her support of this and all my scholarly projects.

# PART ONE

# The History of the New Hampshire Constitution

# INTRODUCTION

To appreciate New Hampshire's constitutional history, we must begin not in 1776, when the state became the first of the original colonies to adopt a constitution, but more than a century before the start of the Revolutionary War. In 1629, King Charles I granted to Captain John Mason an indenture for the territory of New Hampshire, which the crown believed would advance settlement of the region.[1] Mason sought to found "a hereditary principality in America," but the validity of the claims of his heirs proved to be little more than an "endless altercation and political confusion."[2] Mason, and later his descendants, would struggle to make something of New Hampshire, but their various efforts at organizing and running the territory essentially came to naught and there followed, beginning in 1641, several decades in which neighboring Massachusetts exercised jurisdiction over the territory.

---

[1] Scott Douglas Gerber, *A Distinct Judicial Power: The Origins of an Independent Judiciary, 1606–1787* (New York: Oxford University Press, 2011), 94. Mason named the territory "in honor of [his] home county of Hampshire." Elizabeth Forbes Morison & Elting E. Morison, *New Hampshire: A Bicentennial History* (New York: W.W. Norton & Co., 1976), 11.

[2] Morison & Morison, *New Hampshire*, 11–12.

The king declared New Hampshire a royal province in September of 1679. The provincial population was not pleased: "[h]aving long enjoyed the advantages of the union with Massachusetts, they yielded with reluctance to the separation."[3] By 1690, New Hampshire found itself without a government and, in the absence of orders from England, a committee of safety "met, and resolved upon a union with Massachusetts. Their petition was readily accepted at Boston and New Hampshire once more became a part of Massachusetts."[4] The crown reasserted control in 1691 under the charter issued by King William and Queen Mary creating the province of Massachusetts Bay. Save a few brief years in which New Hampshire was a part of the short-lived Dominion of New England,[5] the province would continue to exist as a royal colony until the eve of the Revolutionary War.

## COLONIAL RULE, 1680–1775

New Hampshire's royal governors, selected by the crown, shared executive authority with an appointed council. The official legislative body was the assembly. The last of the royal governors was John Wentworth, who served from 1767 to 1775; he was the nephew of Benning Wentworth, who had served as royal governor from 1741 to 1767—as Scott Douglas Gerber has noted, Benning Wentworth served "the longest term of any governor in colonial America."[6] Benning's father had been Massachusetts lieutenant governor from 1723 to 1728; though he was a Massachusetts official, he resided in and oversaw New Hampshire.[7] New Hampshire would not have its own governor until Benning, in 1741. After the Masons, no family is more prominent in New Hampshire's colonial history than the Wentworths.

Though the system of representation in the provincial assembly favored those towns whose populations were sympathetic to the royal government, Governor John Wentworth struggled in his effort to secure his authority amidst growing discontent and disorder. By May 1774, Wentworth's popularity was waning, and the assembly appointed a committee of correspondence to communicate with similar committees in other provinces. Wentworth

---

[3] George Barstow, *The History of New Hampshire, From Its Discovery, in 1614, to the Passage of the Toleration Act, in 1819* (Boston: Little & Brown, 1853) (2d ed.), 93.

[4] Ibid, 104.

[5] James Duane Squires, *The Granite State of the United States: A History of New Hampshire from 1623 to the Present* (New York: American Historical Association, 1956), Vol. 1, 35–36.

[6] Gerber, *A Distinct Judicial Power*, 105.

[7] Fletcher Haulley, *A Primary Source History of the Colony of New Hampshire* (New York: The Rosen Publishing Group, Inc., 2006), 53.

responded by dissolving the assembly, but it met illegally the next month in Portsmouth—first in the assembly hall, then in a tavern.[8]

From these meetings came a call to all of the towns in New Hampshire to choose delegates to a provincial congress, which would elect representatives to send to the Continental Congress and coordinate resistance in the towns. The first provincial congress met in Exeter on July 21, 1774. Governor Wentworth had by this time ordered new elections for the official assembly, but the assembly refused to seat three members who had been "chosen" under royal election writs by "constituencies" established without its approval.[9] In July, when the assembly refused still to "rescind its vote excluding the three members," Wentworth adjourned it and scheduled it for the end of September.[10] He issued this order from the Fort of William and Mary in New Castle, to which he and his family had fled seeking the protection of the British warship *Scarborough*.

The governor's situation had by this time become increasingly desperate. When in August 1775 the *Scarborough* sailed to Boston to resupply, the Wentworth family went with it. The ship's departure with Wentworth aboard marked the effective end of royal government in New Hampshire, though Wentworth would return one last time shortly before the assembly was due to meet again: from the Isle of Shoals on September 25, 1775, he sent word to adjourn the assembly until the following spring. As one commentator put it, "[t]his was the closing act of his administration. It was the last receding step of royalty."[11] Perhaps needless to say, the assembly took little heed of the order.

New Hampshire found itself at this time without an official government. Unlike the other New England colonies, New Hampshire had no royal charter that could serve as the basis for a system of government.[12] The province had been governed by a series of royal commissions and instructions that gave broad centralized authority to the crown's appointed governor.[13] Concerned for what might happen once the royal court system no longer existed—as well as its own lack of formal authority—the fourth of the provincial congresses sent a request for advice in October 1775 to the Continental Congress in Philadelphia. The Continental Congress responded on November 3, 1775, with a recommendation that New Hampshire convene a "full and fair representation of the people" which could, if necessary, "establish such a form of

[8] Richard Francis Upton, *Revolutionary New Hampshire: An Account of the Social and Political Forces Underlying the Transition from Royal Province to American Commonwealth* (New York: Octagon Books, 1971), 19.

[9] Ibid, 25.

[10] Ibid, 28–29.

[11] Barstow, *The History of New Hampshire*, 236.

[12] Lynn W. Turner, *The Ninth State: New Hampshire's Formative Years* (Chapel Hill: University of North Carolina Press, 1983), 12.

[13] Jere R. Daniell, *Colonial New Hampshire: A History* (Millwood, N.Y.: KTO Press, 1981), 119.

government, as...will best produce the happiness of the people...during the continuance of the present dispute between Great Britain and the Colonies."[14]

The fourth provincial congress took steps to ensure that the next congress would be elected according to a new system of representation, one based upon a census that would lead to more proportional representation than elections past.[15] As well, the fourth congress expanded voting rights beyond the severe restrictions that had been in place prior to the Revolution. For example, the election law of 1728 required all voters for representatives to the royal assembly be possessed of real estate valued at £50. The fourth provincial congress resolved to reduce the requirement to £20 and to allow all taxpayers to vote, a system that prevailed throughout the Revolutionary period.

The subsequently elected fifth congress consisted of eighty-nine delegates from the one hundred fifty incorporated towns of New Hampshire.[16] On December 28, 1775, as authorized by its election precepts, the fifth provincial congress resolved itself into a house of representatives. Meeting in Exeter, this legislative body adopted New Hampshire's first constitution on January 5, 1776, some six months before the signing of the Declaration of Independence. The people of the state were not given the opportunity to ratify the constitution; the new house of representatives—the first legislative body independent of the crown—presented it to them as a necessity of the times.[17]

## THE TEMPORARY CONSTITUTION OF 1776

The house of representatives intended the 1776 constitution—the "Form of Government"—to be a temporary measure, in effect only "during the present unhappy and unnatural Contest with Great Britain."[18] But, due to the many complications associated with finding agreement on a permanent constitution, this "temporary" period lasted nearly eight and a half years. Part of the preamble describes the emergency situation:

> The Sudden & Abrupt Departure of his Excellency John Wentworth Esq: our Late Governor, & Several of the Council, Leaving us Destitute of Legislation,—and no Executive Courts being open to Punish Criminal Offenders; whereby the Lives & Propertys of the Honest People of this Colony, are Liable to Machinations & Evil Designs of wicked men.

---

[14] Worthington C. Ford, ed., *Journals of the Continental Congress* (Washington, D.C.: Government Printing Office, 1904–1931), Vol. III, 319.

[15] Upton, *Revolutionary New Hampshire*, 43

[16] Turner, *The Ninth State*, 13.

[17] Turner, *The Ninth State*, 14. Turner notes that the authority of the Constitution of 1776 rested upon its adoption by an extralegal convention (the fifth provincial congress) that had been elected according to precepts issued by a preceding extralegal body (the fourth provincial congress).

[18] N.H. Const. (1776); *see* Appendix X.

The framers of the 1776 constitution appeared to assume the possibility that the war would result in reunification with Great Britain, as the constitution stated: "[W]e Never Sought to throw off our Dependence upon Great Britain, but felt ourselves happy under her Protection... [W]e Shall Rejoice if Such a Reconciliation between us and our Parent State can be Effected."

As in the other former colonies, certain individuals emerged as leaders during the Revolutionary period. Meshech Weare, who likely wrote the final draft of the constitution of 1776, had served on important committees in all five provincial congresses and twice as president pro tem.[19] Indeed, during this time Weare served simultaneously as chair of the powerful "committee of safety," chief justice of the superior court—then the state's highest court—and president of the council, the upper house of the legislature created by the new constitution.[20] Though he reportedly discharged all "his various duties with unsurpassed fidelity and wisdom,"[21] he would become a target of the criticism that the legislature was run by "a small clique of leaders" who held all the responsible offices as well as their seats in the legislature.[22]

The governmental structure embraced by the framers of the 1776 constitution relied upon the form of government adopted in Massachusetts as established by the Charter of King William and Queen Mary of 1691,[23] which controlled before the British Parliament enacted the Massachusetts Government Act of 1774.[24] The governmental scheme thus created was not without its deficiencies. Reflecting the deep distrust of the royal government, the 1776 constitution did not provide for a chief executive: the framers concentrated all governmental power in the two branches of the legislature, the house of representatives and the council. The house would appoint the first council for one year, with subsequent councils elected by county. The legislature had the power to appoint most public and military officers, except court clerks, county treasurers, and recorders of deeds. The dozen men who made up the "Committee of Safety"—originally created by the Provincial Congress in May 1775—performed most executive functions.[25] When the legislature was not

---

[19] Jere R. Daniell, *Experiment in Republicanism: New Hampshire Politics and the American Revolution, 1741–1794* (Cambridge: Harvard University Press, 1970), 117.

[20] Turner, *The Ninth State*, 15.

[21] Barstow, *The History of New Hampshire*, 249.

[22] Upton, *Revolutionary New Hampshire*, 48.

[23] *See* Lawrence Friedman & Lynnea Thody, *The Massachusetts State Constitution* (New York: Oxford University Press, 2011), 6–7.

[24] Under its 1691 Charter, Massachusetts had a general court of assembly, the members of which were elected by freeholders at town meetings. The twenty-eight-member council was elected by the assembly. Massachusetts also had a governor and lieutenant governor, but the New Hampshire Constitution delegated these functions to the legislature. Benjamin W. Labaree, *Colonial Massachusetts: A History* (Millwood, N.Y.: KTO Press, 1979), 119, 126.

[25] Upton, *Revolutionary New Hampshire*, 43–44.

in session—which was most of the time—the committee assumed numerous governmental responsibilities.[26]

Drafted in extraordinary circumstances, the 1776 constitution lacked many of the elements one would expect to find in a modern constitution. In addition to the absence of an independent executive branch, it contained no bill of rights, no provision for an independent judiciary or separation of powers, and no method for amendment. Further, no provision of the constitution described the basis upon which representatives would be elected to the legislature; indeed, the system of representation used in the election of the provincial congress would remain in effect until the ratification of the permanent constitution in 1784.

Moreover, not all the delegates to the fifth provincial congress approved the adoption of the 1776 constitution. There was discontent among the towns in the Piscataqua area of Portsmouth, on the seacoast. Prior to the war, these towns were dominated by merchants who had exerted a strong influence over colonial politics—influence they used to protect their own economic and social interests. Their economic fortunes diminished as the war continued, and so did their influence. Following the war, representatives of the interior towns exerted control over the new legislature; these representatives had little concern for the interests that preoccupied their seacoast brethren.

The representatives from Portsmouth acted quickly to express their dissatisfaction with the new constitution. On January 10, 1776, when the constitution had been in effect for less than a week, a delegation from Portsmouth and a number of nearby towns presented a petition to the house of representatives questioning the legitimacy of the new legislature. They argued that their "constituents never expected [the house] to make a new form of government, but only to set the judicial and executive wheels in motion."[27] Citizens from the Portsmouth area would later object as well to the "lack of an independent executive" and the proliferation of plural office holding in appointments made by the legislature.[28]

For different reasons, citizens of the mostly smaller towns in the west, near Hanover, also expressed dissatisfaction with the new constitution. Far from the seat of government in Exeter, citizens of the upper Connecticut River valley towns maintained close ties with Connecticut and came to believe they were inadequately represented in the legislature. From the recently founded Dartmouth College, faculty members publicly objected to the adoption of the 1776 constitution and its plan of apportionment of representation in the legislature, as well as the lack of popular ratification of the new constitution. The

[26] Barstow, *The History of New Hampshire*, 248.

[27] *New Hampshire State Papers*, Vol. VIII, 14.

[28] Daniell, *Experiment in Republicanism*, 164–166.

widely circulated "Address from Grafton County," likely written by Bezaleel Woodward, a professor at Dartmouth and the son-in-law of its founder,[29] in July 1776, asserted that the legislature was an illegal body and called upon the people of New Hampshire to exercise their "rights and privileges" by establishing a "supreme legislative court... to lay a foundation and plan of government."[30]

The Address also attacked the apportionment system because it did not allow for at least one representative for each incorporated town. The then-current plan for representation allowed smaller towns to combine to attain the minimum number of one hundred freeholders required for a representative.[31] This system, according to the western dissenters, failed to recognize the sovereignty of the town corporation and to treat all towns equally. The citizens of Hanover and at least thirteen other towns in the area expressed their displeasure by boycotting the elections held in 1776.

In addition, Woodward and others organized a group from town committees of safety in Grafton County called the "United Committees," which advocated for more adequate representation of the western towns in the legislature. The Committees also sought to have the seat of government moved from Exeter to the center of New Hampshire, as the journey to the seacoast often proved to be arduous. The United Committees met with Meshech Weare, the council president, and other council members in February 1777, but failed to reach an agreement. To further complicate matters, the councilors discovered that settlers in the areas of the New Hampshire grants, just across the Connecticut River from the western towns, had organized themselves into what they called "New Connecticut"—now the state of Vermont.

In the fall of 1777, Woodward delivered a petition from the United Committees to a committee of the house of representatives. The petition requested that a constitutional convention be called and a new constitution be adopted, one which would give to each town the option of electing at least one representative.[32] The committee soon recommended that a convention be called and, responding to the pressure to replace the temporary constitution, the New Hampshire legislature on February 26, 1778, voted to hold a full and free convention on the tenth day of June of that year "for the sole purpose of forming and laying a permanent plan or system of government for the future Happiness and well-being of the good people of this State."[33]

By that time, many of the western dissenters had decided that political separation better served their interests than a new constitution. As New

---

[29] Ralph Nading Hill, ed., *The College on the Hill, A Dartmouth Chronicle* (Hanover, N.H.: Dartmouth Publications, 1964), 119–121.

[30] *New Hampshire State Papers*, Vol. X, 234.

[31] Upton, *Revolutionary New Hampshire*, 178.

[32] Daniell, *Experiment in Republicanism*, 150–153.

[33] *New Hampshire State Papers*, Vol. VIII, 775.

Hampshire went about the process of creating a new constitution, the United Committees contemplated forming a separate state, "Dresden," and then petitioned to join the new state of Vermont, which had adopted a constitution guaranteeing to each town at least one representative in its legislature.[34] Indeed, Woodward would go on to serve as justice of the Vermont Supreme Court. Notwithstanding their discontent, however, the western dissenters were not long for Vermont: in 1782 the Vermont assembly renounced jurisdiction over the towns in the valley east of the Connecticut River, and the dissenters ultimately "returned their allegiance to New Hampshire."[35] Citizens of rebellious Hanover lingered in their resentment and sent Woodward himself to the New Hampshire General Court in 1784, an ironic symbol of their accession to governance by the state of New Hampshire.[36]

## THE CONVENTION OF 1778

The convention called by the legislature met in Concord in June 1778. At that time, a constitutional convention was still a relative novelty. John Adams, architect of the Massachusetts Constitution, popularized the idea of holding a specially called convention for the purpose of drafting a constitution. Adams believed the people ought to "be all consulted" regarding the formation of a state government, "to erect the whole building with their own hands, upon the broadest foundation," and this could be done "only by conventions of representatives chosen by the people in the several colonies, in the most exact proportions."[37] He recommended that citizens in every one of the former colonies "call such conventions immediately, and set up governments of their own, under their own authority."[38]

Among those whom Adams impressed with his counsel on constitution-making was "Mr. John Sullivan of New Hampshire," who heard "with apparent pleasure" of these "new, strange, and terrible doctrines."[39] Sullivan is another storied figure in New Hampshire history. He had been sent by the first provincial congress to represent New Hampshire in the First Continental Congress; he served as well in the Second Continental Congress and as a general in the Continental Army under George Washington. Following the war, he returned to New Hampshire, where he would serve as the state's attorney general, as a member of the legislature, speaker of the house, and, later, governor. With

---

[34] Daniell, *Experiment in Republicanism*, 153.

[35] Barstow, *The History of New Hampshire*, 268.

[36] Daniell, *Experiments in Republicanism*, 162.

[37] L. H. Butterfield, ed., *Diary and the Autobiography of John Adams* (Cambridge: Belknap Press of Harvard University Press, 4 vols., 1961), Vol. 3, 352.

[38] Ibid.

[39] Ibid.

Meshech Weare and others, Sullivan is credited with having possessed the "skill, wisdom, and patience" necessary "to fashion a state out of what was a loosely defined and disconnected province."[40]

As the sentiment for a special constitutional convention gained strength in New Hampshire, Massachusetts was moving in a like direction. The Massachusetts General Court in the fall of 1776 sought responses from the towns to its proposal to draft a constitution for the commonwealth, and on October 22, 1776, Concord, Massachusetts, was the first to call for the election of a special convention, recognizing the distinction between legislative powers and constitution-making that had been delineated in the Address from Grafton County.[41] In June 1777, the Massachusetts General Court resolved itself into a constitutional convention and appointed a special committee to draft a constitution; that constitution would in 1778 meet with resounding defeat at the polls.[42] Because the Massachusetts General Court would not issue a call for the election of delegates to a constitutional convention until June 1779, New Hampshire may claim the distinction of holding the first convention whose members were elected for the sole purpose of drafting a constitution, to be adopted after submission to the people and approval by popular vote.[43]

Most of the delegates to the New Hampshire convention came from the seacoast area and the Merrimack Valley, with poor representation from the western and northern towns.[44] Their deep involvement in the secession movement kept many towns in the western counties of Grafton and Cheshire from electing delegates. Towns could elect as many delegates as they wished and had to pay their expenses, which favored the wealthier towns nearer to Concord. Though ninety towns were represented by seventy-four delegates,[45] many towns went unrepresented.[46] Some of the smaller towns grouped together and shared a representative.

The constitutional convention elected in the spring of 1778 continued in existence until 1779, during which time it produced one draft constitution, which voters at town meetings rejected by a large margin on June 5, 1779. The draft by its terms required adoption by three-fourths of the voters, an unusually

---

[40] Morison & Morison, *New Hampshire*, 83–84.

[41] Robert J. Taylor, ed., *Massachusetts, Colony to Commonwealth, Documents on the Formation of Its Constitution, 1775–1780* (Chapel Hill: University of North Carolina Press, 1961), 36–37.

[42] Friedman & Thody, *The Massachusetts State Constitution*, 9–10.

[43] Taylor, *Massachusetts, Colony to Commonwealth*, 48–49.

[44] Turner, *The Ninth State*, 18.

[45] James Fairbanks Colby, *Manual of the Constitution of the State of New Hampshire, Compiled from Official Sources and Edited, with Sketch of the Constitutions of the State, the Basis of Representation, and Appendix* (Concord, N.H.: J. B. Clarke, 1912), 77. Colby refers to the list of delegates compiled from town records by G. Parker Lyon (in the *New Hampshire Register* for 1852, of which Lyon was editor), in which it appeared that about ninety towns were represented by seventy-four delegates.

[46] Daniell, *Experiment in Republicanism*, 189

high approval requirement. This draft closely resembled the 1776 constitution, which was not surprising since many of the framers of that constitution were delegates to the 1778 convention.[47] As a result, it did not respond to many of the basic criticisms leveled at the 1776 constitution: it still centered power in the legislature and it still contained a high wealth qualification for membership in the legislature—£300, one half of which had to be in real estate. Under the draft constitution, the council continued as the upper branch of the legislature, with a "president" chosen by the council from among its members who served in place of a governor but with almost no executive authority. Restrictions limited plural office-holding, and the draft allowed one seat in the house of representatives for each one hundred families, while smaller enclaves could band together for representation.

## THE CONSTITUTION OF 1784

After the voters rejected the first draft constitution, the legislature did not move quickly to restart the drafting process, as more immediate and pressing concerns occupied its attention. These concerns included the rebellion of the Connecticut Valley towns and their attempted secession, as discussed above, as well as the problem of inflation and the demands of the Continental Congress for more men and supplies in the prosecution of the war.

In the spring of 1781, the legislature authorized an election for another constitutional convention, to convene on the first Tuesday in June and to remain in session until it had produced a draft constitution which the people had ratified.[48] The convention that met in June 1781 followed the procedure of referring the actual drafting of the constitution to a committee and then reconvening at a later date to vote on the draft that the committee had produced. The drafters used as a model the recently adopted Massachusetts Constitution of 1780, principally written by John Adams. As a member of the Massachusetts constitutional convention's drafting committee, he was primarily responsible for the organization and much of the substance of the Massachusetts Constitution. Many of the basic elements of New Hampshire's constitution of 1784 can be traced directly to its Massachusetts forebear, including the bill of rights, the principle of separation of powers (though with some differences), and a division of government into three independent branches.

The draft presented to New Hampshire voters in 1781 represented a victory for the advocates of an independent executive branch. The draft proposed a governor with a limited veto power to be elected annually by the people, rather than a chief executive with little real authority elected from among the

---

[47] Turner, *The Ninth State*, 19.

[48] Journal of the House, April 5, 1781, printed in *New Hampshire State Papers*, Vol. VIII, 897.

members of the council. A five-member council, elected by joint ballot of the legislature, would give its advice and consent to certain gubernatorial appointments. The draft provided that judges, who would be appointed by the governor and council, would serve "during good behavior," and the constitution prohibited the holding of several important offices by the same person. The draft addressed the issue of representation in the lower house of the legislature by limiting the house to fifty members who would be elected by county conventions composed of delegates from the towns.[49] The draft reduced the electoral margin for adoption from three-fourths of those present and voting to the two-thirds margin that still obtains today.

When the draft was submitted, towns were asked to "state their objection distinctly and the reasons therefor" if a majority of eligible voters did not agree to approve the draft.[50] And majorities in the towns did not approve the draft constitution. Though similar in basic form to the constitution of today, it proved too controversial for the time. Citizens in some towns centered their disapproval on the draft's provision for a strong chief executive and the limits on membership in the house of representatives. Other opponents saw the draft as an attempt to restore to the seacoast merchant class the power it had lost during the war. Evidence in the historical record also indicates there was a lack of public discussion about the draft constitution prior to the vote.[51]

It appears as well that the June 1781 meeting of the convention was poorly attended, for when the convention reassembled in early 1782, after the first draft constitution had been rejected, it placed a notice in the *New Hampshire Gazette* of Portsmouth, New Hampshire, urging towns that had not elected delegates to the convention to "neglect no longer" and towns that had already sent delegates to "add other members" if expedient to do so. The difficulty in getting towns to send representatives to the convention can be explained in part by the rigors of traveling to Concord, as well as the common struggle among citizens to recover from the hardships of wartime.[52]

Upon reconvening in January 1782, the convention produced a second draft, which was submitted to the voters in August of that year. This draft contained many revisions in response to the complaints that had issued from the towns that had rejected the first draft. The revisions included the deletion of

---

[49] This idea was inspired by the system recommended in the "Essex Result," a report of the Essex, Massachusetts, county convention written by Theophilus Parsons of Massachusetts. Daniell, *Experiment in Republicanism*, 172.

[50] *New Hampshire State Papers*, Vol. IX, 895.

[51] Turner, *The Ninth State*, 26.

[52] Karen Bowden, "After the Revolution, The Transformation of New Hampshire Towns, 1780–1800," in William C. Gardner et al., *New Hampshire, the State That Made Us a Nation: A Celebration of the Bicentennial of the United States Constitution* (Concord, N.H.: P.E. Randall, 1989), 81–82.

the indirect election of members of the house of representatives, but the draft retained the more-powerful executive branch. Nonetheless, voters rejected this draft, with many citizens again voicing their objection to the concept of a strong executive.[53]

The convention met once again in June 1783, after the voters at town meetings in March 1783 had approved an extension of the "temporary" constitution of 1776 to June 10, 1784, and it appeared the former colonies would achieve peace with England before a new constitution could be adopted.[54] This time the convention made significant changes in response to the objections from the towns. This draft diminished the position of governor, with all veto power eliminated and his title changed to "president." Further, it changed the scheme of representation: a town with one hundred fifty rateable polls (that is, male inhabitants subject to taxation) could elect a member to the house, and only inhabitants over the age of twenty-one and who paid for themselves a poll tax had the right to vote. This draft also removed any limits on the size of the house, a decision which would have consequences extending into the second half of the twentieth century. Among other changes, the revised draft emphasized the approval of religion and indeed required "chief officeholders . . . to be of the Protestant religion."[55]

Finally, the state had a draft constitution that would meet with popular approval. The third draft received the necessary two-thirds vote, and it took effect on June 2, 1784—not a moment too soon, for the one-year extension of the temporary constitution of 1776 was about to expire.

## ■ THE REVISION OF 1792

The framers of the 1784 constitution had the foresight to anticipate that the constitution they created might profitably be reviewed and even revised after a relatively short period of time, and so the constitution required the legislature to call for a convention seven years after its adoption. In 1791, elections were held, and in September of that year the convention assembled in Concord.[56] As

[53] Upton, *Revolutionary New Hampshire*, 184–185.

[54] The New Hampshire House of Representatives adopted to resolve on February 17, 1783, noting that peace was likely to soon be accomplished and that, if this happened before a new constitution was adopted, the "present government" needed to be continued to "guard against the dreadful evils naturally flowing from anarchy." The house requested that the selectmen of the towns place the resolve to continue the present government until June 10, 1784 at their next annual town meeting. The council concurred in the resolve the following day. *Laws of New Hampshire*, Vol. 4 (1776–1784), 507–508.

[55] Jean Yarbrough, "Puritanism and the Moral Foundations of America," in Michael Allen Gillespie & Michael Lienesch, eds., *Ratifying the Constitution* (Lawrence, Kans.: University Press of Kansas, 1989), 241.

[56] Colby, *Manual of the Constitution of the State of New Hampshire*, 124.

the delegates to this convention set to work, they had the benefit of the federal constitution and several examples of constitutional reform in other states as models.

This convention's efforts resulted in a significant revision of the constitution. A number of problems with the constitution of 1784 had become apparent.[57] There was a need, for example, for a clearer separation of powers. Though the bill of rights declared that the three branches "ought to be kept as separate from, and independent of, each other, as the nature of a free government will admit," the executive and judicial branches were effectively weak and subservient to the legislature. The legislature was the court of last resort for both public and private matters and often overruled judicial decisions. Though the election of the chief executive—the "president"—was separate from the election of members of the legislature, he was not truly independent. The president served as commander-in-chief of the state's military forces and had the authority to make certain appointments with the approval of the council, but he had no veto power over legislative actions.[58] There were other problems. For instance, the 1784 constitution assigned to towns and not state government the responsibility for paying the wages of their representatives; amidst the extraordinary inflation and economic distress that followed the war, many towns found this obligation particularly burdensome.[59]

In addition to these issues, the ratification of the federal constitution had rendered several provisions of the 1784 constitution problematic. The New Hampshire Constitution required the legislature, and not the people, to elect representatives to the U.S. Congress, in contravention of Article I of the federal constitution. And the national chief executive was called "president," so it was somewhat confusing to have the state's chief executive hold the same title. As well, the state constitution's lack of restrictions on state officials holding multiple offices simultaneously resulted in many cases of what today would be considered incompatible office holding. John Sullivan served, at the same time, as New Hampshire's chief executive and as a federal judge, and Samuel Livermore served as both chief justice of the state's highest court and as a representative to the U.S. Congress.[60]

About a week after the convention assembled, it directed a committee of ten members to draft amendments based upon proposals submitted by the delegates. William Plumer, of Epping, emerged as the most influential member

---

[57] *See* the discussion in Turner, *The Ninth State*, 126–127.

[58] Upton, *Revolutionary New Hampshire*, 185.

[59] Jere R. Daniell, "Ideology and Hardball: Ratification of the Federal Constitution in New Hampshire," in Patrick T. Conley & John P. Kaminski, eds., *The Constitution and the States: The Role of the Original Thirteen in the Framing and Adoption of the Federal Constitution* (Madison, Wis.: Madison House, 1988), 5.

[60] Turner, *The Ninth State*, 126–127.

of the convention; he was speaker of the house and an ardent advocate of constitutional reform.[61] The competing interest groups on the committee of ten worked over the winter of 1791–1792, and the committee presented its recommendations for amendments in February 1792. The convention modified those recommendations and presented a total of seventy-two amendments to the voters in the May 1792 elections.

Among other changes, the amendments established an independent executive, a department not so closely linked to the legislature. Further, the constitution now required the legislature to divide the state into twelve senatorial districts based upon taxable property; the legislature had the authority to do this under the 1784 constitution, but had not exercised that power. The convention sought to address the seemingly intractable problem of fair representation in the house of representatives, but in the end could agree on no solution, thereby preserving the status quo[62]—as provided in the 1784 constitution, each town with "150 rateable male polls" aged twenty-one and older could elect a representative, as well as another representative for every three hundred additional taxpayers. Under the revision of 1792, the right to vote no longer depended upon the payment of the poll tax, but it did exclude paupers and persons who did not pay taxes at their own request.

In addition, relatively minor amendments relating to the judicial branch set the mandatory retirement age at seventy and made various changes concerning the probate courts, clerks' fees, and "the all too prevalent tendency of officials to confuse their public and their private business."[63] The amendments allowed the general court to establish, within limits, jurisdiction for the probate courts and justices of the peace. The committee of ten had suggested a fuller restructuring of the judicial branch, but the convention had rejected that proposal.

The convention faced the problem of how best to present all of its recommended amendments to the voters in a comprehensible way. It decided to send to each town a copy of the constitution as it would appear if all the amendments were to be adopted, as well as a listing of each amendment to be voted on separately.[64] But the public lacked interest and, perhaps, understanding; the amendments were considered at special town meetings in May, when the press

---

[61] William Plumer, Jr., in his book about his father, *Life of William Plumer* (Boston: Philips, Sampson, & Co., 1857), 124, states that the constitution as amended by the convention of 1791–1792 was known as "Plumer's Constitution." According to Superior Court Judge Samuel Livermore, as quoted by Plumer, the reference was originally meant in a derogatory way, implying that the constitutional revisions were the work of one man rather than the entire convention. Ibid.

[62] Turner, *The Ninth State*, 130–131.

[63] Ibid, 135.

[64] *Journal of the Convention to Revise the Constitution* (1791–1792) as printed in *New Hampshire State Papers*, Vol. X (1877), 164.

of other business left little time for active debate.[65] Indeed, many people chose not to vote: in Moultonborough, for example, only sixteen eligible citizens voted on the amendments in 1792, while in 1778, when the population was smaller, forty-six cast votes in a dispute concerning a local minister. And no votes were cast in the town of Wolfeboro.[66] In the end, the total vote of the persons registered for the final endorsement of the amendments was less than 50 percent of the number who had voted earlier in that year in an uncontested gubernatorial election.[67]

In light of the time that the committee of ten and the convention had devoted to the proposed amendments, there was likely no small amount of frustration expressed when the delegates reconvened to examine the inconsistent and contradictory results of the vote. Though forty-six of the proposed seventy-two amendments had been adopted, a number ran afoul of other provisions of the constitution because voters had rejected the changes that would have made the text internally consistent. As the convention did not view the adoption of an internally inconsistent constitution as a desirable option, it proposed a bold solution: offer a single, omnibus amendment that would cover all the deficiencies, rather than a series of amendments that might result in further contradictory results. In other words, voters would have to decide whether to accept the entire package—which they did, by a margin of 2,112 to 978, just forty-five more votes than the required two-thirds majority.[68]

The revisions made by the 1792 amendments, which took effect in 1793, implemented many of the proposals that had been rejected as too radical in 1781.[69] They restored the position of governor and established gubernatorial succession, which in 1792 made the senate president next in line. The revisions of 1792 made the executive branch more independent of the legislature, by removing the requirement that the governor preside over and vote in the senate and by giving the governor the veto power. Voters over time would reject efforts to further enlarge the chief executive's power: they rejected a four-year term for the governor three times (in 1970, 1982, and 1984) and the item veto three times (in 1912, 1920, and 1930).[70] The 1792 revisions also provided that

---

[65] Turner, *The Ninth State*, 136.

[66] William L. Taylor, "Years of Revolution, Years of Decision: Attitudes and Reactions in the Lakes Region during the 1770s and 1780s," in Gardner et al., *New Hampshire, the State That Made Us a Nation*, 147–148, 150.

[67] Turner, *The Ninth State*, 136.

[68] *New Hampshire State Papers*, Vol. X (1877), 164.

[69] Law of 1792, ch. 15 In *Laws of New Hampshire*, Vol. 6 (1792–1801), the law was entitled "An Act to carry into effect the Constitution of the State as altered and amended by the late Convention, passed Dec. 14, 1792." The act provided that the provisions relating to the choice of members of the legislature, executive officers of the state, county treasurer, and recorder of deeds would take effect February 1, 1793, while the "whole of said Constitution" would take effect on the first Wednesday of June, 1793 (June 5, 1793).

[70] Constance T. Rinden et al., *New Hampshire Constitutional Amendment Proposals* (Concord, N.H.: Law Division, New Hampshire State Library, 1984) (2nd ed.), 14. The proposal for a four-year

council members would be elected from councilor districts instead of by members of the legislature. Further, the legislature would be required to deliberate openly, and the state became responsible for the wages of legislators.

In all, the revisions of 1792 were so extensive that, for many years, the constitution was incorrectly known as the "1792 constitution." The New Hampshire Supreme Court so called it in *Copp v. Henniker* in 1875.[71] In 1889, Supreme Court Justice William Allen sought to correct the record, noting in *State v. Saunders* that, because of the many provisions dating from the 1784 constitution, it was erroneous to refer to the document as the "constitution of 1792."[72] To this day, the amendments resulting from the 1791 convention make up the only general revision of the 1784 constitution; following the adoption of those amendments, there began a long period of satisfaction among the citizens with the basic governmental structure and the constitution that created it.

## THE CONVENTION OF 1850

For eighty-five years, from 1792 to 1877, New Hampshire's constitution remained essentially unchanged, save a single amendment in 1862, this despite the numerous opportunities the voters had to call a constitutional convention: from 1800 to 1850, the people voted down the prospect of such a convention—and, therefore, constitutional change—eight times. The span of years between amendments represents among the longest periods in which the people of a state chose not to amend their constitution.[73]

There were a number of reasons why a convention was not held until 1850. At least in the initial years following the 1792 revision, many people likely recalled the difficulties associated with that effort, including the need to hold two separate votes and to respond to seventy-two separate questions. Further, the state would have to pay the costs of the convention, if one were held. Opponents over the years also expressed some fear that a new convention might go too far and propose unnecessary changes, leading to a drastically changed constitution.

Whether to call a convention became a political issue between Democrats and Federalists in the 1830s and 1840s. The legislature was dominated by Democrats and from 1833 until 1847 supported a vote on whether to hold a convention on average about every two years, in contrast to the previous decades, in which such an opportunity had been presented to the voters in accordance with the constitutional provision that required that a sense of the people "as to

---

term which had not been submitted to the voters at the time of the publication in May of 1984 was defeated in November of the year.

[71] Copp. v. Henniker, 55 N.H. 179, 191 (1875).

[72] State v. Saunders, 66 N.H. 39, 86–87 (1889).

[73] Colby, *Manual of the Constitution of the State of New Hampshire*, 168.

a revision of the constitution" be taken every seven years. The *New Hampshire Patriot and Gazette*, which supported the Democrats, complained that "[t]ime and again within the last twenty years, the Democrats... have called upon the people to convene a Convention... and the federal members of the Legislature always opposed it."[74]

In the spring of 1850, the voters agreed by a large margin that the time had come to consider amendments to the constitution.[75] The convention began its work in November of that year; it met over a six-week period, with a break for Thanksgiving. Public pressure for the convention to complete its work expeditiously was such that, after the delegates returned following Thanksgiving, it met almost every day but Sunday, including Christmas Eve day, Christmas Day, and New Year's Day, as well as in evening sessions.

Franklin Pierce, president of the convention[76]—and later fourteenth president of the United States—and other convention leaders in the legislature believed that the social, economic, and religious changes in New Hampshire over the previous sixty years warranted a restructuring of state government.[77] The convention ultimately elected to bring fifteen questions to the voters, including proposals for changes to each branch of government and the Bill of Rights. The convention combined into a single question two issues that had animated support for calling a convention: abolishing the requirements for office that representatives, senators, executive councilors, and the governor to be "of the Protestant religion" and that they own certain amounts of property.

While proposals like abolishing the religious and property requirements for office were needed, the convention in the end suggested so many radical changes that voters rejected all of its proposals—not one question received a simple majority of the vote. The *New Hampshire Patriot and State Gazette* expressed regret for its support for the convention, noting that it had lasted longer than expected, cost almost $40,000, and produced many more proposed amendments than anticipated. The newspaper characterized the convention's recommendation as a "new Constitution" which left "scarcely a feature of the old one recognizable."[78]

After this defeat at the polls, the convention met again and debated whether to resubmit any of its proposals to the voters. Levi Woodbury, an associate justice of the U.S. Supreme Court and a convention delegate, urged the convention to resubmit three proposals: abolition of the religious test and abolition

---

[74] *New Hampshire Patriot and State Gazette*, April 24, 1851.

[75] The record vote was 28,877 in favor and 14,482 against. Rinden, *New Hampshire Constitutional Amendment Proposals*, 13.

[76] William M. Gardner, Introduction, *The State of New Hampshire Convention to Revise the Constitution: 1850* (Concord, N.H.: State of New Hampshire, Secretary of State, 2005).

[77] Colby, *Manual of the Constitution of the State of New Hampshire*, 170.

[78] *New Hampshire Patriot and State Gazette*, March 27, 1851.

of property requirements for office, as well as adoption of a new mode of constitutional change which would allow the legislature to propose amendments. These questions were resubmitted, but the final result of the work of the 1850 convention was the adoption of just one amendment: the abolition of the property requirement for holding office.

## THE CONVENTION OF 1876

The sense of the people was taken seven times between 1850 and 1876, and majorities in 1861 and 1865 voted to call a constitutional convention, but the Civil War precluded these conventions from meeting. In 1876, New Hampshire, like the rest of the nation, was in the midst of dramatic social, political, and economic change. In the wake of the war, industrialization began to supplant agriculture as an economic engine, while railroads made transportation easier and faster. At the same time, the population was growing more diverse. The time appeared right to consider the constitution, and a majority of voters that year agreed.

The changes wrought by the 1876 convention modernized many aspects of New Hampshire government. The amendments ratified by the voters in 1877 changed the date of elections from March to November and the timing from annual to biennial. Two amendments placed restrictions on the use of public money. One amendment prohibited the legislature from authorizing a town to loan or give funds to benefit a corporation formed to achieve "a divided of profits."[79] Another amendment emphasized the separation of church and state by prohibiting tax revenue from being used to support religious schools.[80] And the voters finally agreed to abolish the religious test for office.

In addition, the amendments made changes to the size of the legislature. The senate doubled in size, from twelve to twenty-four. All subsequent attempts to alter the size of the senate have met with failure.[81] The basis for representation in the house was increased from one hundred fifty rateable polls (essentially, male inhabitants subject to taxation[82]) to six hundred inhabitants. This would not be the last amendment aimed at the structure of the house; as a historical matter, most of the amendments concerning legislative size and apportionment have involved the house, which has always been a large body

---

[79] N.H. Const., Pt. 2, Art. 5.

[80] N.H. Const., Pt. 2, Art. 83.

[81] The people defeated proposals to increase the size of the senate in 1912, 1964, and 1974.

[82] It is hard to arrive at an exact meaning for the term "rateable [ratable] polls." The term was not defined by the courts or by statute for the first half-century after the adoption of the 1784 constitution. A June 1835 opinion clarified that "aliens" (noncitizens residing in the state) were to be included as ratable polls because they were taxable, but persons over the age of seventy were not, because they were excused from taxation. *Opinion of the Justices*, 8 N.H. 573 (1835).

in proportion to the state's population and in comparison to other representative bodies. Indeed, the New Hampshire Legislature today is one of the largest representative bodies in the English-speaking world.

Every convention from 1850 to 1938 considered amendments relating to the size of the house of representatives, and eight separate amendments relating to size appeared on the ballot in 1877, two of which the voters ratified. For many years, there was no limit on the size of the house. The first elected house had 91 members, but by 1876 the house had grown to 391 members. In 1877, the move from rateable polls to population represented a fundamental shift, but it did nothing to limit the size of the house. At the time, the amendment effectively reduced the number of representatives in the house to 280, but that number naturally increased over time as the state's population grew.

## THE CONVENTION OF 1889

Of concern to the convention of 1889 was the representation of citizens of small towns in the General Court. The constitution adopted in 1784 contained a special provision relating to small towns which grouped or "classed" them together for purposes of representation. The citizens of these towns, understandably dissatisfied with this arrangement, sought to have their towns receive equal representation in the legislature. In 1889, voters adopted a compromise, an amendment which ended "classing" and allowed the small towns to be represented in the legislature for a proportional amount of time, based upon population.

This amendment did not fully address the concerns that preoccupied the citizens of small towns, as a very small town would be able to send a representative to the General Court only infrequently, which meant that some form of taxation without representation might well occur.[83] For instance, under this system, with a requirement of one representative for every six hundred inhabitants, a town of sixty inhabitants would be entitled to representation just one-tenth of the time. "Time" was to be calculated by the number of legislative sessions to be held, with representation lasting for the entire session. Thus, representation one-tenth of the "time" translated to representation at every tenth session; at the time of the 1889 convention, legislative sessions were being held only once every two years, meaning that a town of sixty inhabitants effectively

[83] *See, for example,* the remarks of delegates Edith D. Banfield and E. James Winslow in the Journal of the Convention (1938). Delegate Banfield asks the legislature not to "tax [smaller towns] without representation." *State of New Hampshire Convention to Revise the Constitution: Journal of the Convention to Revise the Constitution* (Manchester, N.H.: Granite State Press, 1938), 176. Delegate Winslow expressed his concern over the "lack of representation, or the disfranchisement of many towns, part of the time." Ibid, 183.

would be represented only once every twenty years and "practically the town [wa]s disenfranchised," as one delegate noted.[84]

Other constitutional proposals recommended by the convention of 1889 and later adopted included an amendment providing for compensation for members of the legislature at $200 per biennium, plus mileage—for officers, $250, with $3 per day for special sessions.[85] Another amendment altered the gubernatorial line of succession by placing the speaker of the house of representatives after the senate president.

## THE CONVENTION OF 1902

By 1902, the house numbered 397 members. It appeared that Representatives Hall would soon be too small to accommodate all of them. According to New Hampshire Supreme Court Justice Martin Chase, there were "very few citizens that [*sic*] do not feel that the house is too large to secure the best quality of membership and the best results of deliberation."[86] Nineteen resolutions on the subject were introduced at the 1902 convention, but the convention proposed a variation of the town plan then in effect—which granted a representative to any town with six hundred inhabitants, with an additional representative for each twelve hundred inhabitants—with an element of the district system. It required a minimum of eight hundred inhabitants for one representative, twenty-four hundred for two, and sixteen hundred for every representative thereafter, with a local option feature which would have allowed contiguous towns, wards, and similar places to voluntarily unite into a district. A majority of voters favored this proposal, but it failed to garner the required two-thirds vote necessary for adoption.

The 1902 convention, in response to pressure for additional sources of revenue, proposed an amendment to Part 2, Article 6. Tax reform has been a frequent subject of proposed constitutional amendments, partly in response to the long and complex history of judicial interpretation of the taxation provisions contained in Part 1, Article 12 and Part 2, Articles 5 and 6. In general, the state supreme court interpreted the constitution to prohibit graduated taxes of any kind because all taxes had to be proportional and reasonable. As a result, property, both real and personal, was the principal basis for tax revenue in the nineteenth and early twentieth centuries, and the state property tax remained one of the main components of state tax revenue until the 1930s.[87]

---

[84] *Journal of the Constitutional Convention of the State of New Hampshire* (Manchester, N.H.: J. B. Clarke, 1889), 240.

[85] N.H. Const., Pt. 2, Art. 15.

[86] *Concord Evening Monitor*, November 4, 1902.

[87] Peter J. Loughlin, "The Direct State Property Tax," *New Hampshire Law Bulletin* (October 1999): 27.

The convention's proposal was adopted, extending the taxable classes of property beyond "polls and estates" and allowing the imposition of different flat rates on different classifications of taxable property.

## THE CONVENTIONS OF 1912 AND 1918

By 1912, the year when the next constitutional convention assembled, the house had grown to more than four hundred members, but there was no agreement on an amendment that would reduce its size. Elsewhere, the convention considered, not for the first time, the issue of women's suffrage. For almost 175 years, Part 2, Article 28 of the constitution had provided that only "male inhabitants" could vote for senators. The voters had rejected women's suffrage in 1902, and in 1912 the convention failed to propose a similar amendment.[88]

The 1918 convention, which convened in 1921, elected to submit to the voters an amendment removing the word "male" from Article 28.[89] By this time, the issue of women's suffrage had been resolved by the ratification in January 1920 of the Nineteenth Amendment to the U.S. Constitution; nonetheless, the proposed amendment met defeat at the polls.[90] It would be rejected again in 1938.[91]

As for the recurring problem of a rapidly growing house, the 1918 convention proposed two amendments, which the voters rejected. These proposals would have reduced the size of the house to between 300 and 325 members, with one plan basing representation on the number of votes cast in the last presidential election and the other on population.

## THE CONVENTIONS OF 1930 AND 1938

Issues of representation and voting were taken up again by the 1930 convention. The convention proposed to reduce the number of representatives in the house by reducing representation of the larger areas, an effort rejected by the voters. Eight years later, a new convention proposed an amendment relating to voting by "paupers," but the voters rejected this proposal as well.

---

[88] *State of New Hampshire Convention to Revise the Constitution* (1938), 411, 433.

[89] *State of New Hampshire Convention to Revise the Constitution: Journal of the Convention to Revise the Constitution* (Manchester, N.H.: John B. Clarke Printing Co., 1921), 426–427. (Special Session of January 28, 1921).

[90] Beatrice Ruth Jeffries and Philip A. Hazelton, *New Hampshire Constitutional Conventions* (Concord, N.H.: New Hampshire State Library, Legislative Service, 1956), 36.

[91] In 1938, the reference to "male" inhabitants would have been eliminated as part of an amendment proposed to Article 28 of Part 2 relating to voting by paupers, but the elimination of the "male" reference was not mentioned in the question presented to the voters. *See Journal of the Convention to Revise the Constitution* (1938), 321–322.

The convention, rather than seeking elimination of restrictions on voting by paupers had instead attempted to clarify the legislature's authority to define "pauper" for purposes of voting. According to a statement made during debate about the amendment, the clarification would have responded to the uneven enforcement of the laws defining "pauper."[92]

But the 1938 convention was not wholly unsuccessful. Once again turning to the issue of revenue—and the uses to which the legislature could put it—the convention recommended establishing some constitutional protection for highway funds, to prevent them from being raided by the General Court. In 1938, the voters adopted Part 2, Article 6-a, which provides that motor vehicle revenues must be used for "construction, reconstruction, and maintenance of public highways," and not for other purposes. The voters also approved, in 1942, two narrowly drawn amendments which permitted the classification and taxation of standing timber at a different rate from real property.

When the convention reconvened in 1941, it considered the results of the 1940 census. Under the constitutional formula, the house would again increase in size, from 423 to 443, because of population growth.[93] Some convention members argued that the house would soon become too large to function efficiently—and, as a practical matter, it once again threatened to outgrow its space in Representatives Hall. Various proposals for reducing the size of the house generated much debate at the convention, and the plan it finally endorsed involved a numerical cap on the size of the house. Still in effect at this writing, the constitutional cap adopted by the voters in 1942 allows the house to range in size from 375 to 400 members.[94] As for the perennial concerns of citizens of small towns about their representation in the legislature, the voters approved as part of the cap on the size of the house an amendment that each town, no matter how small, would have a representative in the house at least once every ten years. This "concession to the smaller towns" was made to encourage support for the cap.[95]

Voters in 1942 also supported authorizing the legislature to provide for absentee voting. This amendment allowed for absentee voting at general elections (biennial, city, or state). Similar amendments had failed in the past.

---

92 "Con Con May Give Voters 4 Proposals," *Concord Daily Monitor*, May 28, 1938.

93 *State of New Hampshire Convention to Revise the Constitution: Journal of the Convention to Revise the Constitution* (Manchester, N.H.: Granite State Press, 1941), 64.

94 N.H. Const., Pt. 2, Art. 9.

95 "Convention Given 3 Plans to Reduce Size of House and May Recess Tonight," *Concord Daily Monitor*, September 25, 1941.

## THE CONVENTION OF 1948

Eleven proposed amendments were submitted to the voters between 1948 and 1950. The convention president, Richard Upton, noted that the convention had focused on removing those portions of the constitution "which had ceased to be in harmony with the times," and ultimately recommended relatively few substantive changes because the constitution "embodies in a high degree the fundamental principles essential to free government by free men."[96] Of the six amendments approved by the voters in the 1950 election, all concerned the removal of outdated and obsolete provisions from the constitution.

## THE CONVENTION OF 1956

The 1956 convention sent ten proposals to the voters, of which they approved nine. The amendments concerned such matters as absentee voting,[97] accounting for "non-residents temporarily residing in [the] state" in the census,[98] and allowing the governor to conduct business while not in New Hampshire.[99] Other amendments omitted or altered antiquated language, such as references to "males" being eligible to vote—this nearly forty years after the right to vote had been extended to women under the U.S. Constitution.[100]

The convention president, J. Walker Wiggin, focused on the need to send voters proposals that delegates "honestly believe[d]... [would] in all probability result in a future and continuous benefit to our people."[101] He also warned that the convention rules designed to protect the voice of the minority were only acceptable "up to the point where such minority attempts to substitute unreasonable, dilatory and obstructive tactics for the reasonable parliamentary procedural progress to which the majority is entitled."[102] Perhaps not surprisingly, the next convention, called in 1964, concerned itself with the equal treatment of all delegates, reflecting allegations that the 1956 convention had been conducted unfairly toward some.[103]

---

[96] *The State of New Hampshire Convention to Revise the Constitution: Journal of the Convention to Revise the Constitution* (Manchester, N.H.: Granite State Press, 1948), 19–20.

[97] N.H. Const., Pt. 1, Art. 6.

[98] N.H. Const., Pt. 2, Art. 9-a.

[99] N.H. Const., Pt. 2, Art. 49.

[100] N.H. Const., Pt. 2, Art. 28.

[101] *The State of New Hampshire Convention to Revise the Constitution: Journal of the Convention to Revise the Constitution* (Manchester, N.H.: Granite State Press, 1956), 20.

[102] Ibid.

[103] *The State of New Hampshire Convention to Revise the Constitution: Journal of the Convention to Revise the Constitution* (Manchester, N.H.: Granite State Press, 1964), 22–23.

## THE CONVENTION OF 1964

Between the conventions of 1956 and 1964, an interim commission studied the constitution and issued a report, which was provided to all members of the new convention. Upton, once again serving as convention president, acknowledging that the rules prohibited the chair from addressing "the merits or demerits of the issues presented in [the] report," noted that the report provided "considerable historical perspective and invaluable background material . . . that show[ed] the major choices that [were] open to the Convention."[104] He believed the 1964 convention accordingly would be "better prepared to proceed, than many of its predecessors."[105]

The convention ultimately submitted twenty-one amendments to the voters, the most notable of which sought to reduce the extent to which the people would have to rely upon conventions to amend their constitution. This amendment proposed that the General Court be authorized to propose amendments, and it changed the frequency with which a sense of the voters should be sought in respect to a convention from every seven to every ten years.[106] Prior to 1964, the legislature could not propose amendments, and New Hampshire is one of just four states to have held more than ten constitutional conventions.[107] After 1964, an amendment could be proposed by convention or by a 60 percent majority of the legislature. For a proposal to be adopted, it must be ratified by a supermajority of two-thirds of the persons voting on the question, rather than a simple majority.

The 1964 convention also returned to the issue of representation in the house. Before 1964, whether the requirement for the first representative was one hundred fifty rateable polls or six hundred inhabitants, twice that number was required for the second and any successive representative. This formula worked to advantage the smaller towns that qualified for representation. New Hampshire, like its New England neighbors, had a well-developed system of town government that had survived the original transition from colonial to state governance.[108] Representatives from these towns remained a powerful force and they were scarcely interested in ceding any advantage they might enjoy in the legislature. The inequity resulting from the pre-1964 formula had long been recognized. In an address prior to the 1902 convention, New Hampshire Supreme Court Justice Martin Chase noted that, under the formula, "Bow with a population of 617 is entitled to one representative, while

---

[104] Ibid, 23–24.

[105] Ibid, 23–24.

[106] N.H. Const., Pt. 2, Art. 100.

[107] John J. Dinan, *The American State Constitutional Tradition* (Lawrence, Kans.: University Press of Kansas, 2009), 11.

[108] Daniell, *Colonial New Hampshire*, 237.

Ward Five in Concord, with a population of 2,609—more than four times that of Bow—is entitled to only two."[109]

The long-standing "two for one" formula[110] met its demise after the U.S. Supreme Court established the principle of "one person/one vote" as a matter of federal constitutional law under the Fourteenth Amendment.[111] Just five days after the 1964 convention adjourned, on June 15, a series of decisions from the U.S. Supreme Court made clear that equal protection required election districts throughout the country to afford each voter an equal vote.[112] This rule thus forbade a state constitutional provision that conditioned the election of a second and any additional representative upon twice the population size necessary to elect the first. The president of the 1964 convention recalled the members for a one-day session to address the issue, upon which the convention proposed that representation in the house be "as equal as circumstances will admit."[113] The voters ratified this proposal in November 1964, thereby placing small towns in districts with other towns for purposes of representation.

Though the voters did not in 1964 approve increasing the size of the senate, they did approve a requirement that the senate be apportioned on the basis of population and not taxable property, without dividing any town, city wards, or unincorporated places. At the time, the largest senatorial district had about three times the population of the smallest. New Hampshire was the only state to employ this antiquated method of apportionment and, like the formula for representation in the house, it violated the Fourteenth Amendment to the U.S. Constitution.[114]

In the years following the 1964 convention, voters considered amendments addressing executive authority, home rule, and voting requirements, among other matters. In 1966, Part 2, Article 41 was reworded to clarify the

---

[109] Justice Chase's address to the South Church Business Men's Conference on November 2, 1902, was printed in the *Concord Evening Monitor* of November 4, 1902. The same remarks, entitled "A Review of Organic Law Development," were printed for the benefit of the 1902 convention and were included in the *Journal of the Convention to Revise the Constitution*, December 1902, 208–222. Associate Justice William Martin Chase served on the New Hampshire Supreme Court from March 24, 1891, until his retirement on December 28, 1907, at age seventy.

[110] The *Concord Daily Monitor* of July 7,1964, explained the "two for one" formula as a system requiring that a "town or ward have twice as many residents to elect a second representative—and all subsequent ones—than were required to elect a first."

[111] *Baker v. Carr*, 369 U.S. 186, decided in 1962, and *Wesberry v. Sanders*, 376 U.S. 1, decided in early 1964, preceded the "one-person/one-vote" cases decided in June of 1964.

[112] The six decisions, all decided on June 15, 1964, were *Reynolds v. Sims*, 377 U.S. 533, the principal case (Alabama); *Lucas v. Forty-Fourth General Assembly of Colorado*, 377 U.S. 713 (Colorado); *Maryland Committee v. Tawes*, 377 U.S. 656 (Maryland); *Roman v. Sincock*, 377 U.S. 695 (Delaware); *Davis v. Mann*, 377 U.S. 678 (Virginia); and *WMCA, Inc. v. Lomenzo*, 377 U.S. 633 (New York).

[113] N.H. Const., Pt. 2, Art. 9.

[114] In re Below, 151 N.H. 135, 144–45, 855 A.2d 459 (2004).

governor's authority. The voters that year also approved an amendment relating to home rule; Part 1, Article 39 would prohibit the legislature from changing a town or city charter without a local referendum approving such change. A 1968 amendment limited the governor's powers as commander-in-chief.[115] As well, the voters in 1968 further refined the rules of gubernatorial succession to address issues relating to succession in the event of the governor's physical or mental incapacity.[116]

Finally, in 1968, the people eliminated the literacy requirement for voting contained in Part 1, Article 11, which dated from 1902. The constitution had required that voters or office-holders be able to read the constitution in the English language and write their names, with certain exceptions related to age or disability. Likewise, until 1968 the exercise of the franchise was tied in some instances to the payment of taxes; the 1968 amendment brought Article 11 into conformity with federal constitutional decisions prohibiting the denial of voting rights for nonpayment of taxes.[117]

## THE CONVENTION OF 1974

Though the people adopted an amendment providing for alternative means with which to amend the constitution, the 1974 convention entertained 169 proposals,[118] more than twice the number debated at any of the previous five conventions. The convention sent twenty-seven amendments to the voters, ten of which they approved. In addition, pursuant to the changes adopted in 1964, the General Court sent twelve proposals to the voters, six of which they approved.

Among the proposals which voters rejected in 1976 was one that would have eliminated the governor's authority to make a pocket veto under Part 2, Article 44. Voters also refused an amendment that would have eliminated the governor's power to "prorogue," or prevent, the legislature from going back into session for up to ninety days following an adjournment. And voters rejected the substitution of the senior member of the executive council for the other state officers in the line of gubernatorial succession. In 1990, they rejected a proposal that would have prohibited the senate president or house speaker from voting in the legislature while serving as active governor, though

---

[115] N.H. Const., Pt. 2, Art. 51.

[116] N.H. Const., Pt. 2, Art. 49-a.

[117] *See* Harper v. Virginia State Bd. of Elections, 383 U.S. 663 (1966) (holding that "wealth or fee paying has, in our view, no relation to voting qualifications," abolishing the state poll tax as a violation of the Fourteenth Amendment).

[118] *The State of New Hampshire Convention to Revise the Constitution: Journal of the Convention to Revise the Constitution* (Manchester, N.H.: Granite State Press, 1974), 594.

the voters would later adopt this proposal as part of an amendment addressing gubernatorial incapacity.[119]

Other amendments considered by the people addressed voting rights. Voters in 1974 and 1976 brought the New Hampshire Constitution into conformity with the federal constitution[120] with amendments clarifying the minimum voting age as eighteen years old.[121] The voters expanded absentee voting rights in 1976 to allow the absentee ballot in town elections by official ballot, as well as in general or primary elections.[122] Voters in 1976 acted to repeal provisions tying the right to vote to payment of taxes for inhabitants of unincorporated places who had elected not to assess local taxes on themselves; by the time they were repealed, these disqualifications were rarely enforced.

## THE CONVENTION OF 1984

Voters amended Part 1, Article 11 for the last time in the twentieth century in 1984 to require that registration and polling places be easily accessible to disabled persons. In that same year, voters refined home rule with an amendment limiting the state's power to impose programs on local governments absent their consent. As well, they approved an amendment adding a new provision to Part I to protect the retirement funds of public employees. This provision requires that public retirement funds be used exclusively for the benefit of the appropriate retirement system and that such systems be fully funded each fiscal year.[123] In 1990, after the General Court had created a lottery designed to benefit the state's educational system, voters approved an amendment requiring that lottery revenues be used to aid education.[124]

## TWENTY-FIRST CENTURY CONSTITUTIONAL AMENDMENT

In 2006, the voters ratified two amendments to the New Hampshire Constitution. Part I, Article 12-a conditions the government's exercise of the power of eminent domain by prohibiting the taking of property "directly or indirectly" for "the purpose of private development or other private use." This amendment was a response to the U.S. Supreme Court's controversial decision in *Kelo v. City of New London*,[125] in which the Court held that "a city's decision

---

[119] N.H. Const, Pt. 2, Art. 49-a.
[120] U.S. Const., Amend. 26.
[121] N.H. Const., Pt. 1, Art. 11; Pt. 2, Art. 28.
[122] N.H. Const., Pt. 1, Art. 11.
[123] N.H. Const., Pt. 1, Art. 36-a.
[124] N.H. Const., Pt. 2, Art. 6-b.
[125] 545 U.S. 469 (2005).

to take property for the purpose of economic development satisfies the 'public use' requirement of the Fifth Amendment."

In addition, voters in 2006 once again tinkered with the method by which the citizens of smaller towns would be represented in state government. As amended, Part II, Article 11 states that, "[w]hen the population of any town or ward, according to the last federal census, is within a reasonable deviation from the ideal population for one or more representative seats, the town or ward shall have its own district of one or more representative seats." The amendment also allows the use of floterial districts—that is, legislative districts "which includes within [their] boundaries several separate districts or political subdivisions which independently would not be entitled to additional representation but whose conglomerate population entitles the entire area to another seat in the particular legislative body being apportioned."[126]

## ■ JUDICIAL ENFORCEMENT OF THE CONSTITUTION

Constitutional change, of course, does not occur exclusively through the formal processes of amendment but also through judicial interpretation; accordingly, it is worth considering separately the role of the New Hampshire judiciary and its historical enforcement of the constitution. Like its Massachusetts counterpart, the New Hampshire Constitution of 1784 created a permanent and independent judicial branch, recognizing that "[i]t is essential to the preservation of the rights of every individual, his life, liberty, property, and character, that there be an impartial interpretation of the laws, and administration of justice." Part I, Article 35 accordingly provided that the judges of the state's highest court would serve so long as they behaved well, and it guaranteed they would enjoy "honorable salaries, ascertained and established by standing laws." This arrangement stands in stark contrast to what had come before: under the 1776 constitution, the legislature had the authority to appoint judges and to remove them at will. Indeed, the legislature often found judges from among its own members, who would then serve in both capacities.[127]

But the adoption of the constitution of 1784 changed relatively little about the relationship between the branches, as the legislature continued to dominate the judiciary in various ways: "[t]he new constitution might proclaim separation of powers, William Plumer later pointed out, but the legislature not only adjourned courts, it also voided judgments rendered even by the tribunals of last resort."[128] And yet, in the 1780s a lower court took the first steps toward a truly independent judiciary and the unquestioned exercise of what

[126] Davis v. Mann, 377 U.S. 678, 686 n.2 (1964).

[127] John Phillip Reid, *Legislating the Courts: Judicial Dependence in Early National New Hampshire* (DeKalb: Northern Illinois University Press, 2009), 25–26.

[128] Ibid, 27.

today we would recognize as judicial review—"the power of a court to void a government act as inconsistent with the organic law of the polity."[129] The U.S. Supreme Court famously exercised this power in *Marbury v. Madison* in 1803,[130] but state courts had invalidated legislation as unconstitutional prior to *Marbury*. In 1799, for example, the Massachusetts Supreme Judicial Court had ruled unconstitutional an act of the Georgia legislature as a "flagrant, outrageous violation of the first and fundamental principles of social compacts" as well as Article I, § 10 of the U.S. Constitution.[131] And just two years after *Marbury*, that court recorded no hesitation in considering the validity of a law under the state constitution.[132]

In the "Ten Pound Cases," decided nearly twenty years before *Marbury*, a New Hampshire court had asserted its authority to determine the constitutionality of legislative acts.[133] Pursuant to the Ten Pound Act, passed in November 1785, justices of the peace could "try and determine all pleas and actions of Debt and trespass where title of Land is not concerned" when the claim did not exceed ten pounds; the act stripped the lower trial courts of jurisdiction in claims worth less than five pounds, unless heard on appeal.[134] The legislature intended the act "to help debtors by reducing the costs of defending small civil actions filed by creditors in the state."[135] Because justices of the peace did not preside over jury trials, the law effectively deprived debtors owing less than ten pounds a jury trial as guaranteed by Article 20 of the constitution, which provided that "in all suits between two or more persons, except in cases in which it has been heretofore otherwise used and practiced, the parties shall have a right to trial by jury; and this method of procedure shall be held sacred."

In 1786, Williams Wallace, Jr., brought a claim against Richard Tarlton, for whom he had worked, for nine pounds—"the reasonable value of his work"—and Justice of the Peace Thomas Bartlett granted him the "nine pounds 'damage' plus costs."[136] Tarlton, through his attorney, appealed to the Rockingham County Inferior Court of Common Pleas and received the traditional de novo

---

[129] Gerber, *A Distinct Judicial Power*, 115.

[130] 5 U.S. 137 (1803).

[131] Reported as *Derby v. Blake* in a supplement to the *Massachusetts Reports*, 226 Mass. 619, 115 N.E. 978 (1917), the case anticipated the U.S. Supreme Court's decision in *Fletcher v. Peck*, 10 U.S. (6 Cranch) 87 (1810).

[132] Mountfort v. Hall, 1 Mass. (1 Will.) 443 (1805).

[133] Much of what we know about the "Ten Pound Act Cases" is thanks to the work of Richard Lambert, who unearthed the historical evidence of these early instances of judicial review in New Hampshire. Richard Lambert, "The 'Ten Pound Act' Cases and the Origins of Judicial Review in New Hampshire," *New Hampshire Bar Journal* 43 (2002): 37.

[134] *See* Philip Hamburger, *Law and Judicial Duty* (Cambridge, Mass.: Harvard University Press, 2008), 423.

[135] Gerber, *A Distinct Judicial Power*, 117.

[136] Hamburger, *Law and Judicial Duty*, 425.

jury trial, after which the judgment was significantly reduced. Tarlton's lawyer then "moved for arrest of [the larger] judgment" on constitutional grounds.[137] The judges took the case under advisement and later ruled for the defendant. The motion in Tarlton's case would become the first of many in similar cases, with the judges repeatedly finding the Ten Pound Act to be contrary to the state constitution. "The court may have been inferior," the legal historian Philip Hamburger has observed, "but the judges understood their duty, even down to the standard of contradiction—that the statute was 'Manifestly Contrary to the Constitution of this State.' "[138]

There followed no small amount of discussion and debate in the legislature and among the citizenry about the act and the actions of the judges in Rockingham County. Legislative efforts to repeal or revise the act failed, as did efforts to eliminate the Inferior Court's appellate jurisdiction.[139] In June 1787, the house appointed a committee to consider whether the judges should be impeached; the committee reported that "the said Justices are not Impeachable for Mal-administration as their conduct is justified by the constitution of this State."[140] The house soon moved to repeal the act, with which the senate agreed. One local newspaper summed up this legislative action thus: "The General Court, during their late session, repealed the *Ten Pound Act*—and thereby justified the conduct of the Justices of the Inferior Court, who have uniformly opposed it as *unconstitutional* and *unjust*."[141]

Notwithstanding the Ten Pound Cases, by the turn of the century the legislature was still effectively controlling the courts. For instance, as John Phillip Reid reported, "of the six statutes published as *Sessions Laws* for June 1797, five had to do with regulating the courts."[142] Further, the prevailing view held that the General Court had the authority to "legislate" judges out of office; indeed, this was a relatively simple process: "The legislature simply repealed the statute that had created the current court. If the governor concurred and signed the bill, the court was abolished and the judges were removed from office."[143] Thus in 1813 did the General Court legislate out of office the New Hampshire Superior Court (now the Supreme Court).[144] The constitution of 1784 may have contemplated an independent judiciary, but Article 35 was not seen as protecting the institutional integrity of the courts as permanent institutions.

---

137 Ibid, 426.

138 Ibid, 428.

139 Gerber, *A Distinct Judicial Power*, 120.

140 Hamburger, *Law and Judicial Duty*, 435.

141 Ibid, 435 (quoting Correspondence (July 3), *New-Hampshire Spy* (July 3, 1787)).

142 Reid, *Legislating the Courts*, 54.

143 Ibid, 119.

144 Ibid.

Still, popular and political attitudes toward the judiciary were changing,[145] and in an 1818 case called *Merrill v. Sherburne*,[146] the supreme court famously exercised the authority to determine the constitutionality of legislative acts.[147] A year earlier the court had affirmed the principle that it is the General Court's responsibility to determine the necessity for laws and that all such enactments not repugnant to the constitution are "the law of the land."[148] The court in *Merrill* held that the legislature had exceeded its authority when it granted a new trial to an unhappy litigant who had challenged the outcome of a probate dispute. Writing for the court, Justice Levi Woodbury stated that "[o]ne prominent reason for creating the judicial, distinct from the legislative department, was, that the former might determine when laws were thus 'repugnant,' and so operate as a check upon the latter, and as a safeguard to the people against its mistakes or encroachments." "But," he continued, "the judiciary would in every respect cease to be a check on the legislature, if the legislature could at pleasure review or alter any of the judgments of the judiciary."[149]

Though *Merrill* has come to be seen as establishing judicial review in New Hampshire, Woodbury's decision did not go so far as to fully embrace the doctrine, at least as we understand it today. Rather, the decision is primarily concerned with the legislature's practice of meddling in the work of the courts, and it consequently articulates a strong commitment to the separation of legislative and judicial powers. In hindsight, of course, it is difficult to read *Merrill* as about anything other than judicial review, but "it would be better to say," as Reid has suggested, that *Merrill*'s legacy "is that it created a 'new relationship between New Hampshire's judiciary and the legislature.' With Woodbury's decision, the principle of legislative supremacy began to pass from New Hampshire constitutional law."[150] Or, as Timothy Lawrie put it, *Merrill* "instituted an unspoken peace treaty between the branches."[151]

As the relationship between the judiciary and legislature changed and legislative supremacy began to ebb, the judiciary grew progressively more confident

---

[145] Ibid, 160–164.

[146] 1 N.H. 199 (1818).

[147] *Merrill* was not the first time the high court had declared that a legislative act could not be enforced; for example, the Superior Court of Judicature in *Gilman v. M'Clary* had ruled an act "ineffectual and inadmissible." Timothy A. Lawrie, "Interpretation and Authority: Separation of Powers and the Judiciary's Battle for Independence in New Hampshire, 1786–1818," *American Journal of Legal History* 39 (1995): 322.

[148] *Trustees of Dartmouth College v. Woodward*, 1 N.H. 111 (1817). This was the famous "Dartmouth College Case," which the New Hampshire Supreme Court resolved in favor of the state controlling the college's charter, a decision the U.S. Supreme Court reversed in *Dartmouth College v. Woodward*, 17 U.S. 518 (1819).

[149] 1 N.H. 199, 210.

[150] Reid, *Legislating the Courts*, 167.

[151] Lawrie, "Interpretation and Authority," 327.

in its ability to act as a truly independent governmental department, without fear of legislative interference. In 1851, for example, the supreme court held, in *State v. Tenney,* that it possessed the power to punish a person for obstructing the administration of justice.[152] A decade later, in *State v. Matthews,* the court concluded that the judiciary's contempt power is a "necessary incident inherent in the very organization of all legislative bodies and of all courts of law and equity independent of statutory provisions."[153] In 1873, the court struck down a legislative act seeking to affirm the fraudulent sale of a corporation because such an act would be judicial in nature.[154] And, by the early part of the twentieth century, the court could state with some confidence that the constitution essentially prohibited the legislature from enacting "laws which impair the ability of the courts to function as courts."[155]

But it was not until 1966 that the people amended the constitution to expressly protect the integrity of the court system. That amendment states that "[t]he judicial power of the state shall be vested in the supreme court, a trial court of general jurisdiction known as the superior court, and such lower courts as the legislature may establish."[156] A 1978 amendment further provided that the chief justice of the supreme court would be the administrative head of the court system and empowered, with the support of the associate justice of the supreme court, to craft rules governing the administration of the state's courts.[157]

Notwithstanding these textual amendments, perhaps no development better exemplifies the modern independence of the New Hampshire judiciary than its embrace of the "new judicial federalism" beginning in the 1970s. "The new judicial federalism" refers to "the development of state court interpretations of some state constitutional rights provisions to be more protective than the same or similar federal Constitutional provisions."[158] The New Hampshire Supreme Court has been at the vanguard of this movement.[159] In its 1983 decision in *State v. Ball,* the court declared that, "[w]hen State constitutional issues have been raised, this court has a responsibility to make an independent interpretation of the protections afforded under the New Hampshire Constitution."[160] Accordingly, when a litigant raises an individual rights claim,

---

[152] State v. Tenney, 23 N.H. 162 (1851).

[153] State v. Matthews, 37 N.H. 450, 453 (1859).

[154] White Mountain Railroad v. White Mountain Railroad, 50 N.H. 50 (1870).

[155] Richard B. McNamara, "The Separation of Powers Principle and the Role of the Courts in New Hampshire," *New Hampshire Bar Journal* 42 (2001): 76.

[156] N.H. Const., Pt. 2, Art. 72-a.

[157] N.H. Const., Pt. 2, Art. 73-a.

[158] Robert F. Williams, *The Law of American State Constitutions* (New York: Oxford, 2009), 111.

[159] Arpian G. Saunders, Jr., "The New Hampshire Constitution and Individual Rights: 'Developed Advocacy' Required," *New Hampshire Bar Journal* 28 (1987): 327.

[160] State v. Ball, 124 N.H. 226, 231, 471 A.2d 347, 350 (1983).

the court will look first to the New Hampshire Constitution, and only if it concludes the state constitution affords no relief will it go on and examine the claim under the federal constitution. U.S. Supreme Court Justice John Paul Stevens praised this approach for the way in which it facilitates "the independent role of state constitutions and state courts in our federal system."[161]

The New Hampshire Supreme Court has continued to follow this "first things first" approach to the interpretation and application of state constitutional individual rights protections.[162] In *State v. Canelo,* for instance, the court determined that the state constitutional protection against unreasonable searches and seizures embodied in Part I, Article 19, unlike the Fourth Amendment to the U.S. Constitution, requires the exclusion of illegally seized evidence at trial even when a police officer acting in good faith believed a search warrant to be valid. Reviewing the state constitutional text and its history, as well as state and federal precedents regarding the exclusionary rule, the *Canelo* court confirmed—contrary to the U.S. Supreme Court—that the exclusionary rule is "a logical and necessary corollary to achieve the purposes for which prohibitions against unreasonable searches and seizures were constitutionalized."[163]

As the U.S. Supreme Court moved to limit the extent of many individual rights protections under the federal constitution at the end of the twentieth century—particularly in the area of criminal procedure—litigators in state cases began with increasing frequency to raise state constitutional arguments.[164] Many state courts embraced their role as independent interpreters of these state constitutional guarantees. But perhaps no court has so consistently asserted that it will independently examine the state constitution in these cases as has the New Hampshire Supreme Court. In addition to promoting the dual protection of individual rights under state and federal law that the framers of the U.S. Constitution contemplated, the court's unwavering approach to state constitutional interpretation in individual rights cases marks in a concrete way the judiciary's standing as a co-equal branch of New Hampshire government.

## ■ CONCLUSION

At this writing, the New Hampshire Constitution has been amended 146 times over the course of its existence. The Tables that precede the Appendix list the state constitutional conventions held since 1776 (Table 1) and show the number of amendments proposed by conventions and the legislature between 1792

---

161 Delaware v. Van Arsdall, 475 U.S. 673, 704 (1986) (Stevens, J., dissenting).

162 Williams, *The Law of American State Constitutions,* 111.

163 139 N.H. 376, 386, 653 A.2d 1097, 1105 (1995).

164 Charles H. Baron, "The Supreme Judicial Court in Its Fourth Century: Meeting the Challenge of the 'New Constitutional Revolution,'" *Massachusetts Law Review* 77 (1992): 40–41.

and 2013 (Table 2). Compared to other states, the people of New Hampshire have made relatively few changes to their constitution. There are several possible reasons for this. First, the constitution adopted in 1784 was based on sound principles, adapted by its framers from the work of John Adams on the Massachusetts Constitution—another constitution that has remained essentially unchanged since its ratification. Second, with few exceptions the constitution does not dwell upon the quotidian details of governmental operations that are commonly found in statutory law, and so there has been little need for frequent amendment to keep the constitution current. Finally, as a practical matter, the New Hampshire Constitution is more difficult to amend than most because of the requirement that amendments be approved by a two-thirds majority.

When the voters ratified the constitution in 1784, they committed to a republican form of government with authority separated and divided among three branches, the better to serve liberty and promote the public good. In the days following the Revolution, New Hampshire was a critical part of a vast national experiment in governance, and the voters accordingly recognized that their constitution might in time require "such alterations... as from experience may be found necessary."[165] Perhaps they would be pleasantly surprised to learn that experience has demonstrated nothing so much as the soundness of their original inclinations: over the course of more than two hundred years, the essential structure of government to which they pledged themselves in 1784 has remained in place, a model of stability among the constitutions of the United States.

[165] N.H. Const (1784) (directing the general court to call for a constitutional convention after seven years from the date that the constitution took effect).

PART TWO

# The New Hampshire Constitution and Commentary

# Introduction to the Constitutional Commentary

Since the 1980s, the New Hampshire Supreme Court has committed itself to the independent interpretation of the state constitution in cases involving government restrictions on individual rights and liberties protected by both the state and federal constitutions. With its decision in *State v. Ball* (1983), the New Hampshire Supreme Court concluded that, when a litigant has made an individual rights claim under both constitutions, the state claim should be addressed first. After all, the U.S. Constitution, through the Fourteenth Amendment, establishes only a floor below which rights protections may not fall, and not the upper limit on the scope of those protections. Only if the litigant would not prevail under the state constitution will the court go on and examine the equivalent federal constitutional guarantee to determine whether that provision would afford the litigant relief. The court in *Ball* made clear, moreover, that when it "cites federal or other State court opinions in construing provisions of the New Hampshire Constitution," it is relying "on those precedents merely for guidance." *Id.*

The commentaries that follow note many of the instances in which the New Hampshire Constitution's bill of rights provisions provide greater protection than their federal counterparts. It is also worth noting that, unlike the federal Bill of Rights, the New Hampshire bill of rights includes several provisions addressing matters not usually found in collections of rights, like the separation of powers and judicial independence, which suggests that the framers of the New Hampshire Constitution viewed these constitutional commitments as integral to the protection of individual rights and liberties.

In the first codification of New Hampshire statutory law, in 1842, article titles were editorially inserted into the constitutional text; since that time, titles have been indicated in brackets in published versions of the state constitution, even when the article title was a part of the text as adopted by the voters. After each article, the date given is the year in which the voters adopted the provision or amendment. The year of adoption is the same as the year the provision or amendment took effect in accordance with action by the legislature or proclamation by the governor, with the exception of the amendments adopted in 1792, which did not take effect until 1793.

Unless the text indicates otherwise, the commentaries use the terms "general court" and "legislature" synonymously, and references to "the court" or "the supreme court" are to the New Hampshire Supreme Court. The term "RSA" refers to the New Hampshire Revised Statutes Annotated, the current codification of the state's statutory law. In the context of a statewide vote on ratification of a constitutional amendment, the term "voters" refers to the qualified voters present and voting at a particular election. Two-thirds of the qualified voters must approve an amendment for ratification. Finally, the constitutional text that follows is the text as printed in The *New Hampshire Constitution Index to Constitutional Provisions Established October 31, 1783 to Take Effect June 2, 1784 as Subsequently Amended and in Force January 2009*, published by the New Hampshire Secretary of State. In the text that follows, several minor typographical errors have been corrected, as noted in brackets.

# Part 1

## *The Bill of Rights*

### ARTICLE 1. [EQUALITY OF MEN; ORIGIN AND OBJECT OF GOVERNMENT.]

All men are born equally free and independent; therefore, all government of right originates from the people, is founded in consent, and instituted for the general good. *1784.*

The origins of this article's first phrase, "All men are born equally free and independent," may be traced to the Virginia Declaration of Rights and is identical to that suggested by John Adams in his draft for the first article of the Massachusetts Constitution of 1780. The Massachusetts convention changed Adams's proposal—to his dissatisfaction—to "All men are born free and independent," the language of Thomas Jefferson in the Declaration of Independence. The remainder of this article reflects a Lockean conception of the social contract, the notion that the people consent to be governed and that they have established government to promote the common good. The preamble to the Massachusetts Constitution of 1780 expresses a similar sentiment.

The principle of equality is also found in Articles 2, 6, 10, 12, and 14 of the bill of rights. The equality guarantee provides that all individuals are entitled to enjoy equal privileges and to be governed by equal laws; in short, those individuals and classes of individuals who are similarly situated must be treated in a like manner. *State v. Amyot* (1979). But this principle does not require equality of treatment in all circumstances. For instance, in *Seabrook Police*

*Association v. Town of Seabrook* (1994), the New Hampshire Supreme Court rejected an equality challenge to a rule requiring members of the police force to live in the town; the court concluded that the role of police officers could be distinguished from that of other town employees, to whom no such requirement applied.

For the most part, the court has relied upon the doctrinal test used by the federal courts to apply the Fourteenth Amendment's equal protection clause. So long as a governmental classification does not affect a fundamental right or group individuals together on the basis of race, creed, color, gender, national origin, or legitimacy, it will receive rational basis scrutiny by the court—that is, the classification need only be rationally related to a legitimate governmental interest. "When determining whether the challenged classifications are reasonable and have a fair and substantial relation to the object of the legislation," the court "will not examine the factual basis relied upon by the legislature as justification for the statute." *Winnisquam Regional School District v. Levine* (2005).

Economic classifications typically are subject to rational basis scrutiny, but the test is not without bite. In *Amyot, supra,* the court struck down a law regulating truck weights on highways. The law contained an exception for truckers transporting unprocessed forest products in certain north sections of the state who obtained a special permit for which other truckers did not qualify. The court deemed this classification arbitrary and irrational, and unrelated to the statutory goal of enhancing public safety and maintaining the highway system.

### [ART.] 2. [NATURAL RIGHTS.]

All men have certain natural, essential, and inherent rights—among which are, the enjoying and defending of life and liberty; acquiring, possessing, and protecting, property; and, in a word, of seeking and obtaining happiness. Equality of rights under the law shall not be denied or abridged by this state on account of race, creed, color, sex or national origin. *1784; amended 1974.*

This article recognizes that all people have certain rights and enumerates some of those rights. The article also prohibits discrimination on the basis of race, creed, color, sex, or national origin. Its first sentence derives from Part 1, Article 1, of the Massachusetts Constitution of 1780, with a slight difference in wording: the New Hampshire Constitution speaks of "inherent" rights, while the Massachusetts Constitution refers to "inalienable rights." The second sentence, prohibiting discrimination, was added in 1974, two years after New Hampshire had ratified a proposed federal Equal Rights Amendment.

Article 2 provides that certain fundamental rights are deemed natural and inherent in all humankind. See *Burrows v. City of Keene* (1981). These rights include the right to defend one's property, see *Aldrich v. Wright* (1873), the right to use and enjoy one's property, see *Buskey v. Town of Hanover* (1990), and the right to hold public office, see *Hale v. Everett* (1868). The court in *Donnelly v. City of Manchester* (1971) held that the state constitution protects as fundamental the right of citizens to travel and to determine their own residency, and in *Angwin v. City of Manchester* (1978), the court concluded that the state constitution affords individuals greater protection than the federal constitution as to those rights.

Parental rights have also been deemed fundamental: biological and adoptive parents have a constitutionally protected interest in raising and caring for their children. *In re Alexis O.* (2008). These rights, however, are not absolute, and often may be regulated so long as the requirements of due process are satisfied. See *In re Doe* (1983). Before a termination of parental rights can be effected, for example, due process requires that the government prove its case beyond a reasonable doubt. See *In re Baby K.* (1998). When in one case a father did not have a fair opportunity to participate in a termination hearing, because he was incarcerated and could communicate with his attorney only by telephone, due process was not satisfied. See *id.*

Equality finds expression in numerous provisions of the New Hampshire Constitution, including Articles 1, 6, 10, 12, and 14. Though the court has rarely specified which of these equality provisions is at play when a party challenges government action as violating the commitment to equality, Article 2 is cited more frequently than most. The equality principle applies only to government action, not to private conduct. Whether state conduct is involved may not always be a simple matter. In *In re Certain Scholarship Funds* (1990), for example, the participation of the school principal, school board, and city trustees in the administration of a private scholarship trust with discriminatory, gender-based provisions amounted to government action. But the court concluded in *In re Dumaine* (1991) that no government action could be found in the implementation of a private trust which benefited only legitimate children and, therefore, that the equality rights of a child born out of wedlock were not violated.

As discussed in respect to Part 1, Article 1, in determining whether there has been a violation of the equality principle, the court will first determine whether government action treats similarly situated persons or classes differently. *Appeal of Marmac* (1987). If it does, the court will examine the scope, purpose, and the classification, as well as any individual rights affected, and apply to it the appropriate level of judicial scrutiny. "Classifications based upon suspect classes or affecting a fundamental right are subject to the most exacting scrutiny; to pass constitutional muster, they must be justified by a compelling governmental interest and must be necessary to the accomplishment of its legitimate purpose." *Petition of Concord Teachers (New Hampshire Retirement System)* (2009) (internal quotations and citations omitted). A suspect classification is one based upon race, creed, color, gender, national origin, or legitimacy. See *LeClair v. LeClair* (1993). Note that sex discrimination receives strict scrutiny under the New Hampshire Constitution, but only intermediate scrutiny under the federal constitution. See, e.g., *Cheshire Medical Center v. Holbrook* (1995) (common law necessaries doctrine which obligated husband to pay for wife's expenses but not a wife to pay for a husband's, violated equality principle).

Classifications involving important substantive rights will receive an intermediate level of review—the discrimination must be "substantially related to an important governmental objective." *Community Res. for Justice v. City of Manchester* (2007). The government has the burden to demonstrate that the challenged action satisfies this test, and it "may not rely upon justifications that are hypothesized or invented post hoc in response to litigation." *Id.* (quotation omitted). Unlike the U.S. Supreme Court, the New Hampshire Supreme Court has not restricted the application of intermediate scrutiny to classifications based upon sex or illegitimacy. Nonetheless, while the New Hampshire Supreme Court has applied intermediate review "to a broader category of rights than do the federal courts," its analysis "when applying this level of review is the same" as federal intermediate review. *Petition of Concord Teachers, supra.*

Intermediate review has been applied to governmental action implicating a variety of constitutional interests, including the right to recover for personal injuries under Part 1, Article 14. See *Rooney v. Fireman's Fund Ins. Co.* (1994) (concluding lien provision of workers' compensation law had a fair and substantial relation to the legitimate legislative objective of preventing double recovery). Intermediate scrutiny has also been applied to the right to use and enjoy real property subject to zoning regulations. See *Asselin v. Town of Conway* (1992). And the court has concluded that intermediate scrutiny applies to a classification that affects the right of eligible public employees to retirement benefits. See *Petition of Concord Teachers, supra.*

That an interest is recognized in the state constitution—like the right to recover for personal injuries or the right to use and enjoy real property—does not necessarily warrant heightened review in a challenge based upon an alleged violation of the state constitutional commitment to equal treatment. In *State v. Wamala* (2009), for example, the defendant argued that a statute allowing attorney-conducted *voir dire*—the process by which prospective jurors are questioned to probe potential conflicts and biases—in certain civil cases, but not in criminal trials, was unconstitutional. He maintained that intermediate scrutiny should apply to the discrepancy because the jury selection process is an important individual interest. The court disagreed, concluding that, while the right to an impartial jury is constitutionally protected, "*voir dire* is but a means to achieve the end of an impartial jury." *Id.* Accordingly, the court applied rational basis review.

Finally, absent some infringement of a fundamental right, an important substantive right, or discrimination involving a suspect class, the court will apply rational basis review. Under rational basis review, a classification will be upheld if it is "rationally related to a legitimate state interest." *Verizon New*

*England v. City of Rochester* (2007). If rational basis review applies, the party challenging the classification "has the burden to prove that [it] is arbitrary or without some reasonable justification" and "to negative every conceivable basis which might support [the classification], whether or not the basis has a foundation in the record." *Id.* It follows that "a least-restrictive means analysis is not part of this test." *Boulders at Strafford v. Town of Strafford* (2006).

The majority of governmental classifications are subject to rational basis scrutiny. For example, in *LeClair, supra,* the court addressed a law permitting a court to require a divorced parent to pay an adult child's college expenses when no similar provision existed for married parents. The court concluded that the law involved no fundamental or important substantive right, and created no suspect classification; accordingly, the court applied rational basis scrutiny and upheld the law. In *State v. Chrisicos* (2008), the defendant challenged a statute allowing certain sentences to be served under home confinement only if the correctional facility to which a defendant was assigned has such a program. The court concluded that the lack of such a program in a particular county did not violate the defendant's right to equal treatment, because the legislature legitimately could have "intended to allow each county to undertake a separate cost-benefit analysis with respect to a home confinement program." Notably, the court reasoned that no equality violation occurred even though the basis for the differential treatment by county was deemed merely to be conceivable.

Though the rationality standard is deferential, it is not necessarily toothless. In *State v. LaPorte* (1991), the court considered a law barring discovery depositions of victims and witnesses under the age of sixteen, to protect these children from being subjected to repeated interrogation without judicial supervision. The law also operated to bar depositions of victims and witnesses who had attained the age of sixteen at the time of the discovery request. This requirement, the court concluded, violated the equality principle because it bore no rational relationship to the statutory goal of protecting children under the age of sixteen; as the court observed, "the words of the statute do not advance its purported goal." *Id.*

### [ART.] 2-a. [THE BEARING OF ARMS.]

All persons have the right to keep and bear arms in defense of themselves, their families, their property and the state. *1982.*

Though many of the original state constitutions protected the right to bear arms, New Hampshire voters did not adopt a similar provision until 1982. This article gives individuals the right to bear arms in defense of themselves, their families, their property, and the state, and is similar to constitutional provisions in many other states. The text notably differs from the Second Amendment to the U.S. Constitution, which the U.S. Supreme Court has held protects an individual's right to bear arms at least for the purpose of self-defense. See *District of Columbia v. Heller* (2008).

The New Hampshire Supreme Court had occasion to interpret Article 2-a in 1990 in *State v. Smith* (1990). The court held that, while the provision guaranteed an individual right to bear arms, that right is not absolute; accordingly, the legislature may place reasonable restrictions on it. In *Smith,* the court concluded that a law that prohibited felons convicted of certain types of crimes from possessing dangerous weapons was reasonable.

In *Bleiler v. Chief, Dover Police Department* (2007), the court addressed the constitutionality of a police department's statutory authority to revoke a permit to carry a concealed weapon. The court agreed "with every other state court that has considered the issue: strict scrutiny is not the proper test to apply when evaluating whether gun control legislation" violates the state constitution. *Id.* The court confirmed that the reasonableness test should be used to determine the validity of such legislation, and in this case concluded that the statute was "a reasonable regulation of the time, place and manner in which the state constitutional right to bear arms may be exercised." *Id.*

### [ART.] 3. [SOCIETY, ITS ORGANIZATION AND PURPOSES.]

When men enter into a state of society, they surrender up some of their natural rights to that society, in order to ensure the protection of others; and, without such an equivalent, the surrender is void. *1784.*

This article reflects John Locke's idea of the social compact, the principle upon which "[a]ll society is founded," as the New Hampshire Supreme Court put it in *Mayo v. Wilson* (1817). Further, the *Mayo* court continued, "[w]hen we become members of society . . . we surrender our natural right, to be governed by our own wills in every case, where our own wills would lead us to counter the general will." *Id.* We also "agree to conform our actions to the rules prescribed by the whole, and we agree to pay the forfeiture, which the general will may impose upon the violation of those rules." *Id.* The constitution grants the general court "the power to declare the general will." *Id.* Thus, individual freedoms "may be subjected to reasonable and nondiscriminatory regulation in order that the constitutional rights of others may be equally protected in the interest of public order and convenience." *State v. Derrickson* (1951).

Article 3 accordingly has been interpreted to uphold as compulsory a variety of public policies. For example, the court has held that the state's interest in maintaining an effective criminal justice system prevails over a prisoner's right to privacy. See *In re Caulk* (1984). As well, the court has upheld against constitutional challenge school attendance laws, see *State v. Jackson* (1902), vaccination laws, see *State v. Drew* (1937), licensing requirements for public meetings, see *Derrickson, supra,* a requirement that people take shelter during civil defense alerts, see *State v. Pinsince* (1963), and a law prohibiting the blocking of a highway by Vietnam war protesters, see *State v. Albers* (1973).

### [ART.] 4. [RIGHTS OF CONSCIENCE UNALIENABLE.]

Among the natural rights, some are, in their very nature unalienable, because no equivalent can be given or received for them. Of this kind are the Rights of Conscience. *1784.*

Article 4 identifies a subset of natural rights that should be considered inalienable. As the New Hampshire Supreme Court stated in *Hale v. Everett* (1868), certain natural rights are inalienable because no government or person can give an equivalent in return. These rights cannot be surrendered to, or taken away by, government or society. One of these is the right recognized in Part 1, Article 5 to worship according to one's own conscience.

As a general matter the court has interpreted this article as applying to freedom of religion issues, in conjunction with Article 5. For example, the court held in *Free v. Buckingham* (1879), that this article protects a witness from inquiry into the details of his religious beliefs—that is, "into the state of his faith and conscience contrary to the spirit of our institutions." On the other hand, the court in 1957—during the McCarthy era—held that this article, along with Article 5, did not save the executive director of a world peace organization from being compelled to provide guest registration information for a facility operated by the organization, and sought by a legislative committee investigating subversive activities. The court concluded that the "atmosphere of religion" surrounding "the defendant's activities [did] not necessarily insulate them from investigation." *Wyman v. Uphaus* (1957).

Individuals charged with breaking various laws have over the years met with little success in seeking protection under Article 4. For instance, Article 4 did not protect an individual's refusal to comply with laws requiring children to be vaccinated before attending school, see *State v. Drew* (1937), or requiring persons to seek shelter during civil defense practice drills, see *State v. Pinsince* (1963). In addition, the court has concluded there is no "inalienable right" to sell liquor, see *State v. Corron* (1905), or lightning rods, see *State v. Stevens* (1916), activities which the state is free to regulate in the public interest.

### [ART.] 5. [RELIGIOUS FREEDOM RECOGNIZED.]

Every individual has a natural and unalienable right to worship God according to the dictates of his own conscience, and reason; and no subject shall be hurt, molested, or restrained, in his person, liberty, or estate, for worshipping God in the manner and season most agreeable to the dictates of his own conscience; or for his religious profession, sentiments, or persuasion; provided he doth not disturb the public peace or disturb others in their religious worship. *1784.*

This article protects an individual's right to the free exercise of religion, so long as one's religious practices do not disturb the peace or interfere with others in their worship. The wording of this article is similar to that of Part 1, Article 2 of the Massachusetts Constitution of 1780. The Massachusetts Constitution refers to religious practice as the "right as well as the duty" to worship the "Supreme Being," while the New Hampshire constitution omits the idea of duty and describes a "natural and inalienable right to worship God according to the dictates of one's own conscience." *Opinion of the Justices (Choice in Education)* (1992).

As interpreted by the New Hampshire Supreme Court, the state cannot make judgments about the truth of different religious beliefs. In *Glover v. Baker* (1912), the son of Mary Baker Eddy, founder of the Christian Science Church, sued after her death to prevent the church from benefiting under her will. Applying Article 5, the court upheld the will, concluding that "the truth of the religious theories inculcated" by Christian Science was of "no concern to the court." *Id.* "Mrs. Eddy," the court continued, "had the constitutional right to entertain such opinions as she chose, and to make a religion of them," and "[h]er legal right to teach was not ended with her death. She might dispose of her property by a gift in public charity for any use that is not illegal." *Id.* (quotation omitted).

Though this article prohibits the state from discriminating against different forms of creeds or worship, it can regulate conduct in accordance with its police powers, so long as the exercise of this power is reasonable. In *State v. Perfetto* (2010), after the defendant's sentence was suspended on the condition that he have no contact with children under seventeen, he filed a motion claiming that this condition interfered with his religious practices as children were often present at community services. The court found the condition "reasonably related to ends of rehabilitation and protection of public from recidivism," and that the "defendant could still practice his religion in ways that did not violate condition." Relying upon *People v. Branson* (1984), the court noted the importance of distinguishing "between freedom of belief, which may not be restricted, and freedom to act, which, as conduct, may be regulated." *Perfetto, supra.* The court has noted in other cases that an assertion that one is practicing religion does not stay the need to comply with other regulatory laws. See *Petition of Smith* (1994); *Appeal of Trotzer* (1998).

The article's final clause, which conditions an individual's religious freedom upon an obligation not to "disturb the peace," has been interpreted in cases testing the limits of the state's police power in certain circumstances. In 1886, the court upheld a law prohibiting the beating of a drum without the command of a military officer in the compact part of a town; the law did not run afoul of Article 5, even when the drum-beating served religious purposes and there was no evidence that anyone was actually disturbed. *State v. White* (1886). As well, the court upheld a state law requiring a permit for an "information march" held by Jehovah's Witnesses, because there was no intent in the statute to restrain freedom of religion. *State v. Cox* (1940).

When protection under Article 5 is asserted, the objection must have a particular religious dimension. In *State v. Drew* (1937), a parent claimed a religious objection to the preschool vaccination of his child, but the court concluded that his objection was based upon a "religious opinion" and did not involve questions of religious liberty. As in *Drew*, an "atmosphere of religion" was insufficient to protect information about guest registration at a world peace conference from subpoena by a legislative committee investigating subversive activities. See *Wyman v. Uphaus* (1957).

### [ART.] 6. [MORALITY AND PIETY.]

As morality and piety, rightly grounded on high principles, will give the best and greatest security to government, and will lay, in the hearts of men, the strongest obligations to due subjection; and as the knowledge of these is most likely to be propagated through a society, therefore, the several parishes, bodies-corporate, or religious societies shall at all times have the right of electing their own teachers, and of contracting with them for their support or maintenance, or both. But no person shall ever be compelled to pay towards the support of the schools of any sect or denomination. And every person, denomination or sect shall be equally under the protection of the law; and no subordination of any one sect, denomination or persuasion to another shall ever be established. *1784; amended, 1968.*

Based upon Part 1, Article 3 of the Massachusetts Constitution of 1780, this article provides that: (1) parishes and religious societies may select their own teachers, contract with them, and pay for their support; (2) no one can be compelled to pay for the support of a religious school of any sect or denomination; and (3) all denominations and sects are equally protected under the law. Both the New Hampshire and Massachusetts provisions sought to address the need for religious instruction to preserve good government and the issue of how to support that instruction; both also provided that no one sect or denomination could be subordinated to another. The text in the version of the New Hampshire Constitution published in 2009 by the New Hampshire Secretary of State's office contains a typographical error: "bodies, corporate" instead of "bodies-corporate," as originally written in the constitution of 1784.

The original 1784 provision empowered the legislature to authorize towns to "make adequate provision at their own expense, for the support and maintenance of public protestant teachers of piety, religion and morality." Article 6 thus permitted the establishment of a tax to support religion, a provision that can only be understood in light of its history: at the time, town-assessed taxes generally supported public religious worship and most citizens belonged to the Congregational church. In 1791, the legislature made this article operational by passing an act "for Regulating Towns and the Choice of Town Officers," which authorized the voters of each town to collect taxes for the support of the local ministry. This act replaced a colonial law from 1714 that allowed voters at town meetings to choose a minister and to pay him a salary to be funded through taxes assessed on the town's inhabitants.

In practice, the 1791 law supported the Congregational establishment: it proved difficult for dissenters to be excused from paying the tax by demonstrating adherence to another faith, even though Article 6 provided that no one of any particular sect or religion could be compelled to pay toward the support of another sect or religion. "Thus," as George Barstow observed, "many of the people were compelled to pay for the erection of churches they never entered, for teachings they never heard, and clerical labors which they conscientiously regarded as tending only to perpetuate the dominion of religious errors over the public mind."[1] Towns enacted and enforced the tax to varying degrees. In 1819, with the passage of the "Toleration Act," the religious tax was repealed; by that time, the number of members of other sects and religions, as well as those citizens who did not practice any particular religion, had grown to such an extent that there existed considerable opposition to a law which favored an established church.

Notwithstanding the Toleration Act, the text of Article 6 from 1784 to 1968 authorized the legislature to allow towns to require support for "Protestant" teachers of "piety, religion and morality," made reference to "public worship of the Deity," and provided only for equal treatment of "Christian" denominations. Every convention from 1850 to 1918 proposed amendments eliminating the references to "Protestant," but without success; conventions from 1930 to 1956 did not even propose such an amendment. An amendment adopted in 1968 finally removed Article 6's sectarian language.

## Powers of Parishes and Religious Societies

The 1968 amendment, crafted by the constitutional convention of 1964, left untouched the right of "parishes . . . or religious societies" to elect "their own teachers" and contract with them for their support. The court has not interpreted this part of Article 6 since its amendment. Prior to its amendment, commentators noted that Article 6's authorization of discriminatory treatment of religions other than Protestant arguably violated the First Amendment to the U.S. Constitution.[2] In 1868, the New Hampshire Supreme Court observed that this article did not forbid the legislature from allowing towns or religious

---

[1] George Barstow, *The History of New Hampshire, From Its Discovery, in 1614, to the Passage of the Toleration Act, in 1819* (Boston: Little & Brown, 1853), 424.

[2] See Henry S. Drinker, "Some Observations on the Four Freedoms of the First Amendment," *Boston University Law Review* 37 (1957): 1; Arthur E. Sutherland, Jr., "Due Process and Disestablishment," *Harvard Law Review* 62 (1949): 1309.

societies to provide for support of religious teachers other than Protestants. *Hale v. Everett*, 53 N.H. 9 (1868).

## Prohibition of Use of Public Money for Sectarian Purposes

The second part of Article 6 prohibits the use of public money for sectarian purposes. In an advisory opinion, the court suggested that this prohibition would make unconstitutional the proposed use of school vouchers to allow parents dissatisfied with their children's school to send them to an alternative school. *Opinion of the Justices (Choice in Education)* (1992). The sending school would have been required to pay up to 75 percent of the tuition at the new school, and no safeguard existed to prevent the application of public tax moneys to sectarian purposes—namely, the payment of tuition at sectarian schools. On the other hand, a proposed law which provided that public money would be used for nursing scholarships did not violate the constitution, even though many hospitals providing the nursing training were conducted under the auspices of religious denominations; the court reasoned that the funds would be devoted to the public purpose of nurse training and not used for sectarian purposes. *Opinion of the Justices* (1955).

## Equal Protection of All Denominations and Sects

The third part of the article was amended in 1968 to remove a sectarian reference to protection under the law for "every denomination of Christians"; the provision now refers to "every person, denomination or sect." The equality of all denominations and religious sects in the eyes of the law has long been recognized. *Union Baptist Society v. Town of Candia* (1819). Connected to this concept is the separation of church and state, a fundamental constitutional doctrine affirmed in *Muzzy v. Wilkins* (1803), a case that predates the formally reported New Hampshire Supreme Court cases, which began in 1816.

The court has relied upon this part of Article 6 in upholding the legislative property tax exemption for churches. In *Warde v. Manchester* (1876), the city of Manchester attempted to tax the property being used as a school for young women run by Roman Catholic Sisters of Mercy, despite the legislature having granted property tax exemptions for "all houses of public worship, school-houses, and seminaries of learning." Noting that "the protestant religion is regarded with peculiar favor" under Article 6, the court reasoned that every denomination of Christians was equally under the protection of the law, so that the school run by the Sisters of Mercy was entitled to the tax exemption. The court later held that a parish house used for some religious and some secular uses qualified for the tax exemption. See *St. Paul's Church v. City of Concord* (1910).

The court has applied the principle of equality of denominations and sects under the law in the family law context, when parents involved in a divorce custody battle have different and conflicting religious beliefs. A court may not favor one party's religious beliefs over the other party's, and may consider religious beliefs only as they relate to "the concerns and temporal welfare" of the child, see *Sanborn v. Sanborn* (1983), but a court may properly consider the manner in which a parent chooses to impart these beliefs to a child, see *Chandler v. Bishop* (1997).

### [ART.] 7. [STATE SOVEREIGNTY.]

The people of this state have the sole and exclusive right of governing themselves as a free, sovereign, and independent state; and do, and forever hereafter shall, exercise and enjoy every power, jurisdiction, and right, pertaining thereto, which is not, or may not hereafter be, by them expressly delegated to the United States of America in congress assembled. *1784.*

This article states that the people of the state are sovereign and is nearly identical to Part 1, Article 4 of the Massachusetts Constitution of 1780. The New Hampshire convention changed "Commonwealth" to "state," and clarified that the people enjoy the rights "pertaining" to state sovereignty. Both articles include the idea that people enjoy these rights except when they are *expressly* delegated to the U.S. Congress.

Sovereign powers are those deemed essential to the maintenance of government and incapable of alienation or impairment. These include the police powers and the powers of taxation and eminent domain. *Trustees of Phillips Exeter Academy v. Exeter* (1940). The people and not their elected representatives are the true sovereign power of the state; accordingly, there are limitations on the powers of the state legislature. For example, the legislature cannot grant an irrevocable tax exemption. *Id.* On the other hand, the New Hampshire Supreme Court held that the legislature does have the power to create an interstate school district, when that district had received all other necessary state and federal approvals. *Dresden School District v. Hanover School District* (1964).

The sovereign power of the state extends only to its borders. Thus a police officer in hot pursuit cannot arrest a person beyond the territorial jurisdiction of the state of New Hampshire. *State v. Goff* (1978). If an officer believed the offender was a fleeing felon, an exception would apply under the Uniform Law on Interstate Fresh Pursuit. *Id.*

In the late 1970s, the court addressed Article 7 in two cases involving federal aid. In *Opinion of the Justices* (1978), the court concluded that the governor could not disregard the legislature's selection of the state's health and human services department as the state health planning and development agency for the purposes of federal funds. The legislative act superseded the governor's executive order, even though Congress had passed a law requiring the governor of each state to designate a state health planning and development agency to administer the use of federal funds. Article 7, the court reasoned, gives the people the exclusive right to govern themselves, subject only to powers or rights "by them expressly delegated to the United States," and New Hampshire had not delegated to the federal government the authority to decide how the state would organize health planning. In a case decided soon after the court issued this advisory opinion, *In re Jack O'Lantern* (1978), the court again noted the potential of federal aid to threaten the state sovereignty. There, the court addressed the concern that a federal highway official may have tainted a state administrative hearing by impliedly suggesting that federal aid could be endangered should the administrative body make the "wrong" decision.

### [ART.] 8. [ACCOUNTABILITY OF MAGISTRATES AND OFFICERS; PUBLIC'S RIGHT TO KNOW.]

All power residing originally in, and being derived from, the people, all the magistrates and officers of government are their substitutes and agents, and at all times accountable to them. Government, therefore, should be open, accessible, accountable and responsive. To that end, the public's right of access to governmental proceedings and records shall not be unreasonably restricted. *1784; amended 1976.*

When originally drafted as a part of the 1784 New Hampshire Constitution, Article 8 consisted of just the first sentence explaining that power derives from the people and government should be held accountable to them. The framers based this article upon the similarly worded provision in Part 1, Article 5 of the Massachusetts Constitution of 1780. The remainder was added upon the recommendation of the bill of rights committee to the 1974 constitutional convention and adopted in 1976. This second part provides that government should be open and the public's access to "governmental proceedings and records" should not be "unreasonably restricted." New Hampshire already had a state law on the subject of the public's right to access, but the committee argued that the right was "extremely important and ought to be guaranteed by a constitutional provision."[3] The amendment accordingly added a constitutional dimension to the state's Right-to-Know Law. See *Lodge v. Knowlton* (1978).

The first part of the article should be read in conjunction with Article 7, which affirms that the people and not their government are sovereign. *Opinion of the Justices* (1971). But the people relinquish some of their power in electing representatives, and the accountability of the magistrates and officers to the people form the foundation of a representative democracy in which legislation of a general character affecting the whole state may be enacted only by

[3] *Journal of the Convention to Revise the Constitution*, May 1974 (Concord, NH: Evans Printing Co., 1975), 170–171.

the legislature, which consists of the agents of the people. Article 8 has long been used to support the proposition that state-wide referenda are not constitutional because only the legislature can enact the laws. As explained by the court in *State ex rel. Pearson v. Hayes* (1881), if the legislature delegated its constitutional law making powers, its purpose "would be entirely frustrated, as it would cease to be a representative body, and would become a mere proposer of laws for the consideration and final action of some third person or body." The court affirmed this reasoning in a 1999 case concerning a proposed referendum that would have allowed voters to decide between two different tax plans to provide state funding for education. *Opinion of the Justices (Tax Plan Referendum)* (1999).

Magistrates and officers are "accountable" under the constitution in that they are often-elected officers and at the time of election the people can choose to withdraw support and replace them. Another question of accountability arose in a case in which proposed legislation would have required the speaker of the house to be elected by a roll call vote. The court concluded that Article 8 created no special method of accountability under the constitution and did not require that the speaker be elected by a recorded vote. *Opinion of the Justices* (1971).

This article has been interpreted as affirming the power of the citizenry to be involved in governmental decision-making. Indeed, the court has found support in Article 8 for the legislature's authority to treat governmental units and private parties differently in tort cases. For instance, the court upheld a monetary limit on tort recovery for bodily injuries against governmental units, reasoning that such limits created incentives to reduce risks. "In the public sector," after all, "citizens can participate in the decisions that create the risk of injuries, including the selection and disciplining of public employees." *Estate of Cargill v. City of Rochester* (1979).

Under Article 8 and the Right-to-Know Law, the public should have the greatest possible access to the actions of all public bodies. *Union Leader Corporation v. City of Nashua* (1996). The legislature has exempted from public disclosure certain specific records. "These categorical exemptions mean not that the information is *per se* exempt, but rather that it is sufficiently private that it must be balanced against the public's interest in disclosure." *Union Leader Corp. v. New Hampshire Hous. Fin. Auth.* (1997).

There is a presumption in favor of disclosure under the Right-to-Know Law, but the court must first determine whether a privacy interest would be invaded. The court has set out procedures and standards to be used when a member of the public or the press seeks access to sealed court records, holding that the burden of proof rests with the party seeking closure or nondisclosure of records to demonstrate some overriding consideration that outweighs the public's right of access. *Petition of Keene Sentinel* (1992). This is a heavy burden, and the defendants in *Petition of Keene Sentinel* who sought to keep sealed divorce records from disclosure were not successful. When a party seeks court records, it does not matter if the records sought are civil or criminal or if they are sought at some time after the final decision. As the court has explained, "the public right of access to court proceedings and records pre-dates the State and Federal Constitutions and is firmly grounded in the common law, which provides that, absent special circumstances, those things which are filed in court in connection with a pending case are open to public inspection." *Associated Press v. State* (2005).

Cases have arisen under the right-to-know section of this article when newspapers sought and were denied access to records. Newspapers have successfully sought access to a police investigative file regarding a driving while intoxicated (DWI) arrest, see *Union Leader Corporation v. City of Nashua* (1996); records of the state housing finance authority in the form of an index, see *Union Leader Corporation v. New Hampshire Housing Finance Authority* (1997); and the names of retired public employees who received payments from public employee retirement plan and amounts of those payments, see *Union Leader Corp. v. New Hampshire Retirement System* (2011). Nonetheless, the right to know is not without limits: the court has held, for example, that Article 8 did not require the house of representatives to provide tapes of a legislative session to a newspaper for the purpose of stress analysis, because the session was open to the public, an official journal was prepared, and written transcripts were available. *Union Leader Corporation v. Chandler* (1979).

### [ART.] 9. [NO HEREDITARY OFFICE OR PLACE.]

No office or place, whatsoever, in government, shall be hereditary—the abilities and integrity requisite in all, not being transmissible to posterity or relations. *1784.*

This article is a more concise version of Part 1, Article 6 of the Massachusetts Constitution of 1780. It embodies the rejection of the tradition of hereditary offices, a tradition citizens of New Hampshire experienced firsthand when they lived under British rule. Though the New Hampshire Supreme Court has not addressed this article, its Massachusetts counterpart has been interpreted to allow the conferral of a benefit, privilege, or right so long as such conferral is an incidental effect of a statute primarily concerned with the public welfare. See, e.g., *Boston & A.R.R. v. Reardon* (1917) (because the real estate of railroads "is in a sense impressed with a public use," the legislature may protect such property from claims of adverse possession).

### [ART.] 10. [RIGHT OF REVOLUTION.]

Government being instituted for the common benefit, protection, and security, of the whole community, and not for the private interest or emolument of any one man, family, or class of men; therefore, whenever the ends of government are perverted, and public liberty manifestly endangered, and all other means of redress are ineffectual, the people may, and of right ought to reform the old, or establish a new government. The doctrine of nonresistance against arbitrary power, and oppression, is absurd, slavish, and destructive of the good and happiness of mankind. *1784.*

The first provision of this article announces the general principle of equality, which "pervades the entire constitution" and generally prohibits discrimination between citizens. *State v. Pennoyer* (1889). But this article is probably best known for its declaration of a "right of revolution" toward the end of the first sentence, with the rationale for this right detailed in the second sentence. The first part of this article is similar to Part 1, Article 7 of the Massachusetts Constitution of 1780. Then, beginning with the phrase "whenever the ends of government are perverted" and through the last sentence, the article is identical to part of Article 4 of the Declaration of Rights of the Maryland Constitution of 1776.

## Common Benefit

Many of the cases decided under this article concern the commitment to equality contained in the "common benefit" clause. In 1873, for example, the New Hampshire Supreme Court noted the provision's hostility "to the creation of discriminating and unreasonable privileges and immunities." *Delancey v. Insurance Co.* (1873). The court relied upon this article in an 1880 case concerning taxation of railroad express companies; the court held the railroad tax law unconstitutional because it provided for unequal division of public expense. *State v. U.S. & Canada Express Co.* (1880).

In the twentieth century, the court highlighted the equality principle contained in Article 10 in numerous cases. In a 1933 advisory opinion, the court interpreted Article 10, in conjunction with Articles 1, 12, and 14 of the bill of rights, to conclude that the principle of equality required that legal remedies must be available to everyone. The court accordingly found unconstitutional a proposed law which set different standards of access to justice for certain employers by denying them equitable relief in court. *Opinion of the Justices* (1933).

In *Rosenblum v. Griffin* (1938), the court made clear that "the organic principle of equality includes within its application a granted privilege as well as a regulated right. Equality of benefit is no less required than equality of burden." In *Rosenblum,* the court applied the equality principle to a granted privilege—that of holding a driver's license—and concluded that the requirement of proof of security or insurance for the registration of a motor vehicle on which a lien existed amounted to an arbitrary classification.

The court again relied upon this article in a 1954 case in which it concluded that a redevelopment project for low-income housing was instituted for the "common benefit . . . of the whole community, and not for the private interest or emolument of any one man, family, or class of men, but for the benefit and welfare of this state." The court upheld the law, which allowed the taking by eminent domain of nonblighted property as part of a redevelopment project. *Velishka v. City of Nashua* (1954).

More recently, in *In re Town of Bethlehem* (2006), the court held that the equality principle "does not require absolute equality of burden in the case of tax exemptions, provided that the statute at issue advances a public purpose and is properly within the legislature's discretion in acting for the welfare of the state." The court similarly reasoned in *In re Town of Rindge* (2008), that a tax exemption granted by the Department of Environmental Services "promoted proper objects of public welfare and public interest, and did not create an unconstitutional unequal benefit."

## Right of Revolution

The "right of revolution" was an expression of the political philosophy from the time the colony of New Hampshire became a state. This provision constitutionalized the common law principles regarding excessive exercise of power and its usurpation, including the right of the people to alter their state government. *Trustees of Phillips Exeter Academy v. Exeter* (1940).

The right of revolution, however, is limited. The court has held that "the right reserved to the people by this Article is not such a broad and unlimited right of insurrection and rebellion as to permit any group which is dissatisfied with existing government to lawfully attempt at any time to overthrow the government by force or violence." Rather, the right to resist and to reform government exists only when "the ends of government" are "perverted, . . . public liberty manifestly endangered, and all other means of redress . . . ineffectual." *Nelson v. Wyman* (1954). Thus Article 10 did not justify resistance to the government during the McCarthy era, for the constitution does not preclude the legislature from proscribing activities aimed at overthrowing the government by force or violence. See *id.*

As well, the court has concluded that the ends of government were not perverted by allowing a city council, rather than the citizens, to vote on the city budget. *City of Claremont v. Craigue* (1992). The court held that such a procedure hardly "perverts" the ends of government or manifestly endangers public liberty, so long as the city's voters retain the right to elect their local representatives. The persons challenging the procedure also had not "exhausted all other means of legal redress."

### [ART.] 11. [ELECTIONS AND ELECTIVE FRANCHISES.]

All elections are to be free, and every inhabitant of the state of 18 years of age and upwards shall have an equal right to vote in any election. Every person shall be considered an inhabitant for the purposes of voting in the town, ward, or unincorporated place where he has his domicile. No person shall have the right to vote under the constitution of this state who has been convicted of treason, bribery or any willful violation of the election laws of this state or of the United States; but the supreme court may, on notice to the attorney general, restore the privilege to vote to any person who may have forfeited it by conviction of such offenses. The general court shall provide by law for voting by qualified voters who at the time of the biennial or state elections, or of the primary elections therefor, or of city elections, or of town elections by official ballot, are absent from the city or town of which they are inhabitants, or who by reason of physical disability are unable to vote in person, in the choice of any officer or officers to be elected or upon any question submitted at such election. Voting registration and polling places shall be easily accessible to all persons including disabled and elderly persons who are otherwise qualified to vote in the choice of any officer or officers to be elected or upon any question submitted at such election. The right to vote shall not be denied to any person because of the non-payment of any tax. Every inhabitant of the state, having the proper qualifications, has equal right to be elected into office. *1784; amended in 1903, 1912, 1942, 1956, 1968, 1976, and 1984.*

This article outlines a number of rights related to voting and elections. The 1784 version of this article was based on Part 1, Article 9 of the Massachusetts Constitution of 1780 and originally provided for free elections and guaranteed to every inhabitant of the state with proper qualifications the right to vote or be elected to office. Over the years, the article has been amended numerous times.

In 1903, the voters supported an amendment to add a test for voting and holding office, to determine whether individuals were able to write and to read the constitution in the English language. The amendment exempted from this requirement persons with physical disabilities and persons sixty years old or older as of January 1904. This amendment remained a part of Article 11 until 1976; by that time, Congress had suspended all literacy tests through an amendment to the federal Voting Rights Act of 1965.

In 1912, the voters adopted an amendment prohibiting any person from voting or being eligible for office who had been convicted of treason, bribery, or willful violation to the election laws, though the state supreme court had the authority to restore such privileges. In 1942, the voters added a provision to allow absentee voting in biennial or state elections and city elections. The absentee voting right was expanded in 1956 to include primary elections.

The voters adopted two separate amendments to Article 11 in 1968. The first added the penultimate sentence to the article, stating that no person could be denied the right to vote because of nonpayment of taxes. The second amendment removed a provision regarding the ability of sixty-year old persons to vote on January 1, 1904; because the provision only could have applied to persons older than one hundred twenty, it was deemed obsolete.

Consistent with the Twenty-Sixth Amendment to the U.S. Constitution (ratified in 1971), the voters amended Article 11 in 1976 to fix the minimum voting age at eighteen. In 1984, the voters amended this article once again to add a sentence requiring all registration and polling places to be accessible.

## Right to Vote and Be Elected to Office

Under this article, the rights to vote and to be elected to office are coextensive: the qualifications for voting are the same as the qualifications for elective office, unless otherwise provided by the state constitution. For example, Part 2, Articles 29, 42, and 61 provide for a minimum age for the offices of governor, senator, and executive councilor that is higher than the minimum age for voting and for holding other elective offices. Relying upon this principle in a 1927 advisory opinion, the New Hampshire Supreme Court held that when the Nineteenth Amendment to the U.S. Constitution afforded women the right to vote, it also afforded them the right to hold elective office. *Opinion of the Justices* (1927).

Under Article 11, to vote or to be elected to office, a person must be at least eighteen years of age, an inhabitant of the state, and not have previously been convicted of treason, bribery, or a willful violation of state or federal election laws. While voting rights under this article are deemed fundamental, they are not absolute; the legislature has the authority to subject the elective franchise to reasonable regulation. *Wilkes v. Jackson* (1958).

### *Age*

Pursuant to Article 11, "every inhabitant of the state of 18 years of age and upwards shall have an equal right to vote in any election." The New Hampshire Supreme Court addressed this seemingly straightforward requirement in advisory opinions on proposals to permit persons aged seventeen to vote in state or presidential primaries preceding a national election at which the person would be eighteen years old. The court concluded in 2008 that a primary election is an "election" within the meaning of the state constitutional provision governing the right to vote, and that "general provisions as to qualifications of voters under the state constitution are applicable to voters at party primaries." *Opinion of the Justices (Voting Age in Primaries)* (2008). In a 2009 opinion, the court reasoned that the constitutional age requirement worked to preserve the "integrity, fairness, and efficiency of the election process, and in having an informed electorate and assuring that those who vote are sufficiently mature to exercise their right to vote meaningfully." *Opinion of the Justices (Voting Age in Primary Elections II)* (2009).

### *Felony Disfranchisement*

The legislature has the authority to deny felons the right to be candidates for or elected to office. Indeed, by its terms Article 11 automatically disqualifies a person convicted of certain felonies from voting and holding public office.

In *Paey v. Rodrigue* (1979), the New Hampshire version of the Uniform Act on Status of Convicted Persons barred a town selectman from holding office. Under the law, a person holding public office forfeited that office when sentenced for a felony defined as a "crime committed against the laws of this state or of the federal government for which a sentence of death or imprisonment in the state prison or federal prison or penitentiary." *Id.* While the selectman was convicted in federal court for interstate transportation of stolen merchandise and conspiracy, he served time in a "jail type institution" for only forty days of his three-year sentence, and then was placed on probation. The court found his disqualification to be proper because it was based on the possible sentence associated with the felony, and not the sentence actually imposed.

In *Fischer v. Governor* (2000), the court addressed a prisoner's challenge to the felony disenfranchisement statutes. The plaintiff, a prisoner incarcerated for the felonies of attempted first-degree assault and witness tampering, argued that only age, domicile, and conviction for the enumerated offenses of treason, bribery, or willful violation of the election laws could be the basis for a restriction on the right to vote. Before Article 11 was amended in 1976, the first sentence of the article had remained the same since 1784 and gave "every inhabitant of the State, having the proper qualifications, [the] equal right to elect and be elected into office." The 1976 amendment restructured the article and moved the "proper qualifications" language to the new, final sentence granting inhabitants an equal right to run for elective office.

The court concluded that the amendment had not been intended to eliminate the historic authority of the legislature to define voter qualifications beyond those listed in Article 11. As presented to the voters in 1976, the constitutional amendment on voting rights involved changes to or repeal of several different articles. In the question stated to the voters, there was no mention of eliminating legislative authority to define voter qualifications. Since the people were never given notice that the amendment would have any effect on the legislature's historic authority to determine voter qualifications, the court concluded the article "was not properly amended to cause the removal of 'proper qualifications' from the voting clause," and, accordingly, the legislature retained its authority to determine voter qualifications. Further, the court could not say it was "unreasonable for the legislature to conclude that a citizen who commits a felony and is incarcerated also abandons the right to participate in voting for those who create and enforce the laws." *Id.*

### *Absentee Voting*

Legislative enactments regarding absentee voting first appeared in the Civil War period. In 1863, the court held unconstitutional a proposed bill that would have allowed a soldier to mark a ballot and send it to a person holding a power of attorney, who would then cast the ballot for him; the court reasoned that such a law would violate the common law rule that every vote must be personally given. *Opinion of the Justices* (1863). A year later, in 1864, the legislature enacted a law which allowed qualified voters in the military service to vote for certain federal offices (president, vice president, representative in Congress) in the places where they were located instead of at their homes. In other words, these soldiers voted in person and not as absentees at specially designated polling places.

In 1921, the court held unconstitutional a proposed act that would have allowed persons absent or who had a physical disability which prevented them from coming to the polls to vote at biennial elections by absentee ballot. The proposed law was modeled on a Massachusetts statute, which had been enacted after an amendment to the Massachusetts Constitution to allow for absentee voting. *Opinion of the Justices* (1921). The court reasoned that the legislature did not have the authority to provide for absentee voting in the absence of an express amendment to the constitution allowing for it. Despite this advisory ruling, the legislature enacted an absentee voting law in 1925. In 1930 and 1938, constitutional amendments allowing absentee voting met with defeat at the polls. But in 1942 the voters approved an amendment allowing for absentee voting in general elections, which presumably ratified the 1925 law.

## Sanctity of the Individual Vote

The court has held that Article 11 guarantees equal weight to the vote of each citizen. The state constitutional foundation for the one person/one vote standard may be found in many redistricting cases. See *Below v. Gardner* (2002) (redistricting of senate); *Burling v. Chandler* (2002) (redistricting of house of representatives). In *Below* and *Burling*, the court held that the then-current system of redistricting failed to meet constitutional standards; further discussion of these cases may be found below in the sections discussing Part 2, Article 26 (senate) and Article 9 (house).

In *Sununu Ballot Law Commission* (1982), the court addressed the issue of "double voting." The case involved a gubernatorial nominee who challenged the validity of nomination papers filed by a second candidate. Voters who had participated in the primary had also signed a petition for the second candidate to be on the ballot for the general election. The court concluded that voting in an election means casting a direct vote—which is not the same as signing a nomination petition. Accordingly, the signing of nomination petitions by individuals who later voted in the state primary did not constitute illegal "double voting."

The court has held that statutes regulating the form of ballots should not be applied to disenfranchise voters because of technical irregularities, and that no voter should be denied the franchise due to a "lack of ballot." *Opinion of the Justices* (1974). The court in a 1997 case concluded that the attempt to vote for a write-in candidate by use of an unapproved sticker on the ballot was invalid, even though voters' intent was clear, because a voter's choice must conform to reasonable regulations concerning the expression of that choice. *Kibbe v. Town of Milton* (1997).

## Violation of Election Laws

Several cases have interpreted the language in Article 11 regarding an individual's "willful violation of election laws" as disqualifying one from holding public office. Typically the cases have been concerned with challenges to the election of a person who has been charged or convicted of some technical violation of campaign laws. A notable example is that of Hugh Gregg, a successful gubernatorial candidate in the 1952 Republican primary, whose report of his campaign receipts and expenditures, as required by law, contained some inaccuracies. The court concluded this was not a "willful violation" of the state election laws so as to disqualify Gregg from nomination, because he had made an honest and reasonable effort to comply with the provisions of the statute requiring the reporting of campaign expenses. *Daniell v. Gregg* (1952).

Another technical violation which did not amount to a "willful violation" occurred when a candidate's posters, which had been purchased for a former primary campaign in 1962, failed to comply with a law requiring that they bear the name and address of the candidate or the candidate's fiscal agent. Since only a small portion of the candidate's total political advertising at the primary election was not in compliance with the law, the court concluded there had been no "willful violation." *Lavoie v. Tufis* (1964).

## Voter Access to Polls and Registration Places

The voters in 1984 approved an amendment adding voter accessibility requirements for elderly and disabled persons to Article 11, the same year that they approved adding Part 1, Article 28-a to the constitution, which essentially prohibits unfunded mandates. In an opinion to the executive director of the Governor's Commission for the Handicapped in 1986, the attorney general stated that Article 28-a did not relieve local officials of the obligation to provide accessible voting and registration places, because that article's requirements only apply to "state" action in the form of legislation; a constitutional requirement, by contrast, expresses the sovereign will of the people. See 1986 *Opinions of the Attorney General*, at 60.

### [ART.] 12. [PROTECTION AND TAXATION RECIPROCAL.]

Every member of the community has a right to be protected by it, in the enjoyment of his life, liberty, and property; he is therefore bound to contribute his share in the expense of such protection, and to yield his personal service when necessary. But no part of a man's property shall be taken from him, or applied to public uses, without his own consent, or that of the representative body of the people. Nor are the inhabitants of this state controllable by any other laws than those to which they, or their representative body, have given their consent. *1784; amended 1964.*

This article declares the reciprocal obligations of the social contract, reiterates the principle of equal treatment of citizens, protects against the taking of property without compensation, and states that individuals are not bound by laws to which they or their representatives did not give consent. The framers based this article on Part 1, Article 10 of the Massachusetts Constitution of 1780. The voters have amended this article once, in 1964, to remove a reference to the ability to pay "an equivalent" instead of yielding necessary personal service—an obsolete reference to buying one's way out of military service. For a full discussion of the equality principle embraced by this article, see the discussions under Articles 2 and 10 concerning the equality protections of the New Hampshire Constitution.

## Reciprocal Obligations of the Social Contract

In an 1829 advisory opinion, the New Hampshire Supreme Court discussed the theory behind the use of taxation as a means of supporting the reciprocal social contract. The court stated that the share of the expense of protection furnished by the state to an individual is that individual's proportionate share of the entire expense, measured according to the amount of the individual's taxable estate. See *Opinion of the Justices,* 4 N.H. 565 (1829). The court further recognized that such tax must not be merely proportional, but in due proportion, so that each individual will pay only his just share. Though the application of this fundamental principle has only become more complicated over time, its basic premise continues to be applied today. See, e.g., *Rollins v. City of Dover* (1945); *First Berkshire Bus. Trust v. Comm'r, New Hampshire Dept. of Revenue Admin.* (2010).

Together with Part 2, Article 5, this article establishes that equality and justice are the guideposts for all taxation consistent with the constitution. *Smith v. New Hampshire Department of Revenue Administration* (1997). Combined with Part 2, Article 6, these provisions require "that taxation be just, uniform, equal, and proportional; in addition, our constitution demands that classifications be made between types of property, not taxpayers." *Id.* Applying these rules, the court has concluded that the legislature may not create two classes of taxpayers paying differing rates on essentially the same class of property. See *Opinion of the Justices* (1989). Further, when a tax is a disproportionate, unequal assessment it becomes confiscatory. *Rollins v. City of Dover* (1945) illustrates this concept; there, the court held the plaintiff had been overassessed given that the ratio of assessed value was higher than the market value of the taxable property.

Taxation is not the only way in which an individual might be required to pay his or her share in fulfillment of the social contract. The state may recoup costs from individuals whose needs become a burden on the state. In *State v. Haas* (2007), for instance, the court upheld a statute that required the defendant to reimburse the state for the costs of his legal representation, reasoning that the law was rationally related to government's interest in recouping costs expended for public defense from defendants who could afford to pay. In *Horner v. Governor* (2008), the court concluded that a fee imposed upon sex offenders for maintenance of a sex offender registry was not a tax but a proper charge upon individuals who create the need for such governmental services.

Finally, a person may be required to pay his share of the expense of government by "yielding his personal service" in exchange for society's protection and benefits. The yielding of one's personal service relates not only to military service, but to an individual's duty to participate in the administration of justice by appearing in obedience to a proper subpoena. *Boston & Maine Railroad v. State* (1910).

## No Taking without Compensation

This article "requires just compensation in the event of a taking." *Burrows v. City of Keene* (1981). Its origins may be traced to *Magna Charta*. The interests protected by this article include the right to use and enjoy a thing, and this protection is not limited to mere possession. *Eaton v. Boston, Concord, & Montreal Railroad* (1872). "A 'taking' occurs when the application of a regulation to a particular parcel denies the owner an economically viable use of his or her land." *Bio Energy, LLC v. Town of Hopkinton* (2005). A compensable taking may be accomplished in different ways. For example, it may be in accordance with eminent domain laws, see *Appeal of City of Keene* (1997) (eminent domain proceedings for an extraterritorial airport taking), or as consequence of a zoning ordinance. See *Sanderson v. Town of Candia* (2001) (taking claim arising out of application of zoning ordinance).

Private property may be taken by eminent domain only for public uses, but the power to take private property for public use may be exercised by the government through the means of a private corporation. See *Concord Railroad v. Greely* (1845). The court applies a balancing test to determine the necessity for a taking: if the social costs exceed the probable benefits of the proposed project, the project cannot be said to further a public use. *Merrill v. City of Manchester* (1985). The court has held that the use of land for each of the following purposes qualifies as a public use: a private toll road open to the public, see *In re Petition of ML Washington Road Co.* (1857); a toll bridge, see *Proprietors of the Piscataqua Bridge v. New Hampshire Bridge* (1834); a public highway, see *Peirce v. Somersworth* (1839); a railroad, see *Concord Railroad v. Greely* (1845); a public cemetery, see *Crowell v. Londonderry* (1884); and an electric company, see *Rockingham County Light & Power Co. v. Hobbs* (1904).

Because the court has deemed the right to property to be fundamental, "all subsequent grants of power, including the taxing power, are limited as to how they adversely affect it." *Thomas Tool Services, Inc. v. Town of Croydon* (2000). In *Thomas Tool Services*, for example, the plaintiff had failed to pay its property taxes and the town had acquired the property under the statutory tax lien procedure for only $370.26—significantly less than the $65,000 the taxpayer had originally paid. The court concluded that the state's tax lien procedure allowed the town to gain a surplus that amounted to an unduly harsh penalty on the delinquent taxpayer, in violation of Article 12.

Under the state zoning act, municipalities enjoy "broad authority to pass zoning ordinances for the health, safety, morals, and general welfare of the community." *Asselin v. Town of Conway* (1993). Though these ordinances are presumed valid, "arbitrary or unreasonable restrictions which substantially deprive the owner of the economically viable use of his land in order to benefit the public in some way constitute a taking." *Burrows, supra* (quotation omitted). For example, in *Burrows v. City of Keene, supra*, the court struck down an ordinance placing a substantial part of the plaintiff's land in a conservation district because "the city and its officials were attempting to obtain for the public the benefit of having this land remain undeveloped as open space without paying for that benefit in the constitutional manner." This article also protects the "grandfathering" in of preexisting, nonconforming uses subsequent to enactment of a zoning ordinance, see *Town of Hampton v. Brust* (1982), so long as the use is not a nuisance or harmful to the public health, see *Cohen v. Town of Henniker* (1991).

## Consent to Be Governed

The final sentence of this article states that individuals can be controlled only by laws to which they or their representatives have given their consent. A particular legislature cannot enact laws of permanently binding force, for this would infringe on the sovereignty of the people. See *Trustees of Phillips Exeter Academy v. Exeter* (1940).

### [ART.] 12-a. [POWER TO TAKE PROPERTY LIMITED.]

No part of a person's property shall be taken by eminent domain and transferred directly or indirectly, to another person if the taking is for the purpose of private development or other private use of property. *2006.*

Under this article, the power of eminent domain cannot be exercised for private purposes. Its origins may be traced to the U.S. Supreme Court's decision in *Kelo v. City of New London* (2005), holding that "a city's decision to take property for the purpose of economic development satisfies the 'public use' requirement of the Fifth Amendment."[4] This article has not been interpreted by the New Hampshire courts.

### [ART.] 13. [CONSCIENTIOUS OBJECTORS NOT COMPELLED TO BEAR ARMS.]

No person, who is conscientiously scrupulous about the lawfulness of bearing arms, shall be compelled thereto. *1784; amended 1964.*

This article prohibits compelling a conscientious objector to bear arms. The article was amended in 1964—along with Article 12—to eliminate a reference to paying an equivalent should a person be excused from military service because he or she is a conscientious objector. The original language of the article is nearly identical to part of Article VIII of the 1776 Pennsylvania Constitution's Declaration of Rights. Though John Adams and the framers of the Massachusetts Constitution of 1780 looked to the Pennsylvania Declaration of Rights for guidance, they did not include this particular provision in the Massachusetts Constitution.

The New Hampshire Supreme Court has yet to interpret this article. In *United States v. Seeger* (1965), the U.S. Supreme Court, construing a federal law, concluded the test for conscientious objector status is whether the individual's belief is commensurate with the "orthodox belief in God of one who clearly qualifies for the [statutory] exemption." The New Hampshire Supreme Court cited this test in *Appeal of Emissaries of the Divine Light* (1995), a case involving tax exemptions for religious organizations under state law; this reliance upon *Seeger* may give some indication of how the court would approach the task of defining conscientious objectors for the purpose of Article 13.

### [ART.] 14. [LEGAL REMEDIES TO BE FREE, COMPLETE, AND PROMPT.]

Every subject of this state is entitled to a certain remedy, by having recourse to the laws, for all injuries he may receive in his person, property, or character; to obtain right and justice freely, without being obliged to purchase it; completely, and without any denial; promptly, and without delay; conformably to the laws. *1784.*

---

[4] See Steven J. Eagle & Lauren A. Perotti, "Coping with *Kelo*: A Potpourri of Legislative and Judicial Responses," *Real Prop. Prob. & Tr. J.* 42 (2008): 799.

This article serves three basic purposes: to make civil remedies readily available without discrimination; to allow individuals to obtain justice without having to pay for it; and to grant criminal defendants the right to a speedy trial. The article closely resembles Part 1, Article 11 of the Massachusetts Constitution of 1780, and the origins of both may be traced to *Magna Charta*. See *State v. Basinow* (1977).

## Civil Remedies

The first part of the article concerns the equality of remedy to which all similarly situated litigants are entitled. *Estate of Cargill v. City of Rochester* (1979). Litigants have the right to appeal to the courts for relief and defense under the same conditions. *Opinion of the Justices (Limitation on Civil Actions)* (1993). The article's last clause—"conformably to the laws"—has been interpreted by the court to mean that remedies must conform to the rules of statutory and common law applicable at the time the injury was sustained. See *Sousa v. State* (1975).

The right to a civil remedy embraced by Article 14 is an "important substantive right." *Carson v. Maurer* (1980). At the same time, it is "necessarily relative" and must be balanced against the need for the practical administration of justice. *McLellan v. Cavanaugh* (1985). In other words, it "does not prohibit all impairments of the right of access." *Minuteman, LLC v. Microsoft Corp.* (2002). The court had held that this article does not prohibit all limitations or, in some circumstances, even a complete bar on access to the courts. In determining whether the right to a remedy has been undermined, the state courts apply a middle-tier standard of review pursuant to which the court must determine whether classifications made by the legislature which restrict recovery are reasonable and based on a difference which has a fair and substantial relation to the object of the legislation. *City of Dover v. Imperial Casualty & Indemnity Co.* (1990).

To justify the complete abolition of the right of any class of persons to recover, the law must provide a satisfactory substitute. In *Petition of Abbott* (1995), for example, the court concluded that employees covered by workers' compensation "are conclusively presumed to have waived the common law rights against their employers in return for the protection and benefits of the statutes." These schemes satisfy Article 14 so long as "they provide *quid pro quo* or an adequate substitute for statutory or common law rights extinguished" by the workers' compensation statutes. *Id.* The court has also concluded that, when a party may obtain relief even though it does not control the strategy of litigation, there is no violation of Article 14. See *State v. City of Dover* (2006).

A plaintiff may not have a remedy in a particular case simply because the injuries claimed are not in fact actionable. In *Welzenbach v. Powers* (1995), for example, the court concluded that the plaintiff had stated no actionable claim against the mother of his child born out of wedlock simply because she had assured him she was using contraception. Public policy would not support such a claim and could, "like Robert Frost's stone wall," be viewed "with a purpose to determine what claims are walled in and what claims are walled out." *Id.*

Examples of cases in which the court held a challenged classification constitutional include *Estate of Cargill, supra* (statute limiting tort recovery from governmental units served legislative goal of defining the liability to which governmental units would be exposed), and *Opinion of the Justices (Limitation on Civil Actions)* (1993) (law would delay defendant's civil action against a criminal sexual assault victim during the pendency of the criminal action, when defendant's case was based upon certain statements or reports made by the victim). Examples of cases in which the court held a challenged classification unconstitutional include *City of Dover v. Imperial Casualty & Indemnity Co.* (1990) (statute giving complete immunity to municipalities for certain actions in negligence denied parties injured on municipal highways and sidewalks opportunity to recover); *Trovato v. Deveau* (1999) (wrongful death statute cannot distinguish for purposes of damages between death causally related to the injury and death unrelated to the injury); and *State v. Brosseau* (1983) (doctrine of sovereign immunity unconstitutional to the extent it prevented an injured person from receiving a just remedy).

## Obtaining Justice without Having to Pay

The court has held that the object of the right "to obtain right and justice freely, without being obliged to purchase it" is to prevent bribery or the appearance of bribery in the judicial system. Avoiding the appearance of bribery, moreover, is as important as avoiding actual bribery. *Christy & Terrier v. Witte* (1985).

Relying upon this provision, the court in *In re Estate of Dionne* (1986) addressed the long-standing practice of probate court judges' special session fees. Though at the time probate court judges received a salary from the state, they also received compensation for hearing cases on days when the court was not sitting in a regularly scheduled session. The court held this rule unconstitutional, because this "method of compensating probate judges for special sessions smack[ed] of the purchase of justice, and [wa]s therefore anathema to the New Hampshire Constitution." *Id.*

This article has been interpreted as prohibiting fees paid to expedite or delay the administration of justice and not ordinary court filing fees. Thus the court concluded that an $8 filing fee required for an appeal from a conviction for a parking violation, when the defendant was not indigent, did not violate the article. See *State v. Basinow* (1977). But a superior court rule requiring a defendant found guilty of a misdemeanor in a district or municipal court to pay an $8 fee to appeal to the superior court for a de novo jury trial did violate this article; because the right to a jury trial is fundamental to the criminal justice system the state could not condition the right upon the payment of even a nominal fee. See *State v. Cushing* (1979).

## Right to Speedy Trial

The right to a speedy trial refers to the right of a person charged with a crime to be free from capricious and oppressive delay in receiving a trial. There is no mechanical rule for determining whether the right to a speedy trial has been violated, because the right is relative and considered with regard to the practical administration of justice. See *McLellan v. Cavanaugh* (1985). In 1978, the court adopted the four-factor balancing test used by the U.S. Supreme Court to assess speedy trial claims under the federal constitution: a court must balance the length of delay, the reasons for the delay, the defendant's assertion of his speedy trial rights, and any prejudice suffered by the defendant, to determine whether the right to a speedy trial was violated. See *State v. Cole* (1978).

The first factor, the length of the delay, is a triggering mechanism, and a court will not "consider the remaining factors unless the delay is presumptively prejudicial." *State v. Locke* (2002). The clock begins to run at the time of arrest, and not at the time of a later indictment. Although there is no specific amount of time between arrest and trial which would qualify as a clear violation of the right to a speedy trial, the court has found prejudicial a delay of more than two years between the date of indictment and the date of trial, see *State v. Stow* (1993), while it concluded that a ten-month delay should not be presumed automatically prejudicial, see *State v. Isaac* (1979).

### [ART.] 15. [RIGHT OF ACCUSED.]

No subject shall be held to answer for any crime, or offense, until the same is fully and plainly, substantially and formally, described to him; or be compelled to accuse or furnish evidence against himself. Every subject shall have a right to produce all proofs that may be favorable to himself; to meet the witnesses against him face to face, and to be fully heard in his defense, by himself, and counsel. No subject shall be arrested, imprisoned, despoiled, or deprived of his property, immunities, or privileges, put out of the protection of the law, exiled or deprived of his life, liberty, or estate, but by the judgment of his peers, or the law of the land; provided that, in any proceeding to commit a person acquitted of a criminal charge by reason of insanity, due process shall require that clear and convincing evidence that the person is potentially dangerous to himself or to others and that the person suffers from a mental disorder must be established. Every person held to answer in any crime or offense punishable by deprivation of liberty shall have the right to counsel at the expense of the state if need is shown; this right he is at liberty to waive, but only after the matter has been thoroughly explained by the court. *1784; amended 1966, 1984.*

This article secures to individuals an array of criminal procedure protections; it also preserves the right not to be deprived of life, liberty, or property without due process of law. The framers of the 1784 constitution based this article on the Part 1, Article 12 of the Massachusetts Constitution of 1780. Since that time, there have been two additions to the original text: in 1966, the voters approved an amendment providing for counsel at the state's expense in criminal cases, upon a showing of need; and, in 1984, they approved an amendment which lowered the legal requirement in criminal insanity commitment hearings from proof beyond a reasonable doubt to clear and convincing evidence.

## Adequacy of Indictments

The New Hampshire Supreme Court has long recognized that Article 15 requires that an indictment provide a full and fair description of the offense charged, *State v. Silverman* (1912), so that a defendant may prepare for trial, see *State v. Rouston* (1929). A defendant, the court has stated, "has a right to rely upon the information contained in an indictment in preparing his defense, and a court cannot permit a defendant to be tried on charges that are not made in the indictment against him." *State v. Erickson* (1987). This protection also serves to prevent a later prosecution for the same offense. *State v. O'Neill* (1962).

The court has defined a valid indictment as one that gives the defendant sufficient information to prepare for trial by setting forth all the elements of an offense, see *State v. Taylor* (1981), and that contains well-pleaded facts, see *State v. Therrien* (1987). "Once a crime has been identified with factual specificity, acts by which the defendant may have committed the crime need not be identified." *State v. Demond-Surace* (2011). Statutory crimes may generally be described in the words of the statute. *State v. Goodwin* (1958). An indictment may not be duplicitous; if the state were permitted to charge more than one offense in a particular count, the defendant would not be adequately informed of the charge he must meet. *State v. Wright* (1985).

The court had an opportunity to explain the dimensions of Article 15 in the indictment context in *State v. Oakes* (2010), in which the lower court permitted the state to amend the indictments against the defendant, who maintained the changes were substantive and not merely "a change in form." The court reasoned that, because the amendment had the effect of "specifying and circumscribing the scope of the crime alleged," to prevail the defendant had to prove it undermined his ability to properly understand the charges or prepare his defense. *Id.* The court held that the defendant had failed to carry this burden: he could not demonstrate prejudice, and his asserted defenses did not depend upon information in the indictment that had changed following the amendment. *Id.*

## Competency

Under Article 15, a criminal defendant cannot stand trial if he is legally incompetent. *State v. Zorzy* (1993). The courts apply a two-pronged test to determine competency. "First, the defendant must have a sufficient present ability to consult with and assist his lawyer with a reasonable degree of rational understanding. Second, the defendant must have a factual as well as rational understanding of the proceedings against him." *Id.* The trial court must examine a defendant's competency to stand trial "whenever a bona fide or legitimate doubt arises" as to whether he is competent. *Id.*

In *State v. Kincaid* (2008), the court applied this test to conclude that a defendant who claimed amnesia was not incompetent to stand trial. The defendant argued that, because he could not remember the events leading up to motor vehicle crash that resulted in a charge of negligent homicide, as well as what transpired immediately thereafter, he lacked the ability to consult with and assist his trial counsel in his defense. The court disagreed, reasoning that, even if the claim of amnesia was genuine, "[t]here are many ways a defendant can consult with and assist his trial counsel with a reasonable degree of rational understanding without necessarily remembering the details or circumstances of an event that led to his arrest." *Id.*

## Right to Counsel

The right to counsel has been deemed a fundamental right. The U.S. Supreme Court held in 1963 that the right to counsel "for an indigent person was guaranteed under the federal constitution." *Gideon v. Wainwright* (1963). At that time, New Hampshire provided a lawyer at public expense to indigent individuals accused of crimes punishable by more than six months in prison. The 1966 amendment to Article 15 guarantees counsel to individuals who could not afford one, no matter the period of potential incarceration.

The New Hampshire Supreme Court has noted that the right to counsel provided by the amendment covers "a broader range of criminal defendants than are granted a right to counsel" by the U.S. Constitution, see *State v. Scarborough* (1983), and at least as much protection as the federal constitution, see *State v. Drewry* (1995). The article guarantees the right to effective assistance of counsel. In order to be effective, the court has held that defense counsel must perform with "within the range of competence required of attorneys representing defendants in criminal cases." *State v. Staples* (1981). To prevail on a claim of ineffective assistance of counsel, a defendant must demonstrate "first, that counsel's representation was constitutionally deficient and, second, that counsel's deficient performance actually prejudiced the outcome of the case." *State v. McGurk* (2008).

## Privilege against Self-Incrimination

The New Hampshire Constitution has protected a privilege against self-incrimination since 1784. Article 15 prohibits a person from being compelled to testify as to his or her own criminality. No person can be required to make admissions tending to prove his or her guilt in respect to any crime with which he or she might later be charged. *State v. Nowell* (1878). The protections of this article accordingly may be claimed by witnesses, who are protected whenever an injurious disclosure could result. *State v. Wheeler* (1986).

Importantly, the privilege applies only to evidence of a testimonial character—that is, the kind of evidence that a witness would by traditional judicial processes be required to give. It does not apply to evidence obtained from fingerprinting, speaking for identification, or introducing evidence in court of a person's refusal to provide a sample for chemical testing. *State v. Cormier* (1985). The privilege, which is personal, see *State v. Cote* (1948), applies not only to answers that would support a conviction but to any information that would supply a link in the chain of evidence needed to prosecute, see *Key Bank v. Latshaw* (1993).

Article 15 protections apply only in the context of custodial interrogation—that is, in the context of a formal arrest "or restraint on freedom of movement to the degree associated with formal arrest." *State v. Jennings* (2007). When the defendant has not been formally arrested, a court must determine "whether a suspect's freedom of movement was sufficiently curtailed by considering how a reasonable person would have understood the situation." *Id.* In *Jennings,* the court concluded that, when three police officers and a prosecutor went to meet the defendant, and the police took his car keys and phone and patted him down, seated him in the interview room far from the door, and proceeded to interview him for nearly two hours, no reasonable person actually would have felt free to leave. *Id.* As the court noted in *Jennings,* "police conduct should be judged in terms of what was done rather than what the office may have called it at the time." *Id.* (quotation omitted).

To introduce into evidence statements made by a defendant during a custodial interrogation, "the State must prove beyond a reasonable doubt that the defendant was warned of his constitutional rights, that he waived those rights, and that any subsequent statements were made knowingly, voluntarily and intelligently." *State v. Zwicker* (2004). The requirement that the state prove a confession or a waiver of *Miranda* rights voluntary beyond a reasonable doubt imposes a heavier burden of proof on the state than does the preponderance of the evidence standard under the federal constitution. *State v. Laurie* (1992); *State v. Monroe* (1998).

The court has held that a voluntary confession is one which is "the product of an essentially free and unconstrained choice and not extracted by threats, violence, or direct or implied promises of any sort, or by exertion of any improper influence." *Zwicker, supra.* Whether a defendant's statement is voluntary is a determination for the trial court, in light of the totality of the surrounding circumstances. *State v. Bilodeau* (2010). The court may consider "a person's mental or developmental condition if it impairs his capacity for self-determination or his ability to resist police coercion." *Id.*

In *State v. Parker* (2010), the court addressed the question whether in an interviewing detective's promise of confidentiality, upon which the defendant relied, made his resulting statement involuntary. "For a confession to be involuntary, . . . an interrogator's promise must induce or cause the defendant to confess." *Id.* In *Parker*, the court concluded that the defendant "did not confess until after the detective's promise of confidentiality," and that there was no support in the record for the state's argument that the confession was "motivated by other factors, such as a private actor exhorting him to tell the truth or overwhelming physical evidence of guilt." *Id.*

## Right to Produce All Favorable Proofs

Under Article 15, a defendant has the right to produce all favorable proofs, but not to demand the introduction of evidence against the rules of evidence, see *State v. Newcomb* (1995), or evidence that confuses the issues or confounds the jury, see *State v. Woodsum* (1993). The defendant may compel witnesses to appear at trial, but cannot compel their testimony. *State v. Taylor* (1978). If a witness's right against self-incrimination conflicts with a defendant's right to produce all favorable proofs, the court must balance these competing interests. *State v. Lavallee* (1979).

Article 15 requires a prosecutor to provide a defendant with any evidence in her possession that is favorable to the accused when the evidence is material either to guilt or to punishment. *State v. Dedrick* (1992). As construed by the court, the right under Article 15 to produce all favorable proofs affords a criminal defendant more protection than the federal constitution because the standard for prosecutorial disclosure under the New Hampshire Constitution is higher than under federal law. Under Article 15, when a defendant demonstrates that favorable, exculpatory evidence has been knowingly withheld by the prosecution, the burden shifts to the state to prove beyond a reasonable doubt that the undisclosed evidence would not have affected the verdict. *State v. Laurie* (1995).

## Right to Be Present at Trial

Under Article 15, a defendant has a right to be present at trial that "derives from the specific guarantees . . . to produce all favorable proofs, to confront witnesses, and to be fully heard in one's defense, as well as the right to due process." *State v. Hannan* (1993) (quotation omitted). A defendant enjoys this right even when he is not confronting witnesses or evidence against him, to the extent that a fair and just hearing would be thwarted by the defendant's absence. In *State v. Castle* (1986), for example, the court concluded that a judge denied the defendant his right under Article 15 to be present at all stages of his trial when the judge held *ex parte* discussions with a juror off the record concerning possible bias and subsequently refused defense counsel's request for a discharge of the juror or additional questioning of the juror in the presence of counsel.

Except in first-degree and capital murder cases, the court has permitted the trial court to hold discussions with individual jurors on the record and outside the hearing of counsel, and then communicate the substance of the discussion to counsel. See *State v. Bailey* (1985). A record of the discussion must be kept, even if the defendant does not request it, and provided to the defendant upon request. See *State v. Brodowski* (1991). Failure to notify a defendant of the discussion is an error of the same magnitude as failing to record the discussion, and the supreme court will deem it a reversible error unless the state can prove it was harmless beyond a reasonable doubt. *State v. Hannan* (1993).

The court has also held that "[j]ury orientation is not the type of proceeding that triggers a criminal defendant's right to be present or right to a record" under the state constitution. *State v. Cosme* (2008). "[A] defendant's presence at orientation, either personally or through legal counsel, would not provide him with any meaningful opportunity to defend against the charges pending against him because during orientation no specific case is ever discussed." *Id.*

## Right to Public Trial

The U.S. Supreme Court made the Sixth Amendment right to a public trial applicable to the states in *Duncan v. Louisiana* (1968). In 1977, the New Hampshire Supreme Court held the due process requirements of Article 15 protected the right to a public trial, although no specific public trial right existed in the state constitution. *Martineau v. Helgemoe* (1977). A defendant may waive the right to a public trial. *Id.*

To determine whether a defendant's right to public trial has been violated, the court has adopted the federal constitutional analysis. *State v. Guajardo* (1992). The right is not violated when a proceeding is closed so long as: (1) the party seeking to close the courtroom advances an overriding interest that is likely to be prejudiced; (2) the closure is no broader than necessary to protect that interest; (3) the trial court considers reasonable alternatives to closing the proceeding; and (4) the trial court makes adequate findings supporting the closure.

In several cases, defendants accused of sexual assault of a minor victim have claimed a violation of their right to a public trial when the court closed the courtroom during the testimony of the minor victim. When a conflict exists between a defendant's right to a public trial and the state's interest in protecting a victim's physical and psychological well-being, the court must balance these interests on a case-by-case basis. *State v. Weber* (1993). The court has held unconstitutional a statute that required a defendant to show good cause why the victim's testimony should be heard in open court, because of the burden it placed on the defendant. *Id.* When a minor victim is involved, the court may consider the victim's age and psychological maturity, the nature of the crime, the desires of the victim, and the interests of parents and relatives. *Guajardo, supra.*

The court has also addressed the issue of open judicial proceedings in the context of a preliminary hearing involving access by the press. See *Keene Publishing Corp. v. Keene District Court* (1977), and *Keene Publishing Corp. v. Cheshire County Superior Court* (1979). In such cases, the party seeking disclosure bears the burden to demonstrate that open proceedings would present a clear and present danger to the fairness of the trial, as well as the necessity of an order for closure and the lack of effectiveness of alternative procedures. In respect to electronic media in the courtroom, the court has stated that the constitution "gives the press a presumptive right of access to judicial proceedings and court records, limited, however, by the necessity that it be balanced against a criminal defendant's right to a fair trial." *Petition of WMUR Channel 9* (2002).

## Right of Confrontation and Cross-Examination

The right to confront witness has been deemed fundamental. *State v. Christensen* (1992). The opportunity to impeach a witness's credibility through cross-examination is an incident of the protections guaranteed by Article 15. *State v. Stowe* (2011). Cross-examination serves to ensure the defendant can "meet the witnesses against him face to face, and be fully heard in his defense." *State v. Ramos* (1981). "This includes the right to expose the possible biases of witnesses." *Stowe, supra.*

The trial court has "broad discretion to fix the limits of proper areas of cross-examination, including attacks upon a witness's credibility." *State v. Brum* (2007). But the court "may not completely deny a defendant the right to cross-examine a witness upon a proper matter of inquiry and must permit sufficient cross-examination to satisfy a constitutional threshold." *Id.* When that threshold is met, the defendant must demonstrate that any limitations on the scope of additional cross-examination are unreasonable to the prejudice of his case. *Id.*

In *State v. Christensen* (1992), the court addressed a statute requiring a defendant charged with selling drugs to demonstrate "specific grounds" for objection to the admission of a certificate of chemical analysis in order to question the analyst at trial who prepared it. The court held that this requirement violated the defendant's right to confront witnesses, because he could not develop the specific grounds required under the statute to require the analyst's presence at trial without first confronting and questioning the analyst.

The right to cross-examine is not absolute. In *State v. Howard* (1981), the court upheld a rape shield law that barred admission into evidence of prior sexual activity of rape victims. The law did not offend Article 15 because the law allowed the defendant an opportunity to demonstrate that the probative value of the statutorily inadmissible evidence in the context of a particular case outweighed any prejudicial effect on the victim.

The court has held, consistent with this article, that the state may proceed by offer of proof in a pretrial detention hearing, without producing all the witnesses supplying the information at the basis of its offer of proof, so long as the state has a witness capable of being effectively cross-examined. *State v. Poulicakos* (1989). This principle also applies in juvenile certification hearings. *In re Eduardo L.* (1993).

## Right to Be Tried by Fair and Impartial Jury

The right to trial by jury has its roots in *Magna Charta,* and the court has deemed it fundamental. *State v. Bilc* (2009). Article 15 applies in all cases in which such a right existed at common law at the time of the constitution's adoption. *State v. Ray* (1885). The court has held that the state constitutional right to a fair and impartial jury provides at least as much protection as its federal counterpart. *State v. Wier* (1994).

In criminal matters, the right to a jury trial extends to "all criminal defendants facing the possibility of incarceration." *Opinion of the Justices (DWI Jury Trials)* (1992). A criminal defendant has a right to a jury of twelve persons who arrive at a unanimous verdict, though the parties may agree to proceed with fewer than twelve jurors should a juror be disqualified. *State v. Dushame* (1992). Criminal defendants have the right to a jury trial whenever there is the possibility of incarceration, either in the first instance or a de novo trial upon appeal to the superior court. Accordingly, the court has held that the legislature may not enact a law that eliminates the right to a jury trial for a second offense charge of driving while intoxicated that provided for a six-month sentence of imprisonment. *Opinion of the Justices (DWI Jury Trials)* (1992).

The constitution provides for no particular manner of selecting a jury, so long as the jury selected is impartial. *State v. Wilson* (1896). The court will first assess the impartiality of jurors during *voir dire*. *State v. Gullick* (1980). A fair trial does not require that a potential juror have no information or impression of the nature of the case; rather, a juror simply must be able to put "aside his or her impression or opinion and render a verdict based on the evidence presented in court." *State v. Laaman* (1974).

The court has recognized that pretrial publicity can prejudice a defendant. *Id.* Inherent prejudice exists when the publicity by its nature has so tainted the trial atmosphere that it will necessarily result in a deprivation of due process. A claim of inherent prejudice does not require the defendant to show actual, identifiable prejudice; it is the adverse nature of the publicity, not merely its quantity, which is critical in finding presumptive prejudice. In *State v. Smart* (1993), the court concluded the evidence did not support the defendant's claim of presumptive prejudice when the court and counsel subjected the jury members to thorough and intensive questioning over five days and the defendant failed to exercise all of his preemptory challenges.

## Standard of Proof in Criminal Insanity Commitment and Involuntary Civil Commitment Proceedings

Between 1976 and 1988, the standard of proof requirements for criminal insanity and involuntary civil commitment proceedings underwent fundamental change. In *Gibbs v. Helgemoe* (1976), the New Hampshire Supreme Court held that, under Article 15, criminal insanity commitment required the state to prove, beyond a reasonable doubt, that the mental condition of a person convicted of a crime but found not guilty by reason of insanity was such that it would be dangerous for him to be at large. Reacting to *Gibbs*, the legislature enacted a statute in 1977 that established the standard of proof required in such proceedings as clear and convincing evidence, rather than proof beyond a reasonable doubt. The court held that law unconstitutional a year later in *State v. Gregoire* (1978), ruling that a change in the burden of proof required a constitutional amendment was required, which the voters subsequently adopted in 1984.

In *In re Sanborn* (1988), the court noted the resemblance between civilly filed commitment petitions and insanity verdicts in criminal cases, and made the standard for involuntary civil commitment the same as the standard in a criminal insanity proceeding—namely, clear and convincing evidence. Nonetheless, individuals subject to civil commitment are not entitled to the same level of due process as individuals subject to incarceration for criminal wrongdoing, despite the fact that the private interests at stake in civil commitment proceedings—loss of liberty and social stigmatization—parallel the interests at stake in the criminal context. *In re Scott L.* (1983). In *In re Richard A.* (2001), the court established procedures for cases involving indigent respondents who seek to appeal an involuntary commitment when counsel for the respondent believes the appeal to be frivolous.

## "Law of the Land" and Due Process

The New Hampshire Supreme Court has held that the term "the law of the land" refers to the process warranted by law, see *Hutchins v. Edson* (1817)—in other words, due process of law, see *Petition of Harvey* (1967). Article 15 guarantees due process to any individual facing the potential deprivation of life or a property or liberty interest. *In re Gamble* (1978). The court has held in several contexts that the protections of the due process clause under the state constitution are at least as protective as those under the U.S. Constitution. See *Bragg v. New Hampshire Director of Motor Vehicles* (1997); *State v. Hoag* (2000).

Under Article 15, the state may not deprive a person of life, liberty, or property unless its actions are in compliance with certain procedural standards. The threshold determination is whether the challenged action concerns "a legally protected interest." *State v. McLellan* (2001) (quotation omitted). If such an interest is at stake, the court will then "determine whether the procedure at issue afforded the requisite safeguards." *State v. Mwangi* (2011). "The ultimate standard for judging a due process claim is the notion of fundamental fairness," which "requires that government conduct conform to the community's sense of justice, decency and fair play." *Id.*

In cases decided by the New Hampshire Supreme Court, legally protected property interests have included an interest in practicing one's profession, see *Appeal of Trotzer* (1998), as well as an interest in maintaining unemployment compensation benefits, see *Appeal of Eno* (1985), the reimbursement of expenses incurred in the care of children in need of services, see *City of Claremont v. Truell* (1985), and the privilege of holding a driver's license, see *Bragg, supra.* The court has held protected liberty interests to include the right not to be civilly committed involuntarily, see *In re Gamble* (1978); the right to be free from compulsory medication, see *Opinion of the Justices* (1983); the interest in continuing to work in an occupation generally open to similarly educated or experienced individuals, see *Petition of Preisendorfer* (1998); and the interest in being free from reputational stigma, see *State v. Veale* (2009).

Once a court has identified a protected property or liberty interest, it must determine what process an individual was due. This determination involves a balancing of the private interests implicated by the government action, the risk of erroneous deprivation, the probable value of additional process, and the government's interest. *Veale, supra.* The constitution does not mandate the same process in all instances in which a property or liberty interest has been implicated by government action; rather, "the requirements of due process are flexible and call for such procedural protections as the particular situation demands." *Id.* "The fundamental requisite of due process is the right to be heard at a meaningful time and in a meaningful manner." *Appeal of Portsmouth Trust Co.* (1980).

The court has identified due process violations in many contexts. In *Petition of Preisendorfer* (1998), for example, the court concluded that due process required that a preponderance of the evidence standard apply in any hearing to determine whether an individual's name should be added to a central registry. In *First NH Bank v. Town of Windham* (1994), the court condemned the lack of notice to mortgagee bank of the extermination of its rights in a property prior to the issuance of tax deeds. In *City of Claremont v. Truell* (1985), the court concluded that a lack of notice to the parents of a child in need of services informing them they could be held liable for certain expenses violated due process. And in *Royer v. Department of Employment Security* (1978), the court reversed the termination of unemployment benefits before notice and hearing.

In addition to procedural due process protections available under Article 15, the court has held that this provision also protects substantive due process interests. Substantive due process prohibits government action that "shocks the conscience, or interferes with rights implicit in the concept of ordered liberty." *State v. Furgal* (2010) (quotation omitted). Though the New Hampshire Supreme Court has not elaborated upon the range of interests protected under the rubric of substantive due process, the U.S. Supreme Court has concluded that federal due process protects, among other interests, the individual right to intimate and procreative decision-making, see *Griswold v. Connecticut* (1965); a woman's right to choose, see *Planned Parenthood v. Casey* (1992); and the individual right to make certain decisions regarding marriage and family, see *Zablocki v. Redhail* (1978), and *Moore v. City of East Cleveland* (1977).

### [ART.] 16. [FORMER JEOPARDY; JURY TRIAL IN CAPITAL CASES.]

No subject shall be liable to be tried, after an acquittal, for the same crime or offense. Nor shall the legislature make any law that shall subject any person to a capital punishment, (excepting for the government of the army and navy, and the militia in actual service) without trial by jury. *1784.*

This article protects individuals from being tried twice for the same crime and, except in military courts, guarantees a jury trial in capital cases. The framers of the of the 1784 constitution adapted the provision guaranteeing a jury trial in capital cases from Part 1, Article 12 of the Massachusetts Constitution of 1780.

Fundamentally, Article 16 secures the same right as that guaranteed under the U.S. Constitution: it prohibits multiple prosecutions for the same offense. *State v. Fitzgerald* (1993). The protection against double jeopardy incorporates the doctrine of collateral estoppel, which bars relitigation of certain factual issues. *State v. Fielders* (1983). The right not to be charged twice for an offense growing out of the same facts has a long pedigree, *State v. Sias* (1845), but it has not been interpreted so as to handcuff the state. For example, the prohibition only bars the retrial of a defendant whose conviction was reversed on appeal if the appellate court reasons that the evidence offered against the defendant was insufficient to support a conviction. *State v. McLellan* (2003) (holding that the state's failure in a criminal prosecution to prove any element of an offense beyond a reasonable doubt precludes a later attempt to prove the element).

In the criminal context, this article has a broad reach; it protects individuals found guilty of criminal contempt as well as those convicted of statutory crimes. *State v. Goodnow* (1995) (assault indictment stemming from behavior for which defendant had already been held in contempt violated double jeopardy). This guarantee applies following conviction as well as acquittal. *State v. Constant* (1992). Like the federal limitation, Article 16 applies in criminal, but not civil, cases. *In re DeLucca* (1981); *State v. Hudson* (1981). In certain circumstances, Article 16 is more protective than its federal counterpart. Under the federal constitution, trying a defendant in state court after his acquittal in federal court for the same crime does not violate his right against double jeopardy, but bringing such a prosecution in a state court would violate the guarantee. *State v. Hogg* (1978).

This article does not prevent prosecution for multiple crimes that stem from the same set of actions; rather, it prohibits charging the defendant twice for the same acts. To determine whether two offenses are the same for the purpose of double jeopardy, the court has developed the "same-in-law-and-fact" and the "same evidence" tests. In applying the "same-in-law-and-fact" test, the court asks whether the multiple charged offenses require proof of any different statutory element. To meet its burden under the "same evidence" test, the state must show that each offense with which a defendant is charged requires the use of different pieces of evidence.

Under the "same-in-law-and-fact" test, the prosecution must show that the multiple offenses with which a defendant is charged require proof of different elements. *State v. Constant* (1992). Accordingly, defendants may not be convicted of both greater- and lesser-included offenses. In *State v. Constant,* for example, the court held the right against double jeopardy violated when the stated indicted the defendant for possession of a controlled drug after he had already been convicted of transportation of a controlled drug in connection with the same series of events. The transportation charge required proof of all the same elements of the possession charge as well as a showing that the defendant drove a motor vehicle on a public road. "Since the possession charge lack[ed] any element that [was] not common to the transportation charge, it [was] a lesser-included offense of the transportation clause," and charging the defendant with both offenses violated Article 16. The court has held that offenses are the same unless each requires proof of a fact that the other does not. *State v. Smith* (1953).

Under the "same evidence" test, the state must show that "proof of the crimes *as charged* will in actuality require a difference in evidence." *State v. Bailey* (1986). In *State v. Stratton* (1989), for example, the state charged the defendant with six counts of being a felon in possession of a firearm. Though the six indictments required proof of the same elements, the court concluded that the state did not violate the defendant's right against double jeopardy because each charge required evidence that the defendant possessed a different firearm.

It may be helpful to think about these tests in terms of the two most common circumstances in which double jeopardy challenges arise: "(1) the simultaneous prosecution of multiple charges for the same offense; and (2) the subsequent prosecution of a charge involving the same underlying conduct previously prosecuted by the State." *State v. Hannon* (2005). The first situation lends itself to the "same evidence" test because so long as proof of the multiple charges requires a difference in evidence—even a small one—the defendant's right against double jeopardy will not be violated. *State v. Hull* (2003) (concluding "reckless conduct indictment required proof that the defendant drove his truck too close to [the victim] and that he struck the [victim] with his truck; the DUI indictment did not"). The second situation lends itself to application of the "same-in-law-and-fact" test because to charge a defendant with a different crime growing out of the same conduct, the state must show that the second offense requires proof of a different statutory element. See *State v. Bailey* (1986).

"When evaluating a double jeopardy claim, a reviewing court must first ask whether jeopardy attached in the original trial court proceeding." *In re State* (2007). Jeopardy attaches in a jury trial when the jury is empanelled and sworn, *State v. King* (1988), and in a bench trial when the judge begins to hear evidence, *State v. Solomon* (2008). Defendants have a right to be tried by a particular tribunal, which means that judges may only grant mistrials without a defendant's consent if basic notions of justice establish a "manifest necessity" to do so. *State v. Pugliese* (2008). For purposes of allowing a new trial after a judge grants a mistrial, "manifest necessity" describes those situations in which "a defendant's valued right to have his trial completed by a particular tribunal must in some instances be subordinated to the public's interest in fair trials designed to end in just judgments." *State v. Ayer* (2003) (quotation omitted).

When a court terminates a trial by granting a defendant's motion for mistrial, double jeopardy generally does not bar a second trial on the same charge. This makes sense in light of the fact that defendants' motions for mistrials are typically based upon structural defects in the original trial. Accordingly, while constitutional concerns demand that the present trial end, the public interest in prosecution mandates the state be given the opportunity to retry its case. Double jeopardy does apply, however, when a defendant's motion for mistrial represents the only reasonable means to avoid becoming the victim of inadmissible evidence or impermissible trial tactics. *State v. Montella* (1992).

Several cases have addressed whether double jeopardy applies when the state uses particular facts to support imposing extended or enhanced sentences after already using those facts to prove the crime itself. The court has held that imposing an extended sentence based upon the victim's age did not constitute double jeopardy, despite the fact that the prosecution had already used the victim's age to elevate the offense from a class B to a class A felony. *State v. Hennessey* (1997), *abrogated on other grounds by State v. Quintero* (2011). The sentence enhancement did not represent an additional offense based upon the facts already used to prove the offense of which the defendant was convicted. In *State v. Elbert* (1986), the court ruled that double jeopardy did not prohibit the state from convicting and sentencing a defendant of both felonious use of a firearm and attempted murder. Despite the fact that the state proved the felonious use of a firearm once it proved attempted murder and proof of the two offenses required the same evidence, the court held that imposing a sentence enhancement for an underlying offense due to use of a firearm as well as charging felonious use of a firearm did not violate Article 16.

### [ART.] 17. [VENUE OF CRIMINAL PROSECUTIONS.]

In criminal prosecutions, the trial of facts, in the vicinity where they happened, is so essential to the security of the life, liberty and estate of the citizen, that no crime or offense ought to be tried in any other county or judicial district than that in which it is committed; except in any case in any particular county or judicial district, upon motion by the defendant, and after a finding by the court that a fair and impartial trial cannot be had where the offense may be committed, the court shall direct the trial to a county or judicial district in which a fair and impartial trial can be obtained. *1784; amended 1792 and 1978.*

Pursuant to this article, a criminal defendant has the right to have his or her case tried in the county or judicial district in which the crime occurred; when a fair trial cannot be obtained where the offense was committed, a defendant may seek to have the location of the trial moved. This article resembles Part 1, Article 13 of the Massachusetts Constitution of 1780, which provides that, "[i]n criminal prosecutions, the verification of facts, in the vicinity where they happen, is one of the greatest securities of the life, liberty, and property of the citizen." Unlike its Massachusetts counterpart, the New Hampshire Constitution makes more specific the right to a trial in criminal cases in the location where the offense occurred.

This article has been twice amended since its adoption. In 1792, the people amended this provision to substitute "legislature" for "assembly." The article was amended again in 1978. Until that time, criminal cases had to be tried within the county in which the crime occurred, except in cases of general insurrection, which created a problem when a defendant contended that a fair trial was impossible in that venue. The 1978 amendment removed the reference to "general insurrection" and provided that venue in a criminal case could be changed when a fair trial could not be obtained in the county or judicial district in which the offense was committed. The 1978 amendment also expanded the concept of "venue" in a criminal case to mean either "a particular county of judicial district." In 1985, the New Hampshire Supreme Court held that Article 17 allows the creation of judicial districts comprised of contiguous municipalities in different counties. *Opinion of the Justices* (1985).

This provision endorses a privilege "designed for the protection of the accused . . . [to] prevent the possibility of sending him for trial to a remote county, at a distance from friends, among strangers, and perhaps among parties animated by prejudices of a personal or partisan character." *State v. Albee* (1881). The framers sought "to protect the subject against an unfair trial at a distance from the vicinity of the alleged crime and at a place selected by officials who might be hostile to the accused." *Id.* The adoption of this protection did not eliminate a defendant's "common-law right to a change of venue whenever a fair and impartial trial could not be had in the county where the fact happened." *Id.* The defendant may waive his or her Article 17 rights, by express statement or, when a defendant knows all the facts underlying his objection to venue before trial, by the "failure to object to venue before trial." *In re State (State v. Johanson)* (2007).

Venue is proper when the state proves that a crime occurred in a town in a particular county. *State v. Huffman* (1992). To obtain a change in venue, a defendant must show that he cannot receive a fair and impartial trial in the county or district in which the offense was committed. See *State v. Sullivan* (1981). This article does not apply to a preliminary examination by a justice of the peace in a county different from the one in which the offense occurred and in which the defendant was later tried. See *State v. Thompson* (1850). The court has also denied the protections of this article to a defendant in a juvenile cases, observing in *In re Kevin E.* (1999), that the juvenile system is separate from—and has different goals than—the adult penal system; juveniles, after all, are not charged with or convicted of crimes, or given the stigmatizing label of "criminal," and juvenile proceedings do not require juries. Accordingly, the court concluded, such proceedings are exempt from the dictates of Article 17.

In a 1974 case in which a defendant claimed he could not receive a fair trial because of media publicity, the court differentiated between inherent prejudice and actual prejudice that might be caused by such publicity. See *State v. Laaman* (1974). In the case of inherent prejudice, where publicity by its nature has so tainted the trial atmosphere that it will necessarily result in lack of due process, a defendant need not show actual identifiable prejudice to obtain a change in venue. But when the defendant alleges that the publicity has so infected the jurors that a fair and impartial trial is impossible, the defendant must demonstrate that the jurors would not be capable of rendering a verdict based upon the evidence presented in court.

## [ART.] 18. [PENALTIES TO BE PROPORTIONED TO OFFENSES; TRUE DESIGN OF PUNISHMENT.]

All penalties ought to be proportioned to the nature of the offense. No wise legislature will affix the same punishment to the crimes of theft, forgery,

and the like, which they do to those of murder and treason. Where the same undistinguishing severity is exerted against all offenses, the people are led to forget the real distinction in the crimes themselves, and to commit the most flagrant with as little compunction as they do the lightest offenses. For the same reason a multitude of sanguinary laws is both impolitic and unjust. The true design of all punishments being to reform, not to exterminate mankind.
*1784; amended 1792.*

This article announces the principle that a penalty should be proportionate to the offense of which the defendant was convicted. An amendment in 1792 made only minor changes to the original wording. In 1921, the New Hampshire Supreme Court concluded that the language indicating that all punishments must be "proportioned" to the offense was likely directory, rather than mandatory. *State v. Foster* (1921). As for the article's final sentence, the court has concluded that it creates no right to parole, *State v. Farrow* (1978), and is best understood as a general statement of principle; in *State v. Evans* (1985), the court reasoned that, while this article creates no substantive right to rehabilitation, it does place a "constitutional imprimatur" upon this goal.

For a sentence to violate Article 18, "it must be grossly disproportionate to the crime." *State v. Bird* (2010) (quotation omitted). The court will presume the validity of the statutory scheme under which the defendant was sentenced and "cannot declare it unconstitutional except upon inescapable grounds." *Id.* Further, Article 18 requires that, when sentencing a defendant, the trial court should consider "all the relevant factors necessary to the exercise of its discretion." *Duquette v. Warden, New Hampshire Prison System* (2007). These may include the gravity of the offense and the harshness of the penalty, the sentences imposed on other criminals in the same jurisdiction, and the sentences imposed for commission of the same crime in other jurisdictions. See *Dayutis*; *State v. Pliskaner* (1986).

In *State v. Dayutis* (1985), the defendant was sentenced to thirty-five years to life for second-degree murder, a sentence greater than that to which the defendant would have been subject for first-degree murder. The court held the sentence unconstitutionally disproportionate because the penalty for the lesser offense was more severe than that for the greater offense. In numerous other cases, the court has upheld sentences alleged to be grossly disproportionate to the crime for which the defendant was convicted. In *State v. Deflorio* (1986), for example, the court concluded that the incarceration of a sixteen- or seventeen-year old minor with adult prisoners for certain motor vehicle misdemeanor charges did not violate this article. And, in *State v. Fraser* (1980), the court held that one defendant receiving a more severe sentence than an accomplice for the commission of the same crime did not violate the state constitution, because Article 18 does not require that all persons convicted of the same crime receive the same sentence; crimes may be identical, but defendants may not be.

## [ART.] 19. [SEARCHES AND SEIZURES REGULATED.]

Every subject hath a right to be secure from all unreasonable searches and seizures of his person, his houses, his papers, and all his possessions. Therefore, all warrants to search suspected places, or arrest a person for examination or trial in prosecutions for criminal matters, are contrary to this right, if the cause or foundation of them be not previously supported by oath or affirmation; and if the order, in a warrant to a civil officer, to make search in suspected places, or to arrest one or more suspected persons or to seize their property, be not accompanied with a special designation of the persons or objects of search, arrest, or seizure; and no warrant ought to be issued; but in cases and with the formalities, prescribed by law. *1784; amended 1792.*

This article safeguards the right of individuals to be free from unreasonable searches and seizures by the state or an agent of the state. The framers of Article 19 intended the warrant requirement to preclude the use of the "general warrants and writs of assistance which had been used by the British to conduct sweeping searches based upon generalized suspicions and without specifying the places to be searched or things to be seized." *State v. Canelo* (1995) (quotation omitted). The 1784 version of this article tracked Part 1, Article 14 of the Massachusetts Constitution of 1780 word for word; the 1792 amendment altered the language, but did not change the provision's basic meaning.

This article protects people, their papers, possessions, and homes from unreasonable searches and seizures, but to receive constitutional protection, the defendant must have "exhibited a subjective expectation of privacy in the area and that expectation must be one that society is prepared to recognize as reasonable." *State v. Smith* (2012). The New Hampshire Supreme Court has recognized that there exists a heightened expectation of privacy in one's dwelling, see *State v. Orde* (2010), which includes certain property around the home known as curtilage. See *Smith, supra*. Curtilage encompasses "those outbuildings that are directly and intimately connected with the habitation and in proximity thereto and the land or grounds surrounding the dwelling which are necessary and convenient and habitually used for family purposes and carrying on domestic employment." *Id.*

If an individual has a reasonable expectation of privacy, any search must be authorized by a warrant issued by a magistrate and based upon probable cause, or the search must fall within one of the recognized exceptions to the warrant requirement. See *State v. Sawyer* (2001). Unlike under federal law, the court has interpreted Article 19 to provide defendants with "automatic standing" to challenge the legality of a search or seizure when charged with a crime that includes possession of any article or thing as an element. *State v. Settle* (1982). The following sections address the requirements for searches and seizures with and without warrants, as well as the standard under the New Hampshire Constitution for excluding evidence seized in connection with a search or seizure that proves to be unconstitutional.

## Warrant Requirements

Assuming the existence of a protected privacy interest, a search or a seizure will be reasonable if conducted pursuant to a warrant that is (1) supported by oath or affirmation; (2) issued by a neutral and detached magistrate; and (3) contains a specific description of the place to be searched or the person to be seized. The requirement that a warrant must be supported by "oath or affirmation" means that the magistrate who issues the warrant must find that it is supported by probable cause. *State v. Daniel* (1997). Probable cause exists "when a person of ordinary caution would justifiably believe that what is sought will be found through the search and will aid in a particular apprehension or conviction." *State v. Grimshaw* (1986) (quotation omitted). If an informant is the source of the information law enforcement provides in support of a warrant application, the court will determine the warrant's validity by applying a "totality of the circumstances" test. *State v. Hazen* (1988).

A valid warrant requires more than just probable cause: the magistrate issuing the warrant must be neutral and detached. *Canelo, supra.* The court has concluded that a magistrate was not "neutral and detached" when he relied on a grand jury's indictment in making the determination whether probable cause existed to search the defendant's bedroom. See *State v. Kellenbeck* (1984). In *Canelo,* the court concluded that anticipatory search warrants do not violate the neutral-and-detached magistrate requirement, but the facts supporting such a warrant must be "ascertainable and preordained" in order for the magistrate's review to serve its constitutional purpose. *Canelo, supra.*

## Warrantless Searches and Seizures

Under Article 19, warrantless searches are per se unreasonable, unless one of a few judicially created exceptions applies, *State v. Thorp* (1976), or the subject of the search consents, see *State v. Pinder* (1985). The recognized exceptions to the warrant requirement for searches or seizures include: (1) "exigent circumstances" requiring an officer with probable cause to take immediate action, *State v. Santana* (1991); (2) searches in unoccupied "open fields" located away from a defendant's dwelling, *State v. Pinder* (1986); (3) officers' observations of items in "plain view," *State v. Davis* (2003); (4) administrative searches, *State v. Turmelle* (1989); (5) searches incident to arrest, see *State v. Murray* (1992); and (6) investigatory stops, *State v. Brodeur* (1985).

Defendants are entitled to "significantly greater protection" against state search or seizure of automobiles under the New Hampshire Constitution than under the Fourth Amendment to the U.S. Constitution. *State v. Koppel* (1985). In *State v. Sterndale* (1995), the court specifically rejected the automobile exception to the warrant requirement because it did not find a reduced expectation of privacy in automobiles. Other motor vehicle searches in which the court has found a higher level of protection under Article 19 include cases involving the seizure of a hand-rolled cigarette from an automobile based upon mere suspicion, *State v. Ball* (1983) (departing from Fourth Amendment analysis in *Texas v. Brown* (1983)); and opening a closed container in a police inventory search of an automobile, *State v. Finn* (2001).

## Searches and Seizures Not Based on Probable Cause

In *Koppel, supra,* the court articulated the standard under Article 19 that must be met for a generalized search—in that case, a roadblock set up by the police to find individuals driving under the influence of intoxicating liquor. The court stated that, to justify such a search absent probable cause or even reasonable suspicion that a criminal offense is being committed, "the State must prove that its conduct significantly advances the public interest in a manner that outweighs the accompanying intrusion on individual rights. It must further prove that no less intrusive means are available to accomplish the State's goal."

While searches conducted by public school officials must be reasonable under this article, they have greater flexibility than law enforcement officers to conduct searches for contraband. In *State v. Drake* (1995), the court adopted the U.S. Supreme Court's test in *New Jersey v. T.L.O.* (1985), which requires that searches by public school officials be reasonable in light of all the circumstances. See also *State v. Tinkham* (1998). This means that (1) the search must be justified at its inception by the official's reasonable grounds to believe that it will give rise to evidence that the student is violating or has violated a law or school rule; (2) the scope of the search is reasonably related to the grounds supporting it; and (3) the search itself is "reasonably related to the objectives of the search and not excessively intrusive in light of the age and sex of the student and the nature of the infraction." *Drake, supra* (quotation omitted).

## The Exclusionary Rule

Evidence seized in violation of this article is inadmissible under the exclusionary rule. *State v. Beauchesne* (2005). Further, the "fruit of the poisonous tree" doctrine "requires the exclusion from trial of evidence derivatively obtained through a violation of Part I, Article 19." *State v. Cobb* (1999). The exclusionary rule does not apply, however, in certain limited circumstances, such as when the state proves the taint of the initial illegality has been purged; when the police have an independent source for the evidence untainted by their misconduct; when the police inevitably would have discovered the evidence; and when a police officer relies upon a presumptively constitutional ordinance or statute. *State v. De la Cruz* (2009). Notably, the court has specifically rejected an exception to the exclusionary rule for a police officer's good faith reliance upon a warrant that proves to be constitutionally invalid, because such an exception would be "incompatible with and detrimental to . . . citizens' strong right of privacy inherent in part I, article 19." *Canelo, supra.*

### [ART.] 20. [JURY TRIAL IN CIVIL CAUSES.]

In all controversies concerning property, and in all suits between two or more persons except those in which another practice is and has been customary and except those in which the value in controversy does not exceed $1,500 and no title to real estate is involved, the parties have a right to a trial by jury. This method of procedure shall be held sacred, unless, in cases arising on the high seas and in cases ["cases" appears in 1792 parchment copy of constitution; the constitution of 1784 used "causes"] relating to mariners' wages, the legislature shall think it necessary hereafter to alter it. *1784; amended 1877, 1960, and 1988.*

This article guarantees a litigant the right to a civil jury trial except in cases in which the amount in controversy is $1,500 or less and does not involve title to real estate. The framers adopted the original 1784 version of this article almost verbatim from Part 1, Article 15 of the Massachusetts Constitution of 1780.

The minimum amount-in-controversy requirement has been increased several times since 1784. In 1877, the voters approved an amendment to allow a jury trial if the amount exceeded $100 and did not involve title to real estate. In 1918 and 1930, conventions considered but did not adopt proposals to increase the amount. The 1956 convention proposed to increase the amount in controversy to $500, and the voters approved that amendment by the necessary two-thirds, but the New Hampshire Supreme Court invalidated the provision because it was not properly worded. *Concrete, Inc. v. Rheaume Builders* (1957). In 1960, voters adopted the reworded proposal and the amount in controversy necessary to trigger a jury trial was changed to $500.

Later proposed increases to the amount in controversy met with resistance from the voters. In 1976, they rejected an attempt to increase the amount to $3,000. And in 1984, the voters rejected an increase to $5,000, despite the argument made by proponents of the change that it was needed to reduce the growing backlog in superior court cases. In 1985, the Constitutional and Statutory Revision Committee reported that delays of one year had become "almost universal," with delays of two to three years occurring in some counties. The legislature again placed a question on the ballot in 1986; the proposed amendment would have allowed the amount in controversy to be determined by statute. Though the voters rejected this effort, they finally approved an amendment in 1988 which, in addition to some grammatical changes, established the modern amount in controversy: to qualify for a jury trial, a civil claim must exceed $1,500. See *Gilman v. Lake Sunapee Properties, LLC* (2009).

The right to a jury trial has been long regarded in New Hampshire as fundamental, and Article 20 confirms the basic guarantee of a right to trial by a jury of one's peers in civil cases. *Copp v. Henniker* (1875). Several other articles of the New Hampshire Constitution protect the right to a jury trial: Article 15 guarantees that no person shall be deprived of his liberty except by the judgment of his peers or the law of the land, and Article 16 guarantees the protection of a jury trial in criminal cases punishable by the death penalty.

The New Hampshire Supreme Court has interpreted this article to extend the right to all civil cases in which it existed at the time of the constitution's adoption. "To resolve whether a party has a right to trial by jury in a particular action," the court generally looks "to both the nature of the case and the relief sought, and ascertain[s] whether the customary practice included a trial by jury before 1784." *Hair Excitement v. L'Oreal U.S.A.* (2009) (quotation omitted). In the court's view, Article 20 guarantees the right "as it then stood and was practiced, guarding it against repeal, infringement, or undue trammel by legislative action, but not extending it so as to include what had not before been within its benefits." *Id.* (quotation omitted). Accordingly, a claim that the right to a jury trial attaches in a particular case requires a historical discussion.

The court has held that the right to jury trial cannot be denied on the basis of the complexity of the case, *Murphy & Sons v. Peters* (1948), and that it does not extend to cases that are special or statutory, or to summary proceedings unknown to the common law. *Opinion of the Justices (SLAPP Suit Procedure)* (1994). For example, the court determined that rights arising under the Unemployment Compensation Act should be viewed as strictly statutory, and entailed no right to a jury trial. See *Pomponio* v. *State* (1965). Similarly, a claim brought under the Consumer Protection Act did not require trial by jury. *Hair Excitement, Inc., supra*. As well, a plaintiff who seeks equitable relief is not entitled to a jury trial. *Dion v. Cheshire Mills* (1943).

The first sentence of Article 20 suggests a right to a jury trial "in all controversies concerning property." In *Gilman v. Lake Sunapee Properties, LLC, supra,* the court upheld the right to a jury trial in a property dispute between co-owners, concluding that "there was a right to a jury trial in partition actions in 1784." In *HSBC Bank USA, Nat. Ass'n, Inc. v. MacMillan* (2010), the court reached the opposite conclusion regarding a quiet title action, holding that "such actions were resolved in equity actions at time the state constitution was adopted."

In a jury trial, the jury determines factual issues. In 1994, the court rejected a proposed bill before the legislature that would have provided for the dismissal of an action identified as a "strategic lawsuit against public participation" (SLAPP suit) unless the plaintiff could show a probability that she would prevail. The court held that such a procedure would violate Article 20 because it would deny the plaintiff the right to have a jury determine factual issues in the lawsuit. *Opinion of the Justices (SLAPP Suit Procedure), supra.* Nonetheless, the legislature may require that certain cases, such as disputes before the department of labor, see *ICS Communications v. Fitch* (2000), must first be adjudicated by an administrative agency, so long as there is a "relatively unfettered" right of appeal to a court where a jury trial may be had.

The right to a jury trial is subject to reasonable regulation. When, for example, a party fails to follow a court rule requiring that she make a timely demand for a jury trial, the right is deemed waived. *Nassif Realty Corp. v. National Fire Insurance Co.* (1966). Further, the court has held that "conduct or acquiescence inconsistent with an intention to insist on a jury trial may constitute a waiver [of the right]." *SNCR Corp. v. Greene* (2005). At the same time, "Absent an express agreement, consent, failure to comply with [a court rule], or conduct manifesting a clear intent to waive this constitutional right, a waiver . . . should not be inferred or presumed." *Jones v. Chase* (1970). If pleadings are amended, any waiver of the right to jury trial applies only to the issues formed at the time of the waiver. *Lucas v. Gate* (1954).

In determining the amount in controversy, the court has found that the amount includes penalty assessments added to a civil penalty. *State v. Corson* (1991). But separate civil penalties that in the aggregate exceed the amount in controversy requirement will not trigger a jury trial, so long as no single civil penalty exceeds the requirement. *Town of Henniker v. Homo* (1992).

## [ART.] 21. [JURORS; COMPENSATION.]

In order to reap the fullest advantage of the inestimable privilege of the trial by jury, great care ought to be taken, that none but qualified persons should be appointed to serve; and such ought to be fully compensated for their travel, time and attendance. *1784.*

Pursuant to this article, only qualified persons may be permitted to serve as jurors, and jurors should be properly compensated. This article has not been the subject of any extended discussion by the New Hampshire Supreme Court. In a 1922 case concerning the impartiality of a juror, the court cited to this article, in conjunction with Article 35, regarding the importance of impartial judges. See *State v. Rheaume* (1922). And in a 1974 case, the court observed that, "[s]ince the days of the Magna Carta the requisite qualifications of jurors have become embedded in the jury system so as to be commonly known and understood." *State v. Fleury* (1974). No cases have interpreted the provision relating to juror compensation; since at least 1791 the legislature has enacted laws providing for compensation of jurors.

## [ART.] 22. [FREE SPEECH; LIBERTY OF THE PRESS.]

Free speech and liberty of the press are essential to the security of freedom in a state: They ought, therefore, to be inviolably preserved. *1784; amended in 1968.*

This article guarantees both freedom of speech and liberty of the press. The 1784 version tracked its counterpart in Part 1, Article 16 of the Massachusetts Constitution of 1780, but the framers of the New Hampshire Constitution placed a greater emphasis on the liberty of the press, demanding that it be "inviolably preserved," as opposed to "not . . . restrained." The people amended this article in 1968 to add the reference to free speech. Though the right to freedom of speech finds protection in the U.S. Constitution's First Amendment, the committee recommending the resolution maintained that this interest should be equally protected under the New Hampshire Constitution.

## Freedom of Speech

Article 22's protection of expression is expansive: "[o]nly narrow categories of speech, such as defamation, incitement and pornography produced with real children, fall outside the ambit of the right to free speech." *Doyle v. Commissioner, Dep't. of Resources* (2012). But the right to free speech is not absolute. In general, regulations of expression must be "content-neutral, narrowly serve a significant governmental interest, and allow other opportunities for expression." *State v. Comley* (1988). State action is an essential prerequisite to finding a violation of Article 22. See *Hippopress, LLC v. SMG* (2003). State action may be attributed to a private actor when (1) there exists a financial or regulatory nexus between the actor and the government which compelled the private actor to regulate speech as it did; (2) the private actor has assumed a traditionally public function; or (3) there exists a symbiotic relationship between the private actor and the government. Applying this test in *Hippopress,* the New Hampshire Supreme Court concluded that a management company was not a state actor when it granted one newspaper exclusive distribution rights within a city arena.

Two cases interpreting New Hampshire's disorderly conduct law illustrate the court's application of the free speech guarantee. In *State v. Nickerson* (1980), the court held unconstitutionally overbroad a part of the law which allowed the police to arrest a person for refusing to comply with a lawful order to move from a public place. The court reasoned that the statute gave the police too much discretion. The legislature responded by amending the statute in 1983 to narrow police discretion. In *State v. Comley,* the defendant disrupted the governor's inaugural ceremonies by running down the aisle of Representatives Hall and shouting antinuclear power statements. The court concluded that the application of the law did not conflict with Article 22 because the law was a reasonable regulation of the time, place, and manner of conduct, with only an incidental effect on speech. The constitutionality of similar regulations in the context of municipal licenses for parades or processions has long been upheld, absent discrimination against any particular applicant. See *State v. Harvey* (1967).

The court has suggested that commercial speech may be subject to a less stringent standard of review than other forms of expression. In *Opinion of the Justices* (1981), the court concluded that a proposed law intended to curb the use of drug paraphernalia went too far because it included a ban on advertising that was broad enough to apply to speech entitled to constitutional protection; had the ban been worded more carefully, it might have passed constitutional muster. The court has been receptive to arguments that a speech regulation may be overbroad in other contexts; in another advisory opinion the court concluded that a proposed law prohibiting the harassment of hunters, trappers, and fishermen, violated Article 22 because it forbade not just speech likely to interfere with lawful activity or provoke breaches of the peace, but mere expressions of a particular point of view that raised no such risks. See *Opinion of the Justices* (1986).

## Liberty of the Press

Article 22 grants the press a constitutional right to gather news. Together with Part 1, Article 8, Article 22 creates a public right to open court rooms and to government records, including access to records of judicial proceedings. See *Associated Press v. State* (2005). Like the freedom of speech, however, this right is not absolute; it may be overcome "when a sufficiently compelling interest for nondisclosure is identified." *Id.* The court presumes records are public, a presumption which must be overcome by the party seeking nondisclosure. See *Douglas v. Douglas* (2001). Even when a court finds a sufficiently compelling interest, a court record may not be kept sealed unless "no reasonable alternative to nondisclosure exists" and "the least restrictive means available" are utilized in the service of that interest. *Petition of Keene Sentinel* (1992).

The court has held that this article creates a qualified privilege for reporters in civil cases. In criminal cases, the reporter's privilege is more tenuous because an individual citizen's rights must also be protected. See *State v. Siel* (1982). The *Siel* court concluded that a criminal defendant may overcome a press privilege to withhold a confidential source when: (1) he or she has attempted unsuccessfully to obtain the information by all reasonable alternatives; (2) the information would not be irrelevant to the defense; and (3) on a balance of the probabilities, there is a reasonable possibility that the information sought as evidence would affect the verdict in the case. The defendant in *Siel* was not able to meet this test.

In the civil context, the court held that this article prevented the governor and council from calling a reporter as a witness in an effort to remove from office the state director of probation. The reporter had interviewed probation employees and written an article containing statements critical of the director, and the governor and council sought to have him disclose his sources. The court noted the importance of a free press to a free state, and reasoned that news gathering should be viewed as an integral part of the process of reporting. See *Opinion of the Justices* (1977).

The court in *Keene Publishing Corp. v. Keene District Court* (1977) adopted standards to govern the closure of pretrial criminal hearings. Preliminary hearings, including hearings on motions to suppress, may be closed to the public or press only if the dissemination of information from the proceeding would create a "clear and present danger" to the defendant's right to a fair trial, and if the prejudicial effect of the information could not be avoided by any reasonable alternative to closure.

A trial court's ability to control courtroom proceedings may be subject to the dictates of Article 22. In *Keene Publishing Corp. v. Cheshire County Superior Court* (1979), the court faced the question whether a trial court's order acted as a prior restraint upon the freedom of the press. That order required a newspaper's legal counsel to be present during a pretrial evidentiary hearing and advise his client about what the newspaper could publish, an effort to avoid a change venue. The court held the requirement an implied "gag" order which improperly required the newspaper's counsel to act as a censor.

[ART.] 23. [RETROSPECTIVE LAWS PROHIBITED.]

Retrospective laws are highly injurious, oppressive, and unjust. No such laws, therefore, should be made, either for the decision of civil causes, or the punishment of offenses. *1784.*

This article prohibits ex post facto laws in criminal cases and the retrospective application of laws in civil cases. *Woart v. Winnick* (1826). Unchanged since 1784, the article articulates the same protection as that contained in Part 1, Article 24 of the Massachusetts Constitution of 1780, and both provisions use the words "unjust" and "oppressive" to describe retrospective laws. This article seeks to prevent the legislature from interfering with the expectations of persons regarding the legal significance of actions they took prior to the enactment of a law. *State v. Vashaw* (1973). The court has held fundamental the principle that the basis for criminal liability cannot be specified after acts are committed. *State v. Akers* (1979). The article's protections apply to individuals and not to the state or its subdivisions. *Hodge v. Manchester* (1920). The application of the article to the "punishment of offenses" has not changed significantly since *Woart*, while, as then–New Hampshire Supreme Court Justice David Souter observed, its application in civil cases has undergone continual evolution. *State v. Ballou* (1984) (Souter, J., dissenting).

## Ex Post Facto Laws

Pursuant to this article, the legislature must specify in advance the acts or omissions that are to be the basis of criminal liability or punishment. *Akers*, *supra*. A law or its application will be deemed to be ex post facto if it "makes an action done before the passing of the law, and which was innocent when done, criminal, and punishes such action; or aggravates a crime, and makes it greater, than when it was committed; or changes the punishment, and inflicts greater punishment, than the law annexed to the crime when committed." *Woart, supra*. Changes that do not affect a defendant's substantive rights, either by enhancing punishment, altering the elements of the offense, or changing the facts required to prove guilt, do not operate ex post facto; this is so even if changes in the law impose some disadvantage upon the defendant. *State v. Matthews* (2008).

It follows that changes in the law that are procedural and do not affect a defendant's substantive rights do not violate this article. Thus in *Matthews* the court held valid a statutory amendment that affected a defendant's appellate rights. Further, a law that operates to mitigate punishment is not an illegal retrospective law; accordingly, a statute that allowed the annulment of a crime could be applied to convictions dating from both before and after the enactment of the statute. *Doe v. State* (1974).

In *State v. Reynolds* (1994), the court considered the application of an amendment to a law limiting when prisoners could petition for a sentence suspension. The court held the law violated Article 23 because the amended law did not exist when the defendant committed the crime for which she was sentenced and inflicted a greater punishment on her by potentially extending her term of incarceration. In another case decided that same year, *State v. Costello* (1994), the court rejected the argument that a requirement to register as a sexual offender operated ex post facto. The court reasoned that the legislature had enacted the registration statute after the defendant was convicted of the offense that triggered the registration requirement and that the legislature designed the requirement to be regulatory, not to impose a greater punishment for the offense of which he was convicted.

## Protection of Vested Rights in Civil Matters

In civil matters, the court has held that a retrospective law is one that takes away or impairs vested rights acquired under existing laws, or that creates a new obligation, imposes a new duty, or attaches a new disability in respect to transactions or considerations already past. *Vashaw, supra*. Before determining whether the application of new legislation to a particular matter would violate this article, the court must ascertain "whether the legislature intended the new law to apply prospectively or retroactively." *In re Goldman* (2005).

When applying Article 23, the court distinguishes between new laws that affect substantive rights and liabilities and "those that solely affect procedures or remedies enforcing those rights." *Goldman, supra*. The court has stated that, "while the demarcation between substantive rights and liabilities and procedures and remedies provides a helpful guidepost," courts ultimately "must discern the nature of the rights affected by the new act to assess whether its application to a particular matter offends the constitution." *Id.* (quotation omitted). In *Eldridge v. Eldridge* (1993), for example, the court concluded that a law establishing new procedures pursuant to which parties could seek modification of a child support order did not affect the defendant's underlying obligation to support his children.

An individual must claim a vested right to invoke the protections of this article. The court has concluded that "a mere expectancy of future benefit, or a contingent interest in property founded on anticipated continuance of existing laws, does not constitute a vested right." *Goldman, supra* (quotation omitted). "A perfect vested right can be no other than such as is not doubted, or depending on any contingency, but absolute, fixed and certain." *Lakeman v. Moore* (1855).

As noted, this article does not apply to statutes that affect only remedies, provided they do not operate in a way that is injurious, oppressive, or unjust. The court in *Smith v. Sampson* (1974), applied this principle in holding remedial a statute allowing a tenant to appeal a district court's decision concerning the tenant's possessory rights, even though the actions that determined the party's substantive rights took place before the law's effective date. As well, a statute enacted at the time a case has been commenced but before it has been decided may apply to the case so long as the law is remedial or procedural in nature. *Gelinas v. Mackey* (1983).

This article has frequently been interpreted in the context of tax assessments. The court has held that Article 23 prohibits the retroactive taxation of utility franchises, see *Opinion of the Justices* (1983), and the creation of a new tax obligation in respect to transactions already past, see *Cagan's, Inc. v. New Hampshire Department of Revenue Administration* (1985). Further, this article, together with Article 1, Section 10 of the U.S. Constitution, provides an individual protection when a law impairs a contract, or when a law abrogates an earlier statute that was itself a contract; accordingly, in *Opinion of the Justices (Furlough)* (1992), the court held a proposed bill requiring state employees to take unpaid leave would violate this article as well as the contract clause of the federal constitution, because the law would have substantially impaired rights contained in the collective bargaining agreement between the state and certain classified employees.

### [ART.] 24. [MILITIA.]

A well regulated militia is the proper, natural, and sure defense, of a state. *1784.*

This article announces the purpose of the militia: defense of the state. The state militia today consists of the New Hampshire National Guard, the state guard, and the unorganized militia.[5] The legislature frequently regulated the militia in the late eighteenth and nineteenth centuries. This article has not been interpreted by the New Hampshire Supreme Court.

### [ART.] 25. [STANDING ARMIES.]

Standing armies are dangerous to liberty, and ought not to be raised, or kept up, without the consent of the legislature. *1784.*

This article requires there be legislative consent before a "standing army" is raised. It resembles Part 1, Article 17 of the Massachusetts Constitution of 1780. This article has not been interpreted by the New Hampshire Supreme Court.

### [ART.] 26. [MILITARY SUBJECT TO CIVIL POWER.]

In all cases, and at all times, the military ought to be under strict subordination to, and governed by, the civil power. *1784.*

This article subordinates the military to civilian authority. It resembles the last part of Part 1, Article 17 of the Massachusetts Constitution of 1780. This article has not been interpreted by the New Hampshire Supreme Court.

### [ART.] 27. [QUARTERING OF SOLDIERS.]

No soldier in time of peace, shall be quartered in any house, without the consent of the owner; and in time of war, such quarters ought not to be made but by the civil authorities in a manner ordained by the legislature. *1784; amended 1980.*

This article limits the authority of government to require its citizens to quarter soldiers. In peacetime, the owner must consent, while in a time of war, the legislature may regulate the manner in which soldiers are quartered. The 1784 version of this article was almost identical to Part 1, Article 27 of the Massachusetts Constitution of 1780. In 1980, the language was updated by changing the reference to "magistrates" to "authorities." This article has not been interpreted by the New Hampshire Supreme Court.

### [ART.] 28. [TAXES, BY WHOM LEVIED.]

No subsidy, charge, tax, impost, or duty, shall be established, fixed, laid, or levied, under any pretext whatsoever, without the consent of the people, or their representatives in the legislature, or authority derived from that body. *1784.*

---

[5] See *Journal of the Convention to Revise the Constitution, May 1964* (Concord, NH: Evan Printing Co., 1964), 218.

This article prohibits taxation absent the consent of the people. In an early case, *Mack v. Jones* (1850), the New Hampshire Supreme Court held that the power of taxation is an attribute of sovereignty belonging to the people, and this power has been delegated under the New Hampshire Constitution to the legislature. Accordingly, no property can be taxed by any subdivision of the state in the absence of legislative authorization. *Town of Canaan v. Enfield Village Fire District* (1908). The legislature may also exempt certain classes of property from taxation, including by omission in a description of property required to be taxed. *Brewster v. Hough* (1839).

In a 1997 case, the court concluded that the state's method of funding education, based upon local property taxes, was disproportionate and unreasonable. *Claremont School District v. Governor* (1997). In 1999, the state senate considered a bill that would have allowed the people, through a binding referendum, to decide on a tax plan to resolve the education funding crisis; proponents of the senate resolution argued that Article 28 appeared to reserve a right for the people of New Hampshire to consent to taxation, a right distinct from, and in addition, to the legislature's authority to establish taxes. The court in *Opinion of the Justices (Tax Plan Referendum)* (1999), rejected this argument. After examining other constitutional provisions, case law, and the relevant history, the court concluded the article represented an express delegation of the taxing power from the people to the legislature, and had never been understood as containing a reservation or exemption from the supreme legislative power granted to the legislature by the state constitution.

In *Caparco v. Town of Danville* (2005), the court addressed a claim that a municipal fee ordinance violated this article by permitting "charges" to be established by a town planning board absent the consent of the people or legislative authority. The court held that such authority existed, as the legislature had "authorized towns to delegate to planning boards the authority to exercise some discretion, under proper standards, in adjusting impact fees in their administration of impact fee ordinances." As well, the residents of the town had voted to accept the impact fee scheme. Accordingly, even assuming impact fees qualified as "charges" under this article, the legislature and residents of the towns had given their consent.

### [ART.] 28-a. [MANDATED PROGRAMS.]

The state shall not mandate or assign any new, expanded or modified programs or responsibilities to any political subdivision in such a way as to necessitate additional local expenditures by the political subdivision unless such programs or responsibilities are fully funded by the state or unless such programs or responsibilities are approved for funding by a vote of the local legislative body of the political subdivision. *1984.*

This article prohibits the state from enacting programs or imposing responsibilities that place additional fiscal obligations upon local governments, unless the local government consents or the state provides the necessary funding. *New Hampshire Municipal Trust Workers' Compensation Fund v. Flynn* (1990). The 1984 constitutional convention recommended passage of the proposal as one needed "to protect political subdivisions from excessive property tax assessments due to unfunded mandates." The article notably does not apply to the many responsibilities assigned local governments by the state prior to its effective date.

"Invoking th[is] constitutional prohibition," the New Hampshire Supreme Court has stated, "requires both a mandate of responsibility to the political subdivision and a requirement of additional local political subdivision expenditures by virtue of the mandate." *Opinion of the Justices (Solid Waste Disposal)* (1992). "[T]o constitute a new, expanded or modified 'responsibility,' the state action must impose some substantive change to an underlying function, duty or activity performed or to be performed by local government." *City of Concord v. State* (2012). "Increased expenditures alone are not dispositive of whether a program or responsibility has been expanded." *Town of Nelson v. N.H. Department of Transportation* (2001).

In *Town of Nelson*, for example, the state's reclassification of a road serving only local traffic from a state highway to a local highway did not create a new program or responsibility for the town: "That the contested segments [of the road] now serve only local traffic may be a new development; the town's responsibility for maintaining roads that serve only local traffic is not new." *Id.*; see also *Opinion of the Justices (Voting Age in Primaries)* (2008) (that proposed law would allow certain seventeen-year-olds to register and vote in primary elections might have been a new development, but municipal responsibility for processing all voter registrations was not new). The court has held that this article does not apply to actions by the state judiciary even though a judicial decision might impose a new, expanded, or modified responsibility upon local government. *New Hampshire Municipal Trust Workers' Compensation Fund, supra.*

The court concluded in *Flynn* that an amendment to the workers' compensation statute violated Article 28-a. The statutory amendment created a prima facie presumption that a fire fighter suffering from cancer incurred the disease on the job; under prior law, the fire fighter had to show not only the absence of cancer upon employment but also that the cancer was work-related. The court reasoned that the law imposed a new responsibility upon local government in part because more fire fighters would qualify for workers' compensation benefits funded by local governments. In contrast, a statutory alteration of percentage of required employer contribution to the state retirement system made no changes to the scope of benefits local political subdivisions were required to provide police officers, fire fighters, and teachers, and therefore did not violate this article. *City of Concord, supra.*

The court has concluded that a proposed law prohibiting the disposal of certain recyclable materials in any landfill, composting facility, or incinerator would not violate Article 28-a. Though the prohibition would have induced most towns and cities to establish or continue resource recovery or recycling operations, the proposed law did not mandate that they do so. *Opinion of the Justices (Solid Waste Disposal), supra.* Likewise, in *Nashua School District v. State* (1995), the court held constitutional an amendment to the special education law which made a sending-district liable for special education costs for a child placed in a residential school, because the amendment did not represent a new, expanded, or modified program or responsibility to the school district in such a way as to necessitate additional local expenditures.

### [ART.] 29. [SUSPENSION OF LAWS BY LEGISLATURE ONLY.]

The power of suspending the laws, or the execution of them, ought never to be exercised but by the legislature, or by authority derived therefrom, to be exercised in such particular cases only as the legislature shall expressly provide for. *1784.*

This article recognizes legislative authority to temporarily suspend the operation of a law; it is virtually identical to Part 1, Article 20 of the Massachusetts Constitution of 1780. The New Hampshire Supreme Court has defined the "suspension" of a statute as the temporary displacement of a valid legislative enactment by the execution of a later statute which is to prevail during its limited operation. *King v. Sununu* (1985).

The court relied upon this provision in *Girard v. Town of Allenstown* (1981) to strike down a town's "fair rental ordinance." The court rejected the argument that "home rule" powers delegated to local governmental units allowed the town to enact such a law; the home rule powers, the court reasoned, are broad but not unlimited, and the legislature remains the supreme legislative authority pursuant to this article and Part 2, Article 2.

### [ART.] 30. [FREEDOM OF SPEECH.]

The freedom of deliberation, speech, and debate, in either house of the legislature, is so essential to the rights of the people, that it cannot be the foundation of any action, complaint, or prosecution, in any other court or place whatsoever. *1784.*

This article preserves the principle that the members of the legislature must be free to both speak and act without fear of criminal or civil liability. It is very similar to Part 1, Article 21 of the Massachusetts Constitution of 1780; the New Hampshire version deletes the reference to immunity from "accusation." The framers intended the privileges afforded debate and deliberation under this article to protect the integrity of the legislative process. The New Hampshire Supreme Court has stated that the privileges secured by this provision "are intended not to protect legislators against prosecutions for their own benefit, but to support the rights of the people, by enabling their representatives to execute the functions of their office, without fear of prosecution, civil or criminal." *Hughes v. Speaker of the New Hampshire House of Representatives* (2005) (quotation omitted).

The court discussed the parameters of this article in *Keefe v. Roberts* (1976). In that case, Keefe refused to return to the house chamber after the speaker of the house had issued a quorum call, whereupon the speaker instructed the house sergeant-at-arms to arrest Keefe and return him to the chamber. The court concluded that a legislator must be acting within the scope of his legitimate legislative function to qualify for the article's protection. Here, the speaker did act within the scope of his responsibilities: the court held the speaker's actions consistent with the proper functioning of the legislative process and part of the legislative process itself.

In *Hughes*, the court faced the question whether the public's constitutional and statutory rights of access to public proceedings outweighed the privileges afforded free legislative deliberation and debate. The plaintiffs alleged a lack of public access to certain private discussions of conferees and the negotiations that ultimately led to a bill concerning school funding. The court concluded that, in the specific factual circumstances, "the legislature could properly have determined that denying the public access to these negotiations was a reasonable restriction on the public's right of access," particularly given the availability of official journals documenting the legislative process in this instance. *Id.*

### [ART.] 31. [MEETINGS OF LEGISLATURE, FOR WHAT PURPOSES.]

The legislature shall assemble for the redress of public grievances and for making such laws as the public good may require. *1784; amended 1792.*

This article articulates the primary purposes for which the legislature is to assemble: to redress public grievances and to make laws for the public good. The framers in 1784 adopted the original language from Part 1, Article 22 of the Massachusetts Constitution of 1780. In 1792, the people amended the text to add the requirement that the legislature assemble to address "public" grievances, and to remove references to "frequent" assembly and "correcting, strengthening, and confirming the laws." Though the New Hampshire Supreme Court in the 1940 case *State v. Cox* (1940) mentioned this article as factoring in its assessment of a challenge to a statute requiring a special license to stage certain public events, the court did not elaborate upon the provision's meaning.

### [ART.] 32. [RIGHTS OF ASSEMBLY, INSTRUCTION, AND PETITION.]

The people have a right, in an orderly and peaceable manner, to assemble and consult upon the common good, give instructions to their representatives, and to request of the legislative body, by way of petition or remonstrance, redress of the wrongs done them, and of the grievances they suffer. *1784.*

This article protects the right to of the people to peaceably assembly for the purpose of calling public attention to a matter of concern to the persons assembled, the right of citizens to instruct their representatives, and the right to petition the legislature for redress. The text is nearly identical to Part 1, Article 19 of the Massachusetts Constitution of 1780.

## Right to Association

The New Hampshire Supreme Court has held that this article "guarantees the same right to free speech and association" as does the First Amendment to the U.S. Constitution. *Opinion of the Justices* (1981). This right includes the interest of citizens in forming political parties "for the advancement of common political goals and ideas." *Opinion of the Justices (Voting Age in Primary Elections II)* (2009) (quotation omitted). But this right is not absolute: "there must be a substantial regulation of elections if they are to be fair and honest and if some sort of order, rather than chaos, is to accompany the democratic process." *Id.* (quotation omitted). In evaluating the constitutionality of such regulation, the court will weigh the character and magnitude of the burden the regulation places on associational rights against the interests the state argues are advanced by the regulation. In *Opinion of the Justices (Voting Age in Primary Elections II),* the court concluded that, while a political party can, consistent with this article, "select its own structure and standard bearer, it does not follow that it also has the right to determine voter qualifications." *Id.*

## Right to Public Assembly

The court has affirmed the right of the people to peaceably assembly and the authority of the legislature to place reasonable restrictions on public assemblies. In a 1963 case, police arrested students who refused to "take to the nearest shelter" during a civil defense drill authorized by state law. See *State v. Pinsince* (1963). The court held the shelter requirement justified as a preventative measure to ensure the protection and welfare of the general public through the establishment of orderly procedures to be followed in the event of emergency or disaster. The court similarly concluded in a 1967 case that a parade license requirement did not violate this article, so long as the local officials administering the licensing acted reasonably and in a nondiscriminatory manner. *State v. Harvey* (1967). In a later case, *State v. Chong* (1981), the court struck down a city ordinance that allowed the chief of police to impose "reasonable limits" on and attach "reasonable conditions" to permits to distribute handbills, notices, or advertising devices; the court reasoned that the ordinance violated this article because it permitted standardless prior approval and thereby unjustifiably inhibited the right to engage in free political discussion.

The court held part of a disorderly conduct law unconstitutionally overbroad in *State v. Nickerson* (1980). The police had arrested antinuclear protestors pursuant to a law criminalizing the failure of a person to move from a public place when asked by a law enforcement officer to do so. The court reasoned that individuals must be afforded a chance to peacefully express their views, and that the police could have used other means to secure public safety and the safety of the demonstrators. The court distinguished this case in *State v. Comley* (1988), in which the defendant disturbed the peace when he ran down the aisle of the house chamber shouting antinuclear statements during the governor's inaugural ceremonies. Individual rights under this article, the court concluded, may be subject to reasonable time, place, and manner restrictions.

The right to peaceably assemble includes the right to engage in public discussion. Two advisory opinions from 1981 focused on this issue. In the first, the court reviewed a proposed bill placing an absolute limit on the total amount of contributions that a candidate could accept, which the court concluded would violate the guarantees of free expression and association under this article. *Opinion of the Justices* (1981). In the second, the court revised a proposed bill which sought to impose a spending limitation on candidates for public office as a condition of access to public funds, which the court concluded did not violate this article. *Opinion of the Justices* (1981). The court viewed as significant the fact that the second bill placed no absolute restriction on candidates, as it permitted them voluntarily to choose to accept public financing as a condition of receiving public campaign financing.

## Right of Public to Instruct and Petition

Townspeople in New Hampshire began giving written instructions to their representatives in the late 1760s.[6] For instance, a number of towns provided instructions to their representatives regarding the ratification of the federal constitution; indeed, at least 30 of the 108 delegates had received formal instructions from the town or towns they represented.[7] The custom of a municipality's giving written instructions on an important issue to an elected representative has since fallen into disuse. Today, the court generally includes the right of the public to instruct their representatives as an aspect of the rights to free speech and free association. See *Opinion of the Justices (Voting Age in Primary Elections II), supra*.

---

[6] See Jere R. Daniell, *Colonial New Hampshire: A History* (Millwood, NY: KTO Press, 1981), 228.

[7] See Jere R. Daniell, "Counting Noses," *New Hampshire, The State That Made Us a Nation* (Portsmouth, NH: P. E. Randall, 1989), 197.

The court addressed the practical limits of the right to petition in *Sousa v. State* (1975). There, the court noted that the availability of the remedy of petitioning the legislature to persons injured by the negligence of state employees, but that pursuing such a course could prove costly and time consuming. Indeed, the court suggested the creation of a state board of claims to hear such cases, and the legislature created just such a board in 1977.

A 1983 case, *Pickering v. Frink* (1983), concerned a petition accusing a particular official of misconduct. Following the dismissal of formal charges, the official brought libel action against the petitioners. The court held that this article provided the petitioners a higher level of protection than the common law in defamation cases, but not an absolute privilege. The court concluded that, if the petitioners were exercising their constitutional right to petition for removal of an official from public office, they could not be held liable unless they actually knew the statements in the petition to be false.

### [ART.] 33. [EXCESSIVE BAIL, FINES, AND PUNISHMENTS PROHIBITED.]

**No magistrate, or court of law, shall demand excessive bail or sureties, impose excessive fines, or inflict cruel or unusual punishments.** *1784.*

This article protects individuals from being subjected to excessive bail, fines, or cruel or unusual punishments. The text is identical to that of Part 1, Article 26 of the Massachusetts Constitution of 1780.

## Excessive Bail

Bail is designed to ensure a defendant's appearance in court, and the New Hampshire Supreme Court has held that the amount may be set no higher than that reasonably required to accomplish this goal. See *Opinion of the Justices* (1977). The legislature has the authority to establish the conditions for bail. In *Evans v. Foster* (1819), the court held that no civil action may be brought against a judicial officer for imposing excessive bail.

The court has addressed the matter of excessive bail in several decisions, concluding in *Opinion of the Justices, supra,* that, once bail has been set in an amount determined to be reasonable, any amount above that figure would be excessive. In an early case, *Opinion of the Justices* (1852), the court held that "excessive bail" relates not just to the amount of the bail, but to limitations placed upon a defendant's access to bail. Accordingly, a proposed bill that would have prohibited a person from being a surety for an accused, directly or indirectly, in more than one case, violated Article 33 because the limitation would have made it more difficult for a person to procure bail. Further, a denial of bail when it might otherwise be reasonably granted would conflict with this article. See *State v. McNab* (1849).

## Excessive Fines

The court has often examined the issue of excessive fines in the context of Part 1, Article 18, rather than under this article. See, e.g., *State v. Corson* (1991). In *State v. Enderson* (2002), the court concluded that fines imposed upon the defendant were not disproportionate to his convictions for gambling. In *Enderson,* the court saw no "great imbalance between the gravity of the offense and harshness of the fines as to make the sentence grossly disproportionate," given that the trial court properly considered "the defendant's financial circumstances, the sophistication of the gambling operation, the long period of time the operation was active and the substantial sums of money wagered." *Id.* (quotation omitted).

## Cruel or Unusual Punishment

Historically, the court has decided cases alleging cruel or unusual punishment under the Eighth Amendment to the U.S. Constitution, or under the Eighth Amendment in conjunction with Part 1, Article 18 of the New Hampshire Constitution. See, e.g., *State v. Deflorio* (1986) (holding incarceration of juveniles with adult prisoners not cruel or unusual punishment); *State v. Evans* (1985) (holding denial of inmate's taking college courses in order to increase his chances for an earlier suspension of his sentence not cruel or unusual punishment); and *State v. Dean* (1975) (holding statute imposing minimum mandatory sentence for habitual offenders not cruel or unusual punishment).

The court has stated that a sentence grossly disproportionate to the crime, so as to constitute an abuse of discretion, might violate this article, *State v. Wentworth* (1978), but there has been no case to date in which this standard has been met. The court has often defined "cruel or unusual punishment" with reference to federal law. For example, in *State v. Farrow* (1978), the court relied upon criteria articulated in federal cases to conclude that punishment cannot be disproportionate to the crime for which it is imposed; it must be appropriate according to contemporary standards of decency and comport with basic notions of human dignity; and, in the case of a death sentence, it must not be imposed arbitrarily and must be administered in a statistically significant number of similar cases. See *Gregg v. Georgia* (1976).

Applying these or like principles, the court has concluded that the sex offender registration law, because it was regulatory and nonpenal, did not constitute punishment for the purposes of this article, *State v. Costello* (1994); that an order committing a witness for contempt did not violate the article because the order would be terminated upon compliance with a prior order for production of documents in a legislative investigation of subversive activities, *Wyman v. Uphaus* (1954); and that it was not cruel or unusual punishment for the attorney general to publish a witness's testimony, though it might result in public censure or damage to the witness's reputation, *Nelson v. Wyman* (1954).

### [ART.] 34. [MARTIAL LAW LIMITED.]

No person can, in any case, be subjected to law martial, or to any pains or penalties by virtue of that law, except those employed in the army or navy, and except the militia in actual service, but by authority of the legislature. *1784.*

The article emphasizes the principle that the military be governed by civilian authority, as provided by Part 1, Article 26. The text of this article is identical to Part 1, Article 28 of the Massachusetts Constitution of 1780. The New Hampshire Supreme Court has not interpreted this article.

### [ART.] 35. [THE JUDICIARY; TENURE OF OFFICE, ETC.]

It is essential to the preservation of the rights of every individual, his life, liberty, property, and character, that there be an impartial interpretation of the laws, and administration of justice. It is the right of every citizen to be tried by judges as impartial as the lot of humanity will admit. It is therefore not only the best policy, but for the security of the rights of the people, that the judges of the Supreme Judicial Court should hold their offices so long as they behave well; subject, however, to such limitations, on account of age, as may be provided by the Constitution of the State; and that they should have honorable salaries, ascertained and established by standing laws. *1784; amended 1792.*

This article recognizes the importance of an independent judiciary and the right of citizens to impartial judges. To secure these ends, judges enjoy tenure so long "as they behave well," subject to mandatory retirement at age seventy pursuant to Part 2, Article 78; and judges are to receive "honorable salaries" set by the legislature. The original article originally was virtually the same as Part 1, Article 29 of the Massachusetts Constitution of 1780; the New Hampshire Constitution speaks of "impartial" judges, while the Massachusetts version refers to "free, impartial, and independent" judges. In 1792, the people amended this article to refer to the age limitation provided for in Part 2, Article 78. The original article referred to the "supreme (or superior) judicial court," presumably to reflect the fact that the highest court in New Hampshire at the time was the superior court of judicature; the 1792 amendment changed the wording to "supreme judicial court," though that name would not refer to the highest court in New Hampshire until 1813.

## Impartial Judges and the Administration of Justice

The right to impartial judges is a touchstone of the common law. See *Moses v. Julian* (1863). This article guarantees not only impartial decision-makers, but also an impartial decision-making process, and one early case suggests that its spirit should be deemed to pervade the entire constitution. See *State v. Webster* (1843). The requirement of impartiality applies to judges in courts, as well as to other bodies that may pronounce judgment upon the rights of a citizen, including juries, see *State v. Sawtelle* (1891); masters, referees, and auditors, see *Tuftonboro v. Willard* (1938); the governor and council when they are conducting hearings on removal of public officers under New Hampshire statutory law, see *King v. Thomson* (1976); and regulatory boards acting in a quasi-judicial capacity, see *Appeal of Town of Bethlehem* (2006). "An act is judicial in nature if officials are bound to notify and hear the parties, and can only decide after weighing and considering such evidence and arguments as the parties choose to lay before them." *Appeal of City of Keene* (1997) (quotation omitted). An appearance of partiality exists when "an objective, disinterested observer, fully informed of the facts, would entertain significant doubt that justice would be done in the case." *State v. Belyea* (2009) (quotation omitted).

Some potential instances of impartiality are clear: a judge of probate who wrote a will cannot preside over its probate, *Moses, supra*; the smallest pecuniary interest disqualifies a party who is to act in a decision on the case, *In re Petition of New Boston* (1870); a biased juror must be disqualified, *State v. Wellman* (1986). Less obvious are instances involving quasi-judicial proceedings. In *City of Keene, supra,* the court held that the chairperson of a county commission considering the necessity of a taking should have recused himself when his law partner had previously represented two of the individuals whose property was to be taken. The court reasoned that the relationship between the chair and his partner's clients created a conflict of interest.

The defendant in *Douglas v. Douglas* (1999) challenged the constitutionality of Supreme Court Rule 38, which provides that, when a judge's neutrality is questioned, the challenged judge, and not someone else, must determine if recusal is appropriate. The New Hampshire Supreme Court held the rule constitutional because it retains the authority to discipline members of the judiciary for misconduct, suspend a sitting judge, or reassign the case to another judge. The test for judicial recusal is whether a reasonable person, not the judge himself or herself, would question the impartiality of the court. See *State v. Ayer* (2003). The guarantee of impartiality may be policed through the judicial disciplinary process. In *In re Thayer* (2000), the court observed that judicial discipline serves the purposes of maintaining the integrity of, and fostering public confidence in, the judiciary; accordingly, a disciplinary action may be pursued even after a judge's resignation to protect the public's confidence in the judiciary's impartiality.

The court has also held that the judicial branch must have control over courtroom security to protect the guarantee of impartiality. The 1998 case *Petition of Mone* (1998) addressed a law making county sheriffs responsible for courtroom security. The court concluded that the transfer of control over court security to the executive branch infringed this article because it could affect the ability of the judicial branch to ensure impartiality in the adjudicatory process. The court reasoned that bailiffs, who guard juries and deliver messages to the presiding judge, should be under the direct supervision of the presiding judge to ensure the impartiality of the process.

The court has concluded in many cases that the right to an impartial judge under this article had not been abridged. In *Belyea, supra*, the court held that the membership of a judge on a drug court team did not warrant his recusal from a hearing to determine whether the defendant's participation in a drug court sentencing program should be terminated. In *State v. Jaroma* (1993), the court concluded that the nonrandom selection of a jury foreperson by a judge did not result in a violation of this article. In *State v. Dufield* (1979), the court held that a judge's involvement in negotiations preceding a defendant's agreement to testify might have been ill-advised, but the judge nonetheless conducted the trial in a fair and impartial manner, such that the rule of impartiality had not been violated.

## Judicial Tenure and Honorable Salaries

This article, along with Part 2, Articles 73 and 78, limits the tenure of judges, who may hold office so long as they behave well, but must retire at age seventy. Good behavior is undefined in the constitution, but the Supreme Court has acknowledged the authority of the legislature to hold the judiciary accountable through the powers of impeachment and address. See *In re Mussman* (1972). Article 35 and Part 2, Article 59, also address the permanent, honorable salaries guaranteed judges. The court has noted the need to ensure the judiciary's independence as the rationale underlying both these constitutional requirements. *Opinion of the Justices (Judicial Salary Suspension)* (1995). Nonetheless, a judge's pay may be suspended by the supreme court as part of its disciplinary authority over judges and such a sanction—which does not amount to a removal—would not violate the tenure and permanent salary provisions of this article.

### [ART.] 36. [PENSIONS.]

Economy being a most essential virtue in all states, especially in a young one, no pension shall be granted, but in consideration of actual services; and such pensions ought to be granted with great caution, by the legislature, and never for more than one year at a time. *1784.*

This article prohibits the granting of pensions, except for the provision of actual services, and limits the granting of a pension to one year at a time. The Massachusetts Constitution of 1780 contains no counterpart to this article.

For many years, the one-year restriction created a budgetary difficulty for the legislature and for public retirees. The legislature met in annual sessions from 1784 to 1877, and could pay pensions on an annual basis during that period. When legislative sessions became biennial in 1877, the legislature appropriated pension funds to cover the two-year budget period, but the pensions had to be paid over a one-year period, because the constitution was interpreted to mean that no payments could be made in the second year. The removal of the one-year restriction on civil pensions under this article has appeared on the ballot five times. Voters rejected the removal of this limitation in 1850 (allowing two-year pensions) and in 1912, 1918, 1974, and 1976 (removing the one-year limitation).

The history of interpretation of this article consists of a series of advisory opinions by the New Hampshire Supreme Court on the constitutionality of proposed legislation. The court has made clear that the article prohibits the grant of a pension based solely upon age, and that it applies both to the state and its political subdivisions. Further, pensions may be granted only in exchange for actual services; the article prohibits the grant of "mere gratuities." See *Opinion of the Justices* (1917).

As to the meaning of the term "pension," the court has concluded that supplemental allowances to be paid under the former teachers' retirement system constituted "pensions" for purposes of the article because they rewarded individuals for services already rendered. *Opinion of the Justices* (1959). The "pensions" for past services reviewed in this *Opinion of the Justices* should be distinguished from the "deferred compensation" for present and future services discussed in another advisory opinion issued that same year, *Opinion of the Justices* (1959). That second advisory opinion concerned contributions made by the state to the teachers' retirement system to provide for future retirement allowances; the court concluded these funds were not pensions and therefore not subject to the constitutional one-year limitation.

The court in 1977 addressed the application of this article to a new state retirement system, holding that the one-year restriction did not apply to supplemental retirement allowances (cost-of-living increases) or additional annuities to be paid to retirees under the new law. The court noted that the framers designed this article as a response to various abuses and meant it to deter the "boons, bounties and favors" granted by the former royal government or, later, the committee of safety. *Opinion of the Justices* (1977). The court's narrowing of the constitutional meaning of "pension" under this article has greatly diminished, if not extinguished, the article's contemporary relevance.

### [ART.] 36-a. [USE OF RETIREMENT FUNDS.]

The employer contributions certified as payable to the New Hampshire retirement system or any successor system to fund the system's liabilities, as shall be determined by sound actuarial valuation and practice, independent of the executive office, shall be appropriated each fiscal year to the same extent as is certified. All of the assets and proceeds, and income therefrom, of the New

Hampshire retirement system and of any and all other retirement systems for public officers and employees operated by the state or by any of its political subdivisions, and of any successor system, and all contributions and payments made to any such system to provide for retirement and related benefits shall be held, invested or disbursed as in trust for the exclusive purpose of providing for such benefits and shall not be encumbered for, or diverted to, any other purposes. *1984.*

This article requires that assets of the New Hampshire retirement system, or any retirement system for public officers and employees operated by the state or its political subdivisions, be used exclusively for the benefit of the retirement system and not for any other purpose. In addition, this article requires that these retirement systems be fully funded each fiscal year. The 1984 constitutional convention proposed this amendment to protect the integrity of the state retirement system and the future benefits for retirees. The convention feared that the funds in the retirement system would become a source of temptation to the legislature, and that the legislature would not fund the system to the extent recommended by sound actuarial practice.

The New Hampshire Supreme Court cited to Article 36-a in *Day v. New Hampshire Retirement System* (1993), in support of its conclusion that the retirement system was not in "privity" with executive agencies of the state because it had a distinct identity, constituency, and interests. The court reasoned that, in accordance with Article 36-a, the funds of the retirement system should not be considered as a part of the state treasury and could only be used for providing retirement benefits.

In a 2010 case, the court addressed the constitutionality under this article of a statute requiring the state retirement systems to divest themselves of certain investment funds. See *Board of Trustees of the New Hampshire Judicial Retirement Plan v. Secretary of State* (2010). The court addressed the argument that this article "requires only that retirement system funds be used for the sole object of providing retirement benefits." As the challenged law did not require that the systems' funds be used for any other purpose, but simply prohibited one investment option, the plain meaning of this article did not render the law unconstitutional. The court confirmed that the legislative history of the amendment demonstrated that that the framers sought "only to prohibit the legislature from allocating retirement system funds to other areas."

In 2011, the court addressed the question whether this article prohibits the state from directing the retirement systems to deduct health care premiums from pension benefits. See *State Employees' Association of New Hampshire v. State* (2011). Here again, the court concluded that retirement system assets were being used to pay benefits to retirees, and not for any other purpose: the state deducted health benefits only from those retirees who opted to receive them, and there was no diversion of funds to other state operations.

## [ART.] 37. [SEPARATION OF POWERS.]

In the government of this state, the three essential powers thereof, to wit, the legislative, executive, and judicial, ought to be kept as separate from, and independent of, each other, as the nature of a free government will admit, or as is consistent with that chain of connection that binds the whole fabric of the constitution in one indissoluble bond of union and amity. *1784.*

This article provides for the separation of the three departments constituting the New Hampshire state government—executive, legislative, and judicial. This is one of the few articles whose origin cannot be traced to the Massachusetts Constitution of 1780; the New Hampshire provision envisions a more plastic relationship between and among the branches than that embraced by the framers of the Massachusetts Constitution. The central purpose nonetheless remains: to limit governmental authority by allowing each of the three departments of government to act as a check on the others, so that one, alone, cannot exercise unbridled power.

The separation of powers mandated by Article 37 is not absolute; as the New Hampshire Supreme Court has observed, this article is a "provision of interrelation." *Ferretti v. Jackson* (1936). The court accordingly has approached the separation of powers from a practical perspective: "the three branches of government, while distinct, must move in concert whenever possible, as the practical and efficient operation of government is not served by the erection of impenetrable barriers between the branches." *State v. Merrill* (2010) (quotations omitted). As interpreted by the court, this article essentially forbids one branch from imposing its constitutional duties upon another, see *Attorney General v. Morin* (1943), or from encroaching upon another's constitutional function, see *Merrill v. Sherburne* (1818).

The legislature historically has been the dominant branch of government in New Hampshire, and the majority of cases decided under this article have considered the limits of legislative powers. Many of these cases concern alleged legislative encroachment upon the judicial branch. In *Merrill*, for example, the court determined that the legislature had exceeded its constitutional authority by granting new trials via legislative enactment, a practice known as restoring parties to their law. *Barney v. Leeds* (1874). In *Merrill*, the legislature had granted a new trial following judicial settlement of a probate dispute, and the court held the enactment to this article's commitment to the separation of powers:

> One prominent reason for creating the judicial, distinct from the legislative department, was, that the former might determine when laws were thus "repugnant," and so operate as a check upon the latter, and as a safeguard to the people against its mistakes or encroachments. But the judiciary would in every respect cease to be a check on the legislature, if the legislature could at pleasure revise or alter any of the judgments of the judiciary. The legislature too would thus become the court of last resort.

Though the judiciary has confirmed the constitutional authority of the courts to control their own proceedings, *State v. LaFrance* (1983), the legislature has made numerous attempts to encroach upon the judicial power. In *Petition of Mone* (1998), the court invalidated a legislative effort to remove the ultimate control over courtroom security from the judiciary. In *Opinion of the Justices (Judicial Salary Suspension)* (1995), the court held the legislature could not require the court to suspend the salary of every judge suspended for misconduct, and in *Opinion of the Justices* (1933), that it could not set a specific fine and maximum period of imprisonment for punishment for indirect contempt. More recently, the court reiterated that the legislature may not enact procedural rules for the courts "that compromise the core adjudicatory functions of the judiciary to resolve cases fairly and impartially and to protect the constitutional rights of all persons who come before the courts." *Petition of Southern New Hampshire Medical Center* (2012).

When an asserted violation of Article 37 concerns the relationship between the legislative and executive branches, the court will begin by examining the respective constitutional powers of each. *Opinion of the Justices (Requiring Attorney General to Join Lawsuit)* (2011). This examination may require the court to look beyond the text to the purpose and intent of a particular provision, as well as to give some attention to the circumstances in which provisions became a part of the constitution. Relying upon this methodology in *Opinion of the Justices (Requiring Attorney General to Join Lawsuit)*, the court concluded that a proposed bill compelling the attorney general to join a lawsuit challenging a federal law would violate this article by "divest[ing] the executive branch entirely of its authority to decide whether to initiate a particular civil action on the part of the State." *Id.*

The court has in the past resolved numerous separation of powers matters in a like manner. In *Opinion of the Justices* (1976), for example, the executive and legislative branches came into conflict when the governor and council adopted a conflict-of-interest policy that precluded an elected state official from being appointed to an executive branch position. The court concluded that the policy violated the separation of powers because the enactment of such policies was the prerogative and responsibility of the legislature. And in *Opinion of the Justices* (1978), the court examined the constitutionality of a proposed bill requiring the governor to designate a particular agency as the health planning agency for the purpose of complying with federal block grants. The court held the requirement would not violate Article 37 because the health planning agency was not of constitutional dimension.

It is possible, of course, that the judiciary, in the process of resolving a case or controversy, may itself tread too closely upon the powers of one of the coordinate branches of government. To avoid this possibility, the court has adopted a justiciability doctrine which limits judicial review "of certain matters that lie within the province of the other two branches." *Baines v. New*

*Hampshire Senate President* (2005). Because justiciability is jurisdictional in nature, the court may address the issue even if raised for the first time on appeal. In *Baines*, for instance, the court concluded that the question whether legislation violated the state constitution's origination clause was justiciable, but the question whether legislation violated nonconstitutionally mandated procedural rules was not.

### [ART.] 38. [SOCIAL VIRTUES INCULCATED.]

A frequent recurrence to the fundamental principles of the constitution, and a constant adherence to justice, moderation, temperance, industry, frugality, and all the social virtues, are indispensably necessary to preserve the blessings of liberty and good government; the people ought, therefore, to have a particular regard to all those principles in the choice of their officers and representatives, and they have a right to require of their lawgivers and magistrates, an exact and constant observance of them, in the formation and execution of the laws necessary for the good administration of government. *1784.*

This article expresses a preference that state legislators and government officials adhere to "justice, moderation, temperance, industry, frugality, and all the social virtues." The article's origins may be traced to Part 1, Article 18 of the Massachusetts Constitution of 1780, with New Hampshire substituting "all the social virtues" for "piety."

This article does not impose any specific requirements, but "merely advises or admonishes." *State v. Elbert* (1984). Legislative good faith cannot be a subject of judicial review. *Trustees of Phillips Exeter Academy v. Exeter* (1940). The New Hampshire Supreme Court in *Opinion of the Court* (1879), cited to this article in considering the constitutionality of a proposed law authorizing towns to exempt certain manufacturing concerns from taxation for up to ten years. The court concluded that the duty to "inculcate and constantly adhere to honesty and justice as necessary to preserve the blessings of liberty and good government" applied to the court, which could not conclude that this duty "would not be illegally violated by allowing the state or any of its municipal agencies to be guilty of the fraud and tyranny of breaking such contracts of ten-years exemption as have been made."

### [ART.] 39. [CHANGES IN TOWN AND CITY CHARTERS, REFERENDUM REQUIRED.]

No law changing the charter or form of government of a particular city or town shall be enacted by the legislature except to become effective upon the approval of the voters of such city or town upon a referendum to be provided for in said law. The legislature may by general law authorize cities and towns to adopt or amend their charters or forms of government in any way which is not in conflict with general law, provided that such charters or amendments shall become effective only upon the approval of the voters of each such city or town on a referendum. *1966.*

The voters ratified this article in 1966, intending it to limit the legislature's plenary authority over cities and towns. The New Hampshire Supreme Court has interpreted the first part of this "home rule" provision as prohibiting legislative alteration of the charter or form of municipal government absent a referendum of the people affected; it has interpreted the second part as authorizing the legislature to permit municipalities to adopt or amend their charters or forms of government, provided that any such changes are approved by local referendum. *Opinion of the Justices* (1969). The second part did not become operative until the legislature detailed the charter adoption and amendment procedures. *Harriman v. City of Lebanon* (1982).

The court has made clear that this article does not require a local referendum "on general legislation which affects alike all cities and towns, or all cities or towns in the same class" and does not affect "special acts which do not literally change the charter or form of government of a city or town." *Opinion of the Justices (Municipal Bonds)* (2001) (quotation omitted). Thus a proposed law that would establish a uniform statewide supermajority voting requirement for the issuance of bonds and notes would not run afoul of this article because it applied to all cities, towns, school districts, and village districts in the state, "not to a particular city, town, school district, or village district." *Id.*

The extent of the constitutional "home rule" power is "the prerogative to choose one of the statutorily specified forms of municipal government." *Id.* Article 39 does not extend supreme legislative authority to cities and towns. *Opinion of the Justices (Weirs Beach)* (1991). Municipal corporations remain subdivisions of the state, possessed only of the powers granted them by legislative grace. *City of Claremont v. Craigue* (1992). Cities and towns may make changes in the charter provisions establishing their form of government, but such changes must conform to the home rule statutes. In *Appeal of Barry* (1998), for example, the court rejected the city of Manchester's argument that it could amend its retirement system because it was part of the city's form of government; the court concluded the home rule statute was intended only to provide a means by which cities and towns could alter their actual form of government. In *Craigue, supra*, the court invalidated a change to a city charter provision relating to direct voter approval of the budget; the measure would have effectively created an impermissible form of government, because the home rule statute allowed a direct vote by citizens on the budget only under the town form of government.

# Part 2

*The Form of Government*

## NUMBERING OF ARTICLES IN PART 2

For a period of time in the late nineteenth and early twentieth centuries Articles 11 through 101 of Part 2 were renumbered, creating a potential source of confusion for lawyers and researchers. The 1842 edition of the *Constitution and Laws of the State of New-Hampshire,* which included the Revised Statutes, the first codification of the New Hampshire statutory law, editorially divided the "Form of Government" into articles consecutively numbered from 1 to 101. In 1889, the voters repealed Part 2, Article 10; when the next published codification of the constitution and statutes appeared, in 1901, Article 10 was noted as having been rescinded with its contents incorporated into Article 11, while Articles 11 through 101 were renumbered as 10–100. Between 1901 and 1926, the New Hampshire Supreme Court and constitutional conventions in 1902, 1912, and 1918–1923 typically referred to the renumbering scheme of 1901, or referred to both numbers, with the 1842 number appearing parenthetically—thus Article 45 of 1842 was referred to as "Article 44 (45)." In 1926, with the recodification of the statutes as the Public Laws, the numbering reverted to the 1842 system. This is the system that appears in the constitution today.

### ARTICLE 1. [NAME OF BODY POLITIC.]

The people inhabiting the territory formerly called the province of New Hampshire, do hereby solemnly and mutually agree with each other, to form themselves into a free, sovereign and independent body-politic, or state, by the name of THE STATE OF NEW HAMPSHIRE. *1784.*

This article declares the formation and the name of the state of New Hampshire. It resembles the preface of Part 2 of the Massachusetts Constitution of 1780, which introduces "The Frame of Government." The New Hampshire Supreme Court referred to this article in *State v. U.S. & Canada Express Co.* (1880) as a constitutional expression of the creation of New Hampshire's government by social contract, observing that the doctrine of social contract, "[w]hether sound or unsound as a theory...being organic law, cannot be officially controverted by either branch of a government thus created." Half a century later, in *Amyot v. Caron* (1937), the court cited to this article in affirming legislative control over local government; the court noted that New Hampshire is not a union of locally organized communities or units, but a "state" formed by "the people inhabiting the territory formerly called the province of New Hampshire."

### [ART.] 2. [LEGISLATURE, HOW CONSTITUTED.]

The supreme legislative power, within this state, shall be vested in the senate and house of representatives, each of which shall have a negative on the other. *1784.*

Pursuant to this article, the general court holds the supreme legislative authority, which is vested in a bicameral legislature consisting of the senate and house of representatives; each of these houses has the power to check the other. This article resembles Part 2, Article 1 of the Massachusetts Constitution of 1780; both provide for a senate and house of representatives, "each of which shall have a negative on the other."

The New Hampshire Supreme Court has long held the general court to be supreme only in its proper legislative sphere of action; other articles of the constitution and in the federal constitution and laws set various limitations on the legislature's authority. See *Opinion of the Justices* (1829). For instance, the legislature cannot act to limit the ability of future legislatures to make laws—in other words, the legislature cannot pass a law that is immune from repeal. *Dow v. Northern Railroad* (1887).

The legislature cannot delegate its constitutional power to enact general state legislation. *State v. Hayes* (1881). The court accordingly held unconstitutional a proposal to allow legislation proposed by the governor to take effect automatically, unless disapproved by the legislature, see *Opinion of the Justices* (1950), and, more recently, concluded a proposal to allow the people to exercise this power through a tax plan referendum would violate the constitution, see *Opinion of the Justices (Tax Plan Referendum)* (1999).

The legislature may, however, empower executive branch administrative agencies with rulemaking authority, and municipalities with the authority to enact local legislation. To be constitutional, such a grant of power must have clear standards and guidelines. For instance, the court in *Ferretti v. Jackson* (1936) struck down a law giving broad authority to the milk board to fix prices. And, in *Guillou v. State Division of Motor Vehicles* (1986), the court held unconstitutional a delegation of authority a law giving the director of motor vehicles authority to suspend or revoke a driver's license for any cause he deemed sufficient.

### [ART.] 3. [GENERAL COURT, WHEN TO MEET AND DISSOLVE.]

The senate and house shall assemble biennially on the first Wednesday of December for organizational purposes in even numbered years, and shall assemble annually on the first Wednesday following the first Tuesday in January, and at such other times as they may judge necessary; and shall dissolve and be dissolved at 12:01 A.M. on the first Wednesday of December in even numbered years and shall be styled THE GENERAL COURT OF NEW HAMPSHIRE. *1784; amended 1877, 1889, 1974, and 1984.*

This article specifies the frequency and timing of legislative sessions and provides the official name of the legislature: the General Court of New Hampshire. The 1784 version of this article derived from Part 2, Article 1 of the Massachusetts Constitution of 1780. In 1784, the Massachusetts legislature assembled annually on the last Wednesday in May, while in New Hampshire the assembly took place on the first Wednesday of June. Both bodies were known as "The General Court."

In its earliest days, the New Hampshire Legislature met in annual sessions beginning in June. In 1877, largely because of concern about the cost of these annual sessions, the voters amended this article to require sessions every two years. In 1889, the meeting time of assembly was changed to January, following a trend toward winter sessions in other states.[1] The members of the legislature who farmed—no small number—preferred January to June, and legislators in general preferred not to be shut indoors on warm June days. By this time, better roads and railroads made winter travel easier, and the installation of steam radiators provided adequate heat in Representatives Hall.

The possibility of returning to annual sessions was frequently considered. Between 1965 and 1976, in only one year (1968) did the general court not hold a regular or special legislative session. In 1966, the voters ratified a change to an annual session, but the New Hampshire Supreme Court invalidated that proposal in *Gerber v. King* (1967), because it deemed the wording of the question

---

[1] *Journal of the Convention to Revise the Constitution, January 1889* (Manchester, NH: John B. Clarke, 1889): 39.

unclear. The voters in 1970 appeared to have adopted annual sessions after the initial count of a proposal indicated its adoption, but the recount revealed that it had been narrowly defeated. By the late 1970s, it had become clear that the legislature almost always had business in the second year of its term that could not wait for the next biennial session, and that the adoption of annual sessions would reduce the need for special sessions. In November 1976, however, a proposal for annual sessions failed to pass. Finally, in 1984, the voters ratified a proposal for annual sessions, after the question had appeared on the ballot for the sixth time in a twenty-year period.

A 1974 amendment changed the organization date of the legislature from the first Wednesday in January to the first Wednesday in December. This change allowed the legislature elected in November to meet for organizational purposes in December, so that it did not need to devote time to the election of officers at the beginning of the January session. See *Chwalek v. Dover School Committee* (1980) (defining "organization" for purposes of this article). The amendment also provided that the old legislature would be dissolved on the same day that the new legislature met in December, instead of dissolving seven days before the first Wednesday in January, thus eliminating the week-long interregnum in which the state would have no legislature. The amendment also set the day of assembly in January as the first Wednesday after the first Tuesday, to avoid the possibility of having to meet on New Year's Day.

The court affirmed the authority of the members of the legislature to assemble at other times "as they may judge necessary," without the consent of governor and council, in *Opinion of the Justices* (1944). The legislature has the authority under this article to call a special session, so long as it follows some orderly method of obtaining the opinions of its members. Part 2, Article 50 also allows for the calling of a special session by the governor and council—and to provide a check on the legislature by postponing its reassembly for up to ninety days.

## [ART.] 4. [POWER OF GENERAL COURT TO ESTABLISH COURTS.]

The general court (except as otherwise provided by Article 72-a of Part 2) shall forever have full power and authority to erect and constitute judicatories and courts of record, or other courts, to be holden, in the name of the state, for the hearing, trying, and determining, all manner of crimes, offenses, pleas, processes, plaints, action, causes, matters and things whatsoever arising or happening within this state, or between or concerning persons inhabiting or residing, or brought, within the same, whether the same be criminal or civil, or whether the crimes be capital, or not capital, and whether the said pleas be real, personal or mixed, and for the awarding and issuing execution thereon. To which courts and judicatories, are hereby given and granted, full power and authority, from time to time, to administer oaths or affirmations, for the better discovery of truth in any matter in controversy, or depending before them. *1784; amended 1966.*

This article gives the legislature the authority to establish courts and to designate their jurisdiction. It is nearly identical to Part 2, Article 3 of the Massachusetts Constitution of 1780. The New Hampshire Supreme Court noted in 1880 that the framers of the Massachusetts provision had relied upon language in the Massachusetts province charter of 1691, which was written in the typical "prolix style" of the time. *State v. U.S. & Canada Express Co.* (1880).

The voters amended this article in 1966 to insert in the first sentence the exception relating to Part 2, Article 72-a, which establishes the supreme and superior courts as constitutional courts. Until 1966, the New Hampshire Constitution did not establish any particular courts, although it did refer to the justices of the superior and probate courts (in Part 1, Article 35 and Part 2, Articles 59, 74, 76, 78, 80, 81). At the time of the adoption of the constitution in 1784, the highest court in the state was called the superior court of judicature.[2]

The court recognized in 1859 that the legislature has the power to constitute new tribunals and provide for new modes of trial, subject to the right to trial by jury guaranteed by the constitution. *Opinion of the Justices* (1859). The legislature may reconstruct the courts, within the limits of the constitution, but this power does not extend to directing the executive branch to perform a function that intrudes upon an essential function of the judiciary, see *Petition of Mone* (1998), or to eliminating an essential attribute of judicial tribunals, such as the power of indirect contempt, see *Opinion of the Justices* (1933). The legislature has frequently exercised its authority to create inferior tribunals, by, for example, granting boards of selectmen the power to assess taxes, see *Boody v. Watson* (1886), or authorizing the insurance commissioner to determine the facts regarding the revocation of licenses, see *Karamanou v. H. V. Greene Co.* (1922). It remains that only judicial officers may exercise judicial jurisdiction, but the legislature can decide which judicial officers should exercise that jurisdiction, see Part 2, Article 76; and it can create special judicial positions, see Part 2, Articles 4, 72-a; *Opinion of the Justices* (1986).

In *Claremont School District v. Governor* (1998), the court held that the legislature's authority to assign a retired justice on a temporary basis implicitly derived from its powers under this article "to erect and constitute judicatories and courts of record, or other courts." This authority allows the legislature to determine the composition of courts and to create mechanisms to facilitate the administration of justice; such mechanisms could include: allowing a temporary justice to be appointed in case of a disqualification; allowing justices retired by reason of age limitation to be appointed as referees, auditors,

---

[2] The name of New Hampshire's highest court went back and forth from superior court of judicature to supreme judicial court (1813), superior court of judicature (1816), supreme judicial court (1855), superior court of judicature (1874), and supreme court (1876). Laws of 1901, ch. 78, established the modern structure of the court system, with a supreme court acting in an appellate capacity and a superior court as the highest trial court.

and masters; and allowing justices retired by reason of age limitation with ten years' service to be appointed as judicial referees.

### [ART.] 5. [POWER TO MAKE LAWS, ELECT OFFICERS, DEFINE THEIR POWERS AND DUTIES, IMPOSE FINES AND ASSESS TAXES; PROHIBITED FROM AUTHORIZING TOWNS TO AID CERTAIN CORPORATIONS.]

And farther, full power and authority are hereby given and granted to the said general court, from time to time, to make, ordain, and establish, all manner of wholesome and reasonable orders, laws, statutes, ordinances, directions, and instructions, either with penalties, or without, so as the same be not repugnant or contrary to this constitution, as they may judge for the benefit and welfare of this state, and for the governing and ordering thereof, and of the subjects of the same, for the necessary support and defense of the government thereof, and to name and settle biennially, or provide by fixed laws for the naming and settling, all civil officers within this state, such officers excepted, the election and appointment of whom are hereafter in this form of government otherwise provided for; and to set forth the several duties, powers, and limits, of the several civil and military officers of this state, and the forms of such oaths or affirmations as shall be respectively administered unto them, for the execution of their several offices and places, so as the same be not repugnant or contrary to this constitution; and also to impose fines, mulets, imprisonments, and other punishments, and to impose and levy proportional and reasonable assessments, rates, and taxes, upon all the inhabitants of, and residents within, the said state; and upon all estates within the same; to be issued and disposed of by warrant, under the hand of the governor of this state for the time being, with the advice and consent of the council, for the public service, in the necessary defense and support of the government of this state, and the protection and preservation of the subjects thereof, according to such acts as are, or shall be, in force within the same; provided that the general court shall not authorize any town to loan or give its money or credit directly or indirectly for the benefit of any corporation having for its object a dividend of profits or in any way aid the same by taking its stocks or bonds. For the purpose of encouraging conservation of the forest resources of the state, the general court may provide for special assessments, rates and taxes on growing wood and timber. *1784; amended 1792, 1877, and 1942.*

This article enumerates and places certain limitations on the lawmaking and appointive powers of the legislature. The 1784 version resembled Part 2, Article 4 of the Massachusetts Constitution of 1780, except that New Hampshire specifically allowed the legislature to impose "fines, mulets, imprisonments, and other punishments," while Massachusetts allowed for the imposition of reasonable "duties and excises." The people amended this article in 1792 to change "president" to "governor." In 1877, when annual sessions became biennial sessions, the reference to election of civil officers "annually" was changed to "biennially," with a proviso added to prohibit towns and cities from making loans or giving credit to corporations. This article operates in conjunction with Part 1, Article 12 and Part 2, Article 6, to ensure the fairness of any tax scheme enacted by the legislature. See *Smith v. New Hampshire Department of Revenue Administration* (1997). A frequently litigated issue is whether a legislative classification for taxation purposes runs afoul of the constitution; this issue is addressed below in the discussion of Part 2, Article 6.

## The Power to Enact "Wholesome And Reasonable" Laws and Define Criminal Acts and Punishments

This article authorizes the general court to make all manner of "wholesome and reasonable" laws; the wisdom and expediency of such laws are within the legislature's discretion and all laws not repugnant to the constitution are "the law of the land." *Trustees of Dartmouth College v. Woodward* (1817). As stated in an early case confirming the right of a dog owner to a hearing on the issue of damages, the constitution does not authorize the legislature to make laws in plain violation of the "fundamental principles of natural justice." *East Kingston v. Towle* (1868). The "reasonableness" of a law depends upon the situation at the time the law is passed. *Carter v. Craig* (1914). Still, setting aside other state and federal constitutional limitations, the legislature, and not the judiciary, ultimately determines what is reasonable and wholesome. *Coleman v. School District of Rochester* (1936).

This article also confirms the legislature's authority to define criminal acts and to prescribe punishments. See *State v. Wong* (1984). In *State v. Dean* (1975), the court considered a claim that a mandatory criminal penalty conflicted with the inherent authority of a sentencing judge to suspend all or part of a sentence. The court upheld the mandatory sentence, reasoning that the constitution does not prohibit the legislature from constricting the independent exercise of judicial discretion by the requirement of mandatory sentences.

## Naming and Settling of Civil Officers

Pursuant to this article, the legislature may provide for the election or appointment of any civil officer in the state, or it may delegate that authority, so long as the constitution does not make some other provision for the election or appointment of the officer in question. For example, Part 2, Article 67 provides for the election of the secretary of state and the state treasurer by the legislature, while Part 2, Article 46 provides that the governor and council appoint judges, the attorney general, and certain military officers; accordingly, the legislature cannot provide for the selection of these officers.

The court has held that the authority to name and settle civil officers provides the basis for the legislative power to divide towns into voting districts or precincts for the election of civil officers; the constitution makes no other provision for these officials. See *Opinion of the Justices* (1905). Further, the power to abolish nonconstitutional positions rests in the general court. *Hunt v. Personnel*

*Commission* (1975). The authority to appoint officers may be delegated by the legislature with appropriate conditions. See *Opinion of the Justices* (1970).

## Proportional and Reasonable Taxes, Abatements, and Exemptions

This article requires that taxes be "proportionate and reasonable, equal in valuation and uniform in rate, and just." *Appeal of Town of Bethlehem* (2006); see *Opinion of the Justices* (1829). A tax must be uniform throughout the taxing district—a state tax must be uniform throughout the state, a county tax throughout the county, and a town tax throughout the town. See *Boston, Concord and Montreal Railroad v. State* (1880). A tax is disproportionate when it is assessed at a greater proportion of a taxpayer's property's true value than the property of other taxpayers in the same taxing district. *Appeal of Town of Bow* (1990). But the constitution does not prohibit the inequality that results when the legislature chooses to tax some property and not other property. *Opinion of the Justices* (1949).

The estates of all residents and inhabitants of the state are taxable. *Town of New London v. Colby Academy* (1898). Revenue need not be called a "tax" to be subject to the requirements of this article. The court has held that licensing authority cannot be used to generate revenues in excess of direct and incidental costs of licensing; any revenues above the costs of licensing are taxes, subject to the constitutional requirements of this article. *American Automobile Association v. State* (1992).

In *Opinion of the Justices (Property Taxation of Telephone Poles)* (1997), the court addressed the question whether the legislature could authorize the taxation of telephone poles and wires consistent with the requirements of Article 5. The court concluded that it could: in acting for the public welfare, the legislature could provide local governments the authority to tax property within their boundaries, which would relate to the legitimate goal of increasing revenues.

Though the constitution does not specifically address tax abatements and exemptions, the court has interpreted this article as granting the legislature broad discretion to provide for abatements and exemptions. *Appeal of Town of Bethlehem, supra.* Abatements must be supported by good cause. *Opinion of the Justices* (1977). In abatement actions, taxpayers must demonstrate that "they paid more than their fair share of taxes." *Gail C. Nadeau 1994 Trust v. City of Portsmouth* (2007).

An exemption must be reasonable and uniform. *Opinion of the Justices* (1989). Classification of property for purposes of an exemption may not be arbitrary, and must reasonably promote a "proper subject of public welfare or interest." *Eltra Corp. v. Town of Hopkinton* (1979). Whether "just reasons" support an exemption "equates to rational basis review." *Appeal of Town of Rindge* (2008).

## Prohibition on Benefit to Private Corporations

This article prohibits the legislature from authorizing any town to loan or give any money or credit to a private corporation. Accordingly, the state cannot reimburse depositors for losses resulting from a bank failure, *Opinion of the Justices* (1959), or pay the expenses of liquidation of a commercial account of an insolvent bank, *Opinion of the Justices* (1961). An exemption for a private entity may be allowable if it is uniform and for the benefit and welfare of the state.

In *Opinion of the Justices* (1949), for example, the court examined a proposed law and concluded that the exemption from taxation of private airports dedicated to public use, as provided in the law, would be constitutional. The court applied similar reasoning in *Town of Hampton v. Hampton Beach Improvement Co.* (1966). There, the court considered whether a provision in a contract between the town and a corporation that benefited the latter violated this article. The court inquired whether the contract over its entire term would primarily benefit a private party or whether it would serve mainly proper public purposes, with incidental benefits to private parties. The provision at issue satisfied the "mainly proper public purposes" test.

## Tax on Standing Timber

The people added the final sentence in 1942 to allow taxation of growing wood and timber at a rate different from that of the full assessed value required for other real property or income, an amendment intended to address the problem of landowners prematurely cutting down timber to avoid paying tax on timber lands appraised at full value. *Opinion of the Justices* (1955). Pursuant to this amendment, the legislature in 1949 enacted a timber yield tax to be assessed on timber when it was cut down. The court approved the tax in *Brown v. Rye* (1957).

### [ART.] 5-a. [CONTINUITY OF GOVERNMENT IN CASE OF ENEMY ATTACK.]

Notwithstanding any general or special provision of this constitution, the general court, in order to insure continuity of state and local government operations in periods of emergency resulting from disasters caused by enemy attack, shall have the power and the immediate duty to provide for prompt and temporary succession to the powers and duties of public offices, of whatever nature and whether filled by election or appointment, the incumbents of which may become unavailable for carrying on the powers and duties of such offices, and to adopt such other measures as may be necessary and proper for insuring the continuity of governmental operations including but not limited to the financing thereof. In the exercise of the powers hereby conferred the general court shall in all respects conform to the requirements of this constitution except to the extent that in the judgment of the general court so to do would be impracticable or would admit of undue delay. *1960.*

The article allows the legislature to take immediate action to temporarily fill governmental vacancies in the case of enemy attack, until such time as proper elections and appointments can be utilized to fill vacancies. The voters added this article to the constitution in 1960, in the midst of the Cold War and attendant fears about governmental continuity in the wake of an enemy attack. The New Hampshire Supreme Court has cited to this article once, in *Claremont School District v. Governor* (1997), noting that it is one of only two articles in the constitution placing an affirmative duty on the legislature; the other is in Part 2, Article 83, relating to public education.

### [ART.] 5-b. [POWER TO PROVIDE FOR TAX VALUATIONS BASED ON USE.]

The general court may provide for the assessment of any class of real estate at valuations based upon the current use thereof. *1968.*

This article allows the legislature to enact laws that allow the taxation of real estate at a special rate based upon the current use of the property. The voters added this article in 1968 to reduce the property tax burden on farmers and individuals who held forest lands by allowing them to pay lower taxes when they keep land in an undeveloped state, at the same time providing an environmental benefit to the state. See *Merrill v. City of Manchester* (1985). Before the passage of current use laws, the assessment of land at its highest economic use resulted in high tax assessments and motivated landowners to sell tracts to developers.

### [ART.] 6. [VALUATION AND TAXATION.]

The public charges of government, or any part thereof, may be raised by taxation upon polls, estates, and other classes of property, including franchises and property when passing by will or inheritance; and there shall be a valuation of the estates within the state taken anew once in every five years, at least, and as much oftener as the general court shall order. *1784; amended 1903.*

This article specifies the kinds of property subject to taxation and requires a valuation of estates at least every five years. The framers of the 1784 version based the original text on similar language in the Massachusetts Constitution of 1780; the Massachusetts provision required a valuation of estates at least every ten years, instead of every five. The constitution originally allowed only for two subjects of taxation—polls and estates; the authority to tax "estates" included taxation based upon the ownership, possession, or enjoyment of every type of property in the state. See *Conner v. State* (1925).

The 1903 amendment worked a radical change in the New Hampshire system of taxation by permitting taxes on classes of property other than polls and estates, including franchises and property passing by inheritance. Following the amendment, the New Hampshire Supreme Court concluded that courts should disregard then-existing constitutional rules regarding equality, proportionality, and double taxation, to the extent they were necessarily in conflict with this new grant authority. See *Thompson v. Kidder* (1906). In 1971, the court observed that even though the 1903 amendment allowed disproportionality in taxes levied on the "classes of property" it made taxable, still the government must respect the requirements of Part 2, Article 5 that taxes be proportional and rates uniform within a class. *Opinion of the Justices* (1971); see *Smith v. Dep't of Revenue Admin.* (1997).

Pursuant to this article, "the legislature has broad discretion to classify property for taxation purposes," and "[a] reasonable classification which is sufficiently inclusive to constitute a distinctive class will be upheld." *Opinion of the Justices (Property Taxation of Telephone Poles)* (1997) (quotation omitted). While the legislature may classify property for tax purposes, it may not classify taxpayers. See *Smith, supra.* The courts limit review under this article to the determination whether "there exist 'just reasons' for the classification," *Opinion of the Justices (Property Taxation of Telephone Poles), supra,* and all subjects of taxation within a class must be taxed at a uniform rate to conform to the equality and proportionality requirements of Part 2, Article 5.

A class created by the legislature for the purposes of taxation must be reasonable and not arbitrary. In *Opinion of the Justices* (1951), for example, the court concluded cigarettes, separate from other tobacco products, could be considered as a distinct class of property within the meaning of Article 6, taxable even when the legislature had exempted other tobacco products from taxation. On the other hand, the court struck down the taxation of cigarettes at a higher rate than other tobacco products "in the absence of a regulatory or just reason" for the difference in rate. *Opinion of the Justices* (1955). Three decades later, in *Cagan's, Inc. v. New Hampshire Dep't of Revenue Admin.* (1985), the court declared unconstitutional a tax on prepared meals dispensed by vending machines because those meals could not be distinguished from the identical, nontaxed items sold in supermarkets. In *North Country Environmental Services v. State* (2008), the court concluded that the legislature could classify as taxable pollution control facilities at landfills while exempting pollution control facilities located elsewhere because, unlike in *Cagan's,* the exemption depended upon a distinction related to the use of the property.

In *Sirrell v. State* (2001), the court addressed the requirement that there be a valuation of the estates within the state at least every five years. The case involved a challenge to the statewide property tax in 2001 and the court concluded this article does not require full physical inspections of all property in the state every five years, but it does require that property be assessed at market value at least every five years. A state law requirement that local assessors and selectmen annually examine all real estate in their cities and towns and reassess any property that has changed in value satisfied this requirement. To be actionable, a municipal failure to so examine property must be shown to have resulted in constitutionally disproportionate taxation and harm to the taxpayer.

### [ART.] 6-a. [USE OF CERTAIN REVENUES RESTRICTED TO HIGHWAYS.]

All revenue in excess of the necessary cost of collection and administration accruing to the state from registration fees, operators' licenses, gasoline road tolls or any other special charges or taxes with respect to the operation of motor vehicles or the sale or consumption of motor vehicle fuels shall be appropriated and used exclusively for the construction, reconstruction and maintenance of public highways within this state, including the supervision of traffic thereon and payment of the interest and principal of obligations incurred for said purposes; and no part of such revenues shall, by transfer of funds or otherwise, be diverted to any other purpose whatsoever. *1938.*

This article prohibits the diversion of "highway funds" for anything other than highway purposes, which could include road construction, maintenance, and improvements. The article's legislative history shows the amendment was proposed "to prevent motor vehicle fees and taxes from being siphoned away from highway uses." *New Hampshire Motor Transport v. State* (2004). The restrictions on highway fund revenues apply to such revenues that accrue to the state and to municipalities, because the latter derive their authority to regulate highways from the state. See *Opinion of the Justices* (1947).

Article 6-a defines highway funds as revenues derived from "registration fees, operators' licenses, gasoline road tolls or any other special charges or taxes with respect to the operation of motor vehicles or the sale or consumption of motor vehicle fuels." Highway funds do not include motor vehicle certificate of title fees, see *American Automobile Association v. State* (1992); motor vehicle fines, see *Opinion of the Justices* (1977); or unrefunded tolls from motor fuel used in boats, see *Opinion of the Justices* (1967). On the other hand, the New Hampshire Supreme Court viewed the use of parking meters as an incident of modern highway travel; accordingly, revenue from the operation of parking meters qualifies as highway funds. *Opinion of the Justices* (1969).

Highway funds must be used for the "construction, reconstruction and maintenance of public highways...including the supervision of traffic thereon." The court has held that highway funds may be used for the construction of public parking facilities, see *Opinion of the Justices* (1969), *supra,* or the relocation of utility facilities necessitated by the relocation of a highway, see *Opinion of the Justices* (1957). The court concluded that the language allowing the use of highway funds for the "supervision of the traffic thereon" encompasses the operation of the detective bureau of the division of state police, provided that the percentage of the bureau's budget coming from the highway trust fund bore a reasonable relation to the time the bureau devoted to the enforcement of traffic laws. *Opinion of the Justices* (1977), *supra.* Nothing in the article suggests that highway funds might be expended on the development of a state rail system. See *New Hampshire Motor Transport, supra.*

### [ART.] 6-b. [USE OF LOTTERY REVENUES RESTRICTED TO EDUCATIONAL PURPOSES.]

All moneys received from a state-run lottery and all the interest received on such moneys shall, after deducting the necessary costs of administration, be appropriated and used exclusively for the school districts of the state. Such moneys shall be used exclusively for the purpose of state aid to education and shall not be transferred or diverted to any other purpose. *1990.*

This article mandates that revenues from a state-run lottery must be used for educational purposes. New Hampshire has the oldest state-run lottery in the nation, having passed a law allowing a state sweepstakes lottery in 1963. The lottery was originally tied to horse races, with its revenues intended to be used for educational purposes. At the time of the lottery's creation, the legislature enacted a law to provide for the distribution of lottery revenues to school districts, but in the 1980s the legislature relied upon those revenues to meet budgetary shortfalls. See *King v. Sununu* (1985). This amendment resulted from the fear that revenues, in a time of fiscal need, would be used for noneducational purposes. It has not been interpreted by the New Hampshire Supreme Court.

### [ART.] 7. [MEMBERS OF LEGISLATURE NOT TO TAKE FEES OR ACT AS COUNSEL.]

No member of the general court shall take fees, be of counsel, or act as advocate, in any cause before either branch of the legislature; and upon due proof thereof, such member shall forfeit his seat in the legislature. *1792.*

This article, added to the constitution in 1792, prohibits legislators from taking fees or acting as counsel or advocate before the house or senate. The framers intended this article to deter the kinds of conflict of interests which had commonly cropped up during the Revolutionary and early constitutional periods. This article has not been interpreted by the New Hampshire Supreme Court.

### [ART.] 8. [OPEN SESSIONS OF LEGISLATURE.]

The doors of the galleries, of each house of the legislature, shall be kept open to all persons who behave decently, except when the welfare of the state, in the opinion of either branch, shall require secrecy. *1792.*

This article provides for the opening of galleries in the house and senate so that the public may observe their proceedings, except when the welfare of the state requires secrecy. This provision has not been interpreted by the New Hampshire Supreme Court.

## [ART.] 9. [REPRESENTATIVES ELECTED EVERY SECOND YEAR; APPORTIONMENT OF REPRESENTATIVES.]

There shall be in the legislature of this state a house of representatives, biennially elected and founded on principles of equality, and representation therein shall be as equal as circumstances will admit. The whole number of representatives to be chosen from the towns, wards, places, and representative districts thereof established hereunder, shall be not less than three hundred seventy-five or more than four hundred. As soon as possible after the convening of the next regular session of the legislature, and at the session in 1971, and every ten years thereafter, the legislature shall make an apportionment of representatives according to the last general census of the inhabitants of the state taken by authority of the United States or of this state. In making such apportionment, no town, ward or place shall be divided nor the boundaries thereof altered. *1784; amended 1877, 1942, and 1964.*

This article permits the size of the New Hampshire House of Representatives to range between three hundred seventy-five and four hundred members, with elections to be held every two years on the basis of equal apportionment. The article also provides that no town, ward, or place may be divided in order to create a district, unless a division has been locally approved under Part 2, Article 11-a. The framers of the 1784 version of this article followed the similar provision in the Massachusetts Constitution of 1780. Representation in 1784 was based upon rateable polls—that is, persons entitled to vote on the basis of property—rather than on population. A town with one hundred fifty rateable male polls earned one representative, with another for each additional three hundred polls—an apportionment scheme that favored small towns. In 1877, the people amended the constitution to change the basis of representation for one representative from one hundred fifty rateable polls to six hundred inhabitants, based upon the most recent census. The constitution still required twice as many inhabitants for each additional representative, the so-called "two for one" requirement. With the change from rateable polls to population in 1877, towns lost the ability to manipulate their property values to inflate the number of representatives to which they were entitled under the constitution. See *Levitt v. Attorney General* (1962).

The people adopted the numerical cap on the membership of the house in 1942 in order to keep the size of the house from continually increasing as the state population increased. In 1964, the U.S. Supreme Court in *Reynolds v. Sims* (1964) and several related cases held that the equal protection clause of the Fourteenth Amendment establishes a "one person, one vote" standard which effectively rendered the "two for one" provision unconstitutional. The people subsequently changed the wording of Article 9 to require that representation be "as equal as circumstances will admit."

The "last general census" referred to in the article is the most recent federal decennial census, as there is no general state census. The legislature makes a reapportionment following each federal census.

## Standard for Apportionment

The New Hampshire Supreme Court has held that "the overriding objective [of legislative apportionment] must be substantial equality of population among the various [legislative] districts, so that the vote of any citizen is approximately equal in weight to that of any other citizen in the State." *In re Below* (2004) (quotation omitted). In 1993, the court concluded that an apportionment may meet the standard of being "as equal as circumstances will admit" even if the legislature "rounds up" or "rounds down" fractional representative numbers for the districts involved, when the division of the population figure by the number of seats in the representative district yields a fractional number. Further, the legislature may legitimately consider population trends in determining whether to "round up" or "round down" an impossible fractional representative figure. *McGovern v. Secretary of State* (1993).

## Permissible Districts

Though redistricting after a federal census is typically a legislative responsibility, the court in 2002 took on the task. The legislature had passed a redistricting plan that year based upon the 2000 federal census, but the governor vetoed the plan and the legislature failed to override the veto. Because the then-current districts violated the federal constitution's "one person, one vote" standard, and because the new districts had to be in place for the 2002 elections, the court established a plan for house districts in *Burling v. Chandler* (2002), and for senate districts in *Below v. Gardner* (2002). In order to meet its goal of "substantial equality" of population among the districts, the court adopted a plan that made significant changes to the house districting system. Indeed, the court concluded that past plans "had not given the fundamental democratic principle of one person/one vote the attention and weight to which it is entitled." *Burling.*

In its redistricting plan, the court used single-member and multimember districts, but not floterial districts. A floterial district is one that includes several separate districts that, by themselves, would not qualify for additional representation but, when combined, the total population would entitle such a district to another legislative seat. The geographic boundaries of a floterial district overlap those of another district in the same representative body. In 1982, the U.S. District Court ruled valid under the federal constitution seventeen floterial districts in the 1982 New Hampshire legislative apportionment plan. *Boyer v. Gardner* (D.N.H. 1982). In *Burling,* however, the New Hampshire Supreme Court rejected the use of floterial districts because they had led to voting right inequities under the state constitution. In a subsequent case, *In re Below, supra,* the court concluded that its decision to craft a redistricting plan in 2002 did not deprive the legislature the authority to amend the court's plan.

The court in 1965 interpreted the provision of Article 9 prohibiting the changing of boundaries of towns, wards, or places when the legislature proposed to redraw the ward lines in the city of Nashua to reflect population changes since the 1960 census. At the same time, the legislature was about to make a reapportionment based upon population because of the 1964 amendment to Article 9 requiring equal apportionment. The court in an advisory opinion directed the legislature to first make the reapportionment, after which it could then subdivide the total number of representatives allocated to Nashua equitably among the new city wards. The legislature could not change ward lines when making the apportionment, because the apportionment had to be based upon the most recent census-established population figures that reflected existing ward lines. *Opinion of the Justices* (1965).

### [ART.] 9-a. [LEGISLATIVE ADJUSTMENTS OF CENSUS WITH REFERENCE TO NON-RESIDENTS.]

The general court shall have the power to provide by statute for making suitable adjustments to the general census of the inhabitants of the state taken by the authority of the United States or of this state on account of non-residents temporarily residing in this state. *1960.*

The people adopted this article in 1960 to allow the legislature to adjust federal census figures to exclude nonresidents from population counts, primarily students attending colleges and military personnel stationed in the state. The New Hampshire Supreme Court considered a challenge to the constitutionality of this article as the legislature began the reapportionment process following the 1970 census. The court concluded that the provision did not violate the federal constitutional guarantee of equal protection: the legislature could adjust federal census figures to exclude college students and military personnel stationed in the state so long as they were bona fide nonresidents and the legislature used a reliable and systematic method to make these determinations. Such adjustment, however, had to be done at the time of the general census; an actual census in a city or town, or an estimate of population changes by the office of state planning, could not be used in between federal censuses as a basis for adjusting population figures to be used in reapportionment or redistricting. *Opinion of the Justices* (1971).

### [ART.] 10. [REPRESENTATION OF SMALL TOWNS.]

(Repealed in 1889)

From 1784 to 1877, this article provided that small towns would be grouped together to make the required one hundred fifty rateable polls for a representative and that the location of the annual meeting would rotate among the towns. In 1877, the people amended this article to refer to one representative for every six hundred inhabitants, and biennial instead of annual meetings. When the people voted to repeal this article in 1889, its provisions were incorporated into Article 11.

### [ART.] 11. [SMALL TOWNS; REPRESENTATION BY DISTRICTS.]

When the population of any town or ward, according to the last federal census, is within a reasonable deviation from the ideal population for one or more representative seats the town or ward shall have its own district of one or more representative seats. The apportionment shall not deny any other town or ward membership in one non-floterial representative district. When any town, ward, or unincorporated place has fewer than the number of inhabitants necessary to entitle it to one representative, the legislature shall form those towns, wards, or unincorporated places into representative districts which contain a sufficient number of inhabitants to entitle each district so formed to one or more representatives for the entire district. In forming the districts, the boundaries of towns, wards, and unincorporated places shall be preserved and contiguous. The excess number of inhabitants of a district may be added to the excess number of inhabitants of other districts to form at-large or floterial districts conforming to acceptable deviations. The legislature shall form the representative districts at the regular session following every decennial federal census. *1784; amended 1792, 1877, 1889, 1942, 1964, and 2006.*

This article addresses the representation of citizens from "small towns" in the house of representatives. Pursuant to this article, the legislature must create districts that combine towns, wards, and unincorporated places, when such an entity has insufficient population for a representative. When creating a district, the legislature must act so as to preserve the boundaries of towns, wards, and unincorporated places, unless the entity affected has approved its division under Article 11-a. The people have amended this article over the years to reflect different solutions to the problem of how the citizens of small towns should best be represented. The framers of the 1784 provision sought to create voting districts by grouping or "classing" towns together to obtain the minimum number for a representative, while rotating the location of elections among the towns. In 1784, that number was one hundred fifty "rateable polls"; the people changed that to six hundred inhabitants in 1877. The formula for representation in the house favored small towns by requiring twice as rateable polls (later inhabitants) for the second and each additional representative.

Dissatisfaction with the classing of towns and the rotation of the annual meetings as provided by Article 10, coupled with long-standing complaints about the problems associated with physically traveling to polling places, spurred a late-nineteenth-century effort to develop a new system. In 1889, the people adopted the "proportional representation" scheme, pursuant to which the citizens of each town could elect their own representative, but only for a proportional amount of time. Because of the number of small towns in New

Hampshire, proportional representation resulted in no representation in the house for years at a time for many citizens.

In 1942, when the people voted to limit the size of the legislature to between three hundred seventy-five and four hundred members, see Part 2, Article 9, each town, no matter how small, was permitted a representative in the house at least once every ten years. At the same time, the amendment eliminated the requirement of six hundred inhabitants for one representative, as the number necessary would be set by the legislature relative to the maximum number of four hundred house members. See *Burling v. Chandler* (2002). As a result of the 1942 amendment, the citizens of some towns enjoyed only part-time representation. The U.S. Supreme Court's decisions in *Reynolds v. Sims* (1964), and several related cases, holding that the equal protection clause of the Fourteenth Amendment sets a "one person, one vote" standard effectively resolved these issues in favor of representation on the basis of population, with representation for everyone, all the time, through the creation of population-based voting districts. See *In re Below* (2004).

This provision grants the legislature considerable latitude in deciding how a district should be constructed, but the legislature must preserve the boundaries of towns, wards, and unincorporated places, unless a division has been approved by local referendum under Article 11-a (adopted in 1978 and allowing towns, wards, or unincorporated places to be divided when forming a district after approval by local referendum). These entities, when combined in a district by the legislature, must be "reasonably proximate" to each other.

The New Hampshire Supreme Court held in 1971 that this article would not be violated if a house reapportionment and redistricting plan provided for some multimember and some single-member districts, or all multimember districts but with differing numbers of members, or districts composed of towns or wards in more than one county, so long as each person's vote was approximately equal to that of any other person. See *Opinion of the Justices* (1971). The legislature may cross county lines when forming a representative district.

As discussed above in respect to Article 9, the court in 2002 established a plan for house districts in *Burling v. Chandler* (2002). In its redistricting plan, the court used single-member and multimember districts, but not floterial districts. In response, the people amended Article 11 in 2006 to allow the use of such districts. See *Town of Canaan v. Secretary of State* (2008). In *City of Manchester v. Secretary of State* (2012), the court rejected an Article 11 challenge in which the plaintiff alleged that the redistricting plan failed to provide a certain number of towns, wards, and places with their own representatives; that the plan improperly divided certain cities, towns, and wards; and that created multimember districts composed of noncontiguous towns, wards, and places. The court essentially concluded that the plan fell within a reasonable deviation and did not otherwise offend the state constitution.

### [ART.] 11-a. [DIVISION OF TOWN, WARD OR PLACE; REPRESENTATIVE DISTRICTS.]

Notwithstanding Articles 9 and 11, a law providing for an apportionment to form representative districts under Articles 9 and 11 of Part Second may divide a town, ward or unincorporated place into two or more representative districts if such town, ward or place, by referendum requests such division. *1978.*

The voters adopted this article in 1978. Articles 9 and 11 did not permit the legislature to divide a town or city ward into separate representative districts; accordingly, before the voters adopted this article, all the representatives of a large town or a large city ward were at-large representatives—that is, each represented the entire district. This provision aims to enhance the legislature's ability to create more local representation in towns, wards, and unincorporated places, so long as those entities request the same through a referendum. Though this article has not been the subject of thorough consideration by the New Hampshire Supreme Court, it did note in *City of Manchester v. Secretary of State* (2012) that neither this, nor Articles 9 or 11, requires that a legislative redistricting plan preserve "communities of interest."

### [ART.] 12. [BIENNIAL ELECTION OF REPRESENTATIVES IN NOVEMBER.]

The members of the house of representatives shall be chosen biennially, in the month of November, and shall be the second branch of the legislature. *1784; amended 1877.*

This article sets the frequency and timing of elections for members of the house of representatives. The corresponding article for senators is Part 2, Article 27. The framers modeled the 1784 version of this article on the similar provision of the Massachusetts Constitution of 1780, but specified a different month for the election. The reference to the "second branch of the legislature" complemented the former Part 2, Article 28, which referred to the senate as the "first branch of the legislature."

The people amended this article in 1877 to change the time of state elections from March to November, the time of elections in nearly all other states. The amendment made elections biennial instead of annual, to be consistent with the change in 1877 from annual sessions to biennial sessions of the legislature. The change was animated by financial considerations, as well as the belief that the business of the legislature could be accomplished by meeting every two years. The legislature returned to annual sessions in 1984, but biennial elections remain the constitutional standard.

This provision has not been interpreted by the New Hampshire Supreme Court.

## [ART.] 13. [QUALIFICATIONS OF ELECTORS.]

(Repealed in 1976)

This article specified the qualifications for voters for representatives were the same as for voters for senators, and that voters were qualified to vote in the district in which they dwelled. The voters acted to repeal this article in 1976 when they adopted an amendment dealing with voting rights, one part of which amended Part 2, Article 30 to make domicile rather than residence a qualification for voting.

## [ART.] 14. [REPRESENTATIVES, HOW ELECTED, QUALIFICATIONS OF.]

Every member of the house of representatives shall be chosen by ballot; and, for two years, at least, next preceding his election shall have been an inhabitant of this state; shall be, at the time of his election, an inhabitant of the town, ward, place, or district he may be chosen to represent and shall cease to represent such town, ward, place, or district immediately on his ceasing to be qualified as aforesaid. *1784; amended 1852, 1877, 1956, and 1964.*

This article outlines the residency requirement for members of the house of representatives: a member must have been a resident of the state for at least two years and a resident of the town, ward, place or district he or she represents at the time of election. If a member moves out of his or her district, the residency requirement is not met and he or she ceases to be a representative. Minor amendments adopted in 1958 and 1964 changed "parish" to "town" and added "district."

This article originally contained both a property requirement and a "religious test" for house members. The framers of the 1784 article used the similar requirement in the Massachusetts Constitution of 1780 as a guide, though the Massachusetts provision contained no religious test. The voters in 1852 eliminated the requirement that house members have estates of £100, at the same time they eliminated the property requirements for senators and governor. In 1877 the voters eliminated the requirement that a member be "of the Protestant religion"; the voters had defeated earlier efforts to delete the requirement in 1792, 1851, and 1852. Whether the "religious test" worked to prevent individuals from serving in the house is debatable; in 1868, the New Hampshire Supreme Court remarked that the religious tests for representative, senator, and governor "have always been, in fact, a dead letter, and the only regret is that they have not been long ago removed by amendment, so as to free our constitution from this just objection." *Hale v. Everett* (1868).

This provision has not been interpreted by the New Hampshire Supreme Court.

## [ART.] 15. [COMPENSATION OF THE LEGISLATURE.]

The presiding officers of both houses of the legislature, shall severally receive out of the state treasury as compensation in full for their services for the term elected the sum of $250, and all other members thereof, seasonably attending and not departing without license, the sum of $200 and each member shall receive mileage for actual daily attendance on legislative days, but not after the legislature shall have been in session for 45 legislative days or after the first day of July following the annual assembly of the legislature, whichever occurs first; provided, however, that, when a special session shall be called by the governor or by a 2/3 vote of the then qualified members of each branch of the general court, such officers and members shall receive for attendance an additional compensation of $3 per day for a period not exceeding 15 days and the usual mileage. Nothing herein shall prevent the payment of additional mileage to members attending committee meetings or on other legislative business on nonlegislative days. *1784; amended 1792, 1889, 1960, and 1984.*

This article sets legislative compensation at $200 per biennium, except for presiding officers, and requires that legislators receive mileage payments as determined by statute. Legislators do not have to actually travel on a particular day when the legislature meets to receive mileage payments, but they must attend the legislative session on that day. Members may also receive mileage payments for "nonlegislative" days when they attend committee meetings or are involved in other legislative business. When a special session of the legislature is called the special session mileage rates apply, with a fifteen-day limit.

The original 1784 text, based upon a similar provision in the Massachusetts Constitution of 1780, required the state to pay a legislator's travel expenses, but the "town, parish or place" the legislator represented bore the responsibility for paying wages. In 1792, the people amended this article to require the state to pay a legislator's wages as well as travel expenses, but the constitution set no specific amount of compensation; legislators were paid a per diem rate, set by statute. Then, in 1887, the legislative session lasted 158 days, beginning in June and continuing into November; critics leveled the blame on railroad lobbyists.[3] Memories of this session were fresh in the minds of members of the constitutional convention of 1889. In the 1887 session, each legislator had received $474 in wages under the constitutional formula. The public believed this pay excessive and a convention delegate proposed wages of $200, noting that this amount nearly equaled the result of multiplying 67 days by the then-current rate of $3 a day. The average annual session length over the previous twenty years had been about 38 days, so allowing for 67 days over a two-year period cut a little time from the average session. The convention set the per diem rate for special sessions in the 1889 amendment at the 1887 statutory per diem rate. The New Hampshire Supreme Court observed several decades later that, by limiting compensation, the convention intended to limit the length of the legislative session. *Opinion of the Justices* (1949). At this writing, New Hampshire's legislators remain by far the lowest paid in the nation.

[3] For a discussion of the tumultuous 1887 session, see Leon W. Anderson, *To This Day: The 300 Years of the New Hampshire Legislature* (Canaan, NH: Phoenix Publishing, 1981), 169–183.

In 1960, the voters acted to limit the number of legislative days for which mileage could be paid. The 1959 legislative session had been the longest in the state's history, running from January 7 through September 7, 1959. Because the constitution contained no limitation on the length of a session, legislators received mileage payments for each session day attended, no matter how long the session lasted. The 1960 amendment limited mileage payments to ninety legislative days. When biennial sessions became annual sessions in 1984, the number of mileage days was equally divided over the two years of the biennium, so mileage was limited to forty-five days each year.

The court in 1949 clarified that this article allows only compensation and mileage to be paid to legislators, and not personal expenses. The court interpreted the article to preclude any payment of expenses of legislators because the article at the time provided for the $200 salary "exclusive of mileage." *Opinion of the Justices, supra.* Though the language "exclusive of mileage" has since been removed, neither the court nor commentators have suggested the underlying intent has changed.

Most of the court decisions concerning this article have addressed various mileage schedules created by the legislature. The court has concluded that the mileage rate need not exactly reflect the cost of travel, but it must bear a "reasonable relation to the cost of travel." *Opinion of the Justices, supra.* The court upheld a proposed graduated mileage scheme in *Opinion of the Justices* (1949), but struck down mileage rates of $4 for the first mile and $0.05 for each successive mile thereafter, concluding that such rates were neither compensation nor mileage under this article.

In 1961 the court rejected a scheme that would have given legislators a minimum $5 payment for daily mileage—$0.25 per mile for the first 45 miles and $0.08 per mile for all miles in excess of 45 miles, with a proviso that mileage would be computed on a minimum basis of 20 miles per round trip. The court reasoned that the constitution did not permit the legislature to use mileage payments to increase its compensation, notwithstanding its view that the $200 compensation was "grossly inadequate" and "antediluvian." *Monitor Publishing Co. v. Hill* (1961).

## [ART.] 16. [VACANCIES IN HOUSE, HOW FILLED.]

All intermediate vacancies, in the house of representatives may be filled up, from time to time, in the same manner as biennial elections are made. *1784; amended 1877.*

This article specifies that vacancies in the house of representatives should be filled in the same manner as biennial elections. The people amended this article in 1877, to change a reference from "annual" to "biennial," when annual elections were changed to biennial elections. This provision has not been interpreted by the New Hampshire Supreme Court.

## [ART.] 17. [HOUSE TO IMPEACH BEFORE THE SENATE.]

The house of representatives shall be the grand inquest of the state; and all impeachments made by them, shall be heard and tried by the senate. *1784.*

Based upon a similar provision in the Massachusetts Constitution of 1780, this article provides that the impeachment of a state officer shall begin in the house of representatives; should the house vote to bring formal charges of impeachment, the senate will then try the case pursuant to Part 2, Article 38. The New Hampshire Supreme Court has stated that, in addition to impeachment, the legislature may "undertake those ancillary activities, such as investigation, that give efficiency to impeachment...proceedings." *In re Judicial Conduct Committee* (2004) (quotation omitted)

The article grants the legislature the power "to remove a judge from office by impeachment." *In re Judicial Conduct Committee, supra.* In 1790, the house impeached Superior Court Judge Woodbury Langdon for failing to regularly attend court; his impeachment did not proceed to trial before the senate because he resigned his office to take an appointment as a federal judge.[4] In 2000, the house impeached Supreme Court Chief Justice David Brock for allegedly interfering in a lower-court case, lying to investigators from the house, soliciting comments from a fellow supreme court judge about that judge's own divorce case, and allowing judges to participate in a case from which they had been disqualified. At trial the senate acquitted Chief Justice Brock of all charges, and he remained on the court. See *Horton v. McLaughlin* (2003) (recounting facts of the 2000 impeachment and investigation).

In the course of the Brock impeachment investigation, the Supreme Court's judicial conduct commission challenged a rule adopted by the House Judiciary Committee which prevented the commission's counsel from attending depositions of supreme court justices and court employees. The supreme court noted that the house had delegated its authority under this article to the judiciary committee to conduct the impeachment investigation and to draft the rules under which its investigation would be conducted. The court recognized the legislature's authority to impeach judges under this article, but affirmed its jurisdiction under Part 2, Article 72-a to hear matters arising in the course of an impeachment proceeding. In the end, however, the court declined to make a decision on the rule because the judicial conduct commission had presented it with a nonjusticiable political question. *In re Judicial Conduct Commission* (2000); see also *Horton, supra* (issue of granting judges attorney's fees for defending against impeachment "belongs in the legislature and not the courts").

---

[4] For a discussion of the Langdon impeachment, see John Phillip Reid, *Legislating the Courts: Judicial Dependence in Early National New Hampshire* (DeKalb, IL: Northern Ill. Univ. Press, 2008), 35–39.

### [ART.] 18. [MONEY BILLS TO ORIGINATE IN HOUSE.]

All money bills shall originate in the house of representatives; but the senate may propose, or concur with amendments, as on other bills. *1784.*

This article requires that the house of representatives initiate bills that impose new means of raising money. This provision is similar to one in the 1776 temporary constitution and the same as its counterpart in the Massachusetts Constitution of 1780.

Cases arising under this article have addressed the meaning of the term "money bill." In 1901, the New Hampshire Supreme Court recognized that at least since 1784 the term had been interpreted to mean direct taxation upon the people. Thus an income tax bill would have to originate in the house, but a bill making an appropriation of state money, see *Opinion of the Justices* (1959), imposing or increasing a license fee, see *Opinion of the Justices, supra,* or imposing a direct tax on parimutuel pools or a payment in lieu of taxes, see *Opinion of the Justices* (1976), would not constitute money bills.

### [ART.] 18-a. [BUDGET BILLS.]

All sections of all budget bills before the general court shall contain only the operating and capital expenses for the executive, legislative and judicial branches of government. No section or footnote of any such budget bill shall contain any provision which establishes, amends or repeals statutory law, other than provisions establishing, amending or repealing operating and capital expenses for the executive, legislative and judicial branches of government. *1984.*

This article prohibits the legislature from inserting footnotes or other sections in budget bills that do not relate to the operating and capital expenses of government. Footnotes or sections may be used, however, to establish, amend, or repeal statutes relating to operating or capital expenses for state government. The people adopted this article in 1984 to prevent the state budget from being used to carry unrelated pieces of lawmaking through the legislative process. Because the governor has no item veto, when the state budget comes to the governor at the end of the fiscal year, he or she must sign or veto the budget as a whole. Failure to enact a budget on time could result in a state fiscal crisis. The committee report adopted by the 1984 constitutional convention referred to "the infamous footnotes which have appeared in increasing numbers in recent years . . . [which] have enacted midnight department head pay raises, unconstitutional minimum business profits taxes, [and] Sunday dog racing in Seabrook contrary to the town's wishes."[5]

---

[5] *Journal of the Convention to Revise the Constitution, May 1984* (Concord, NH: Evans Printing Co., 1984), 299–300.

The year after the adoption of this article, the house of representatives asked the New Hampshire Supreme Court to examine the biennial budget bill and determine whether any of its provisions violated the article's provisions. In *Opinion of the Justices* (1985), the court concluded that budget sections may attach certain conditions to expenditures or make fiscal events contingent upon certain happenings, so long as those sections do not effectuate a change in general statutory law. For example, different spending levels could be authorized at the state prison, depending on the number of inmates. As well, the court concluded that the prohibitions of Article 18-a applied when a provision of law is suspended, notwithstanding that the article refers only to establishing, amending, or repealing statutory law; in the court's view, a suspension of law is a temporary repeal. Further, when the phrase "notwithstanding any other provision of law" precedes a provision, it is not allowable if there is a conflicting provision of general statutory law, whether or not the law is specifically mentioned, but it is allowable if the provision relates only to an expenditure or fiscal matter.

At the time the people ratified this article, the legislature met in biennial session and adopted a biennial budget, and the article accordingly was understood to apply to the biennial operating and capital budget bills. After 1984, the legislature met in annual rather than biennial sessions, but it still adopted a biennial budget, with the enactment of a supplemental budget in the second year to amend the original budget. The question arose in *Warburton v. Thomas* (1992) whether this article applied to an omnibus appropriations bill, enacted as a companion bill to the supplemental budget. The court held that the article arguably applied to the supplemental operating budget bill, but not to an omnibus appropriations bill, because the omnibus bill did not have the "content, structure, or essential characteristics to qualify as a budget bill" under the article and it did not primarily serve to revise the financial program established by the biennial budget.

## [ART.] 19. [ADJOURNMENT.]

The house of representatives shall have the power to adjourn themselves.

*1784; amended 1948 and 1966.*

Under this article, the house of representatives may suspend its session to another time; Part 2, Article 36 provides the senate the corresponding power. The 1784 original tracked the similar provision in the Massachusetts Constitution of 1780, granting the house the power to adjourn, but not for more than two days at a time. In 1948, the people amended the time limit on adjournment from two to five days. Prior to that amendment, the house would adjourn from Thursday to Tuesday, and, to get around the two-day requirement, meet in mock session on Saturdays with just a few members in attendance. An amendment in 1966 removed any limitation on the ability of the house to adjourn itself. The power of the house to adjourn itself under this article is independent of the power of the governor and council to adjourn the house and senate under Part 2, Article 50, when the two houses so desire. The New Hampshire Supreme Court has held that the adoption of the 1966 amendment allowing the house to adjourn itself did not by implication limit the power of the governor and council under Part 2, Article 50 to call the general court into session, if the welfare of the state so required. *Opinion of the Justices* (1975).

### [ART.] 20. [QUORUM, WHAT CONSTITUTES.]

A majority of the members of the house of representatives shall be a quorum for doing business: But when less than two-thirds of the representatives elected shall be present, the assent of two-thirds of those members shall be necessary to render their acts and proceedings valid. *1784.*

This article provides that the quorum requirement for the house of representatives is a majority of the house; nonetheless, whenever fewer than two-thirds of the members are present, a supermajority of two-thirds of the members present and voting is required for any official action.

The New Hampshire Supreme Court in *Pollard v. Gregg* (1914) addressed the question whether the quorum should be computed on the basis of members elected or members active and qualified. The court concluded that the computation of the number required for a quorum should be based upon the number of members elected who are then qualified and recognized as constituting the body of the house for the transaction of business. That number does not include members who have died, resigned, or been disqualified since their election.

Implicit in the constitutional principle that the house and senate cannot act in the absence of a quorum is the requirement that the legislative authority of the general court cannot be exercised except by a quorum of both bodies. Accordingly, the legislature may not delegate its lawmaking authority to a smaller legislative body, as in a bill allowing "legislative veto" of administrative rules that would have essentially granted legislative committees in the house and senate the authority to review and disapprove of such rules. See *Opinion of the Justices* (1981).

### [ART.] 21. [PRIVILEGES OF MEMBERS OF LEGISLATURE.]

No member of the house of representatives, or senate shall be arrested, or held to bail, on mesne process, during his going to, returning from, or attendance upon, the court. *1784.*

Based upon a similar provision of the Massachusetts Constitution of 1780, this article recognizes the importance of the legislative process by protecting members of the house of representatives from arrest and detention while they are going to, returning from, or attending a session of the general court; "mesne process" refers to the intermediate process between the beginning and end of a lawsuit. In *Keefe v. Roberts* (1976), the New Hampshire Supreme Court concluded that this article did not prohibit the Speaker of the house from sending the sergeant-at-arms to compel a member of the house to be present for roll-call votes; the article was not intended to prevent that kind of detention.

### [ART.] 22. [HOUSE TO ELECT SPEAKER AND OFFICERS, SETTLE RULES OF PROCEEDINGS, AND PUNISH MISCONDUCT.]

The house of representatives shall choose their own speaker, appoint their own officers, and settle the rules of proceedings in their own house; and shall be judge of the returns, elections, and qualifications, of its members, as pointed out in this constitution. They shall have authority to punish, by imprisonment, every person who shall be guilty of disrespect to the house, in its presence, by any disorderly and contemptuous behavior, or by threatening, or illtreating, any of its members; or by obstructing its deliberations; every person guilty of a breach of its privileges, in making arrests for debt, or by assaulting any member during his attendance at any session; in assaulting or disturbing any one of its officers in the execution of any order or procedure of the house; in assaulting any witness, or other person, ordered to attend, by and during his attendance of the house; or in rescuing any person arrested by order of the house, knowing them to be such. *1784; amended 1792.*

This article provides the house of representatives the authority to determine internal matters of procedure—to select its speaker and other officers, determine its own rules of procedure, and judge the elections and qualifications of its members. It also gives the house the authority to punish anyone who interferes with its business or house members when attending to such business. Part 2, Article 35 provides the senate similar authority. The framers of the 1784 article followed a similar provision in the Massachusetts Constitution of 1780; in 1792, the people amended this article to provide that the house shall be judge of the returns, elections, and qualifications of its members.

The New Hampshire Supreme Court confirmed in an 1891 decision, *Bingham v. Jewett* (1891), that the house and not the court has jurisdiction to determine the returns (officially attested election results), elections, and qualifications of its members. In *Opinion of the Justices* (1971), the court ruled that a law requiring that the speaker of the house be elected by a roll-call vote would violate this article; this article prohibits the senate from infringing upon the authority of the house to elect its speaker.

Further, no statute can infringe upon the house's authority to determine its own rules of proceedings. No law could require, for example, that the house give advance notice to individuals who might be affected by petitions under consideration in a session. See *Opinion of the Court* (1885). On the other hand, the house cannot use its rulemaking authority to determine a matter that affects both branches of the legislature; in *Opinion of the Justices* (1959), the court concluded that the house could not submit mileage claims that differed from the standard mileage table set by statute because the matter concerned members of both branches of the legislature.

The legislature alone "has complete control and discretion whether it shall observe, enforce, waive, suspend, or disregard its own rules of procedure." *Hughes v. Speaker of the House of Representatives* (2005) (quotation omitted). Whether the legislature violated rules or statutes prescribing legislative procedure generally presents a nonjusticiable political question. See *Baines v. N.H. Senate President* (2005). *Bednar v. King* (1970), for example, concerned a challenge to the validity of votes taken by the house and senate to place a proposed constitutional amendment on the ballot. The court held that each house has the authority to determine the procedure by which the three-fifths vote could be obtained, and that violation of such rules in the process of arriving at the constitutionally required "three-fifths vote" would not invalidate the result of the vote.

There have been no cases interpreting the house authority under this article to punish persons who interfere with its business or its members. When a demonstrator interrupted the inauguration ceremonies of Governor John H. Sununu in 1987, the state charged him with disorderly conduct under the criminal code. See *State v. Comley* (1988). Though that event was not a proceeding of the house, it seems likely a person could similarly be charged under the criminal code for interfering with house proceedings or house members.

### [ART.] 23. [SENATE AND EXECUTIVE HAVE LIKE POWERS; IMPRISONMENT LIMITED.]

The senate, governor and council, shall have the same powers in like cases; provided, that no imprisonment by either, for any offense, exceeds ten days.

*1784; amended 1792.*

This article provides that the senate, and governor and council, have the same authority as the house of representatives under Article 22 to punish any person who interferes with its business or its members when they are attending to such business. It limits imprisonment for any such offense to ten days. The provision of the Massachusetts Constitution of 1780 upon which the framers based this article limited imprisonment to thirty days. In 1792, the people amended this article to substitute "governor" for "president." This provision has not been interpreted by the New Hampshire Supreme Court.

### [ART.] 24. [JOURNALS AND LAWS TO BE PUBLISHED; YEAS AND NAYS; AND PROTESTS.]

The journals of the proceedings, and all public acts of both houses, of the legislature, shall be printed and published immediately after every adjournment or prorogation; and upon motion made by any one member, duly seconded, the yeas and nays, upon any question, shall be entered, on the journal. And any member of the senate, or house of representatives, shall have a right, on motion made at the time for that purpose to have his protest, or dissent, with the reasons, against any vote, resolve, or bill passed, entered on the journal.

*1784; amended 1792 and 1966.*

This article requires each house to keep and publish a journal, the official record of each house's legislative acts and proceedings. It also provides that a member, when duly seconded, may request a roll-call vote that will be recorded in the journal. A member also has the right to have his or her dissent against any vote, resolution, or bill recorded in the journal. The original 1784 provision required the printing and publication of these journals, and granted a single member the right to ask for a roll call. A 1792 amendment permitted members to enter a protest or dissent with reasons in the journal, and required that "public acts" as well as "proceedings" be published. A 1966 amendment mandated that requests for roll-call votes had to be "duly seconded." This amendment resulted from the use of roll calls to delay legislative proceedings; a single member in the house of representatives could effectively filibuster by calling for successive roll calls, each of which—before electronic voting—occupied about twenty-five minutes.

As the New Hampshire Supreme Court has noted, the journals provide a means by which the public and the courts can ascertain what each house has actually done, allowing for public scrutiny of legislative action and ensuring conformity to constitutional requirements. *Bezio v. Neville* (1973). Both the house and the senate have the inherent authority to correct their journals. See *Opinion of the Justices* (1959).

The court presumes published acts to be valid, but that presumption may be overcome by evidence from the journals that the legislation was not constitutionally enacted. In one instance, the court, after examining the journals, held an act invalid due to a lack of evidence that the house had concurred with a senate amendment that appeared in the published act. See *Opinion of the Justices* (1857). In another instance, the court held an act invalid because the requisite quorum of senators was not present for a required vote. See *Opinion of the Justices* (1959), *supra.* Nullification of a vote does not necessarily result in the act being deemed invalid: in *Bezio, supra,* the court nullified a senate vote to return a bill to second reading because the senate journal showed that action lacked the requisite quorum, but the court still held the bill valid because, even absent that vote, the bill met the necessary requirements for enactment.

Under this article, a member may ask for a roll call on any "question" to be entered in the journal. "Question," as used in this sense, does not include the election of the house speaker, so that a member does not have the right to ask for a roll-call vote on the election of the speaker. *Opinion of the Justices* (1971).

### [ART.] 25. [SENATE, HOW CONSTITUTED.]

The senate shall consist of twenty-four members. *1784; amended in 1792, 1877, 1889, and 1974.*

This article sets the size of the senate at twenty-four members. The senate originally consisted of twelve members, which an 1877 amendment increased to twenty-four. A 1974 amendment deleted from the text information relating to the terms of senators (amended in 1792 and 1889). Largely because of the wide disparity between the size of the house of representatives and the size of the senate, and the corresponding amount of power wielded by a single senator, there have been over the years numerous efforts to increase the size of the senate; voters rejected three specific proposals in 1912, 1964, and 1974. This provision has not been interpreted by the New Hampshire Supreme Court.

### [ART.] 26. [SENATORIAL DISTRICTS, HOW CONSTITUTED.]

And that the state may be equally represented in the senate, the legislature shall divide the state into single-member districts, as nearly equal as may be in population, each consisting of contiguous towns, city wards and unincorporated places, without dividing any town, city ward or unincorporated place. The legislature shall form the single-member districts at its next session after approval of this article by the voters of the state and thereafter at the regular session following each decennial federal census. *1784; amended 1792, 1877, and 1964.*

This article sets the rules governing senatorial districts: the legislature must divide the state into twenty-four single-member districts, equally based upon population, after each decennial federal census without dividing any town, city ward, or unincorporated place, unless such a division has been approved by local referendum pursuant to Article 26-a. The framers of the 1784 article followed Part, 2, Chapter 1, Section 2, Article 1 of the Massachusetts Constitution of 1780. At the time, election districts in both Massachusetts and New Hampshire were to be based upon the proportion of public taxes paid by the district. The people amended the constitution in 1792 to require the legislature to create twelve senatorial districts; an 1877 amendment increased that number to twenty-four, accompanying an increase in the size of the senate. Representation continued to be apportioned on the basis of taxable property until 1964, when certain U.S. Supreme Court decisions interpreting the Fourteenth Amendment to the U.S. Constitution made that method of apportionment suspect. The 1964 amendment to this article based apportionment upon population. New Hampshire was at the time the only state to use property rather than population for such purposes.

As discussed above in respect to Part 2, Article 9, in 2002 the New Hampshire Supreme Court redistricted the senate according to state constitutional standards. See *Below v. Gardner* (2002).

### [ART.] 26-a. [DIVISION OF TOWN, WARD OR PLACE; SENATORIAL DISTRICTS.]

Notwithstanding Article 26 or any other article, a law providing for an apportionment to form senatorial districts under Article 26 of Part Second may divide a town, ward or unincorporated place into two or more senatorial districts if such town, ward or place by referendum requests such division. *1978.*

This article allows the legislature to divide a town, city ward, or unincorporated place when forming senatorial districts, notwithstanding the prohibition in Article 26, so long as the town, city ward, or unincorporated place requests such a division by referendum. The corresponding article for the house of representatives is Part 2, Article 11-a. This provision has not been interpreted by the New Hampshire Supreme Court.

### [ART.] 27. [ELECTION OF SENATORS.]

The freeholders and other inhabitants of each district, qualified as in this constitution is provided shall biennially give in their votes for a senator, at some meeting holden in the month of November. *1784; amended 1792 and 1877.*

This article sets the time for senatorial elections as November, every two years. In 1784, town meetings elected senators annually in March. A 1792 amendment reworded but did not substantively change this provision. In 1877, the people ratified an amendment changing elections from annual to biennial, and the time of such elections from March to November. The New Hampshire Supreme Court referred to this article in a 1914 decision holding that a blank ballot was not a "vote." *Attorney General v. Bickford* (1914).

### [ART.] 28. [SENATORS, HOW AND BY WHOM CHOSEN; RIGHT OF SUFFRAGE.]

(Repealed in 1976)

This article provided that male inhabitants twenty-one years of age and older who paid their own poll tax were eligible to vote for senators; individuals so qualified could also vote for representatives, the governor, and councilors. A 1958 amendment removed the reference to "male" inhabitants as being the only persons qualified to vote. The people voted to repeal this article in 1976 because other articles covered its requirements relating to elections and voter qualifications.

### [ART.] 29. [QUALIFICATIONS OF SENATORS.]

Provided nevertheless, that no person shall be capable of being elected a senator, who is not of the age of thirty years, and who shall not have been an inhabitant of this state for seven years immediately preceding his election, and at the time thereof he shall be an inhabitant of the district for which he shall be chosen. Should such person, after election, cease to be an inhabitant of the district for which he was chosen, he shall be disqualified to hold said position and a vacancy shall be declared therein. *1784; amended 1852, 1877, and 1976.*

This article establishes age and residency requirements for senators: a person must be at least thirty years old and have been an inhabitant of the state for at least seven years immediately preceding election, and be an inhabitant of the district he or she represents. A senator is disqualified from office if he or she moves out of the district. The original 1784 article followed the general outlines of its counterpart in the Massachusetts Constitution of 1780, and required that a senator own property in his own right and be of the Protestant religion. A 1952 amendment eliminated the property requirement and an 1877 amendment the religious qualification. In 1976, the people amended this article to disqualify senators from continuing to represent their districts after moving out of those districts, bringing senators in line with the rules governing representatives and executive councilors.

The requirement that a senator be an "inhabitant" of the state requires that the person be a citizen. In *Barker v. Young* (1922), a person who had resided in New Hampshire for more than seven years but was not naturalized as a citizen until 1920 challenged his disqualification to run for the senate in 1922. The court reviewed prior judicial interpretations of "inhabitant," and concluded that, as used in this article, the two preceding articles, and the three succeeding articles, the term meant "citizen," and not all residents. In 1974, John H. Sununu unsuccessfully challenged the seven-year residency requirement in federal court. *Sununu v. Stark* (D.N.H. 1974). The court ruled that the state residency requirement did not infringe upon Sununu's rights under the First Amendment, equal protection, or due process, and that the state had a compelling interest in imposing durational residency requirements upon those who seek state elective office.

### [ART.] 30. [INHABITANT DEFINED.]

And every person, qualified as the constitution provides, shall be considered an inhabitant for the purpose of being elected into any office or place within this state, in the town, or ward, where he is domiciled. *1784; amended 1958 and 1976.*

This article defines "inhabitant" for the purposes of voting or running for elective office. Based upon a similar provision of the Massachusetts Constitution of 1780, this article originally provided that a person was an inhabitant "where he dwelleth and hath his home." A 1958 amendment changed a reference from "parish and plantation" to "ward." A 1976 amendment redefined "inhabitant" to refer to a person's domicile rather than his or her residency. The Commission to Study the Constitution in 1974 recommended the change because it concluded that the term "domicile" had a more certain meaning: it could be defined as a permanent place of abode to which one intended to return, as opposed to "residence," which had a more transitory quality. In light of *Felker v. Henderson*

(1917), this amendment did not work a dramatic change in the law. In that case, the New Hampshire Supreme Court interpreted the meaning of residency in this article to be the place where a person had settled with an intention to stay indefinitely, notwithstanding any floating intention to move to another place at some indefinite time in the future, much like the modern understanding of "domicile." Indeed, the court would later point to *Felker* as defining the traditional concept of domicile: intention to remain, coupled with actual residence. *Bisson v. University of New Hampshire* (1990). This article does not apply to offices that are not elective. See *Opinion of the Justices* (1927).

### [ART.] 31. [INHABITANTS OF UNINCORPORATED PLACES; THEIR RIGHTS, ETC.]

(Repealed in 1976)

This article defined the voting rights of inhabitants of unincorporated places and the time of their annual meetings. Assessors rather than selectmen were responsible for collecting and returning votes. A part of the 1784 constitution, the people amended this article in 1877 to be consistent with the change in time of annual elections and in 1958 to refer to "wards" instead of "plantations" and "parishes." At the time of its repeal, this article contained an obsolete requirement that inhabitants of unincorporated places had to assess taxes upon themselves before they could vote. In *Harper v. Virginia State Board of Elections* (1966), the U.S. Supreme Court held denial of the right to vote for nonpayment of taxes to be unconstitutional. Removal of that provision had been on the ballot in 1968 but the people did not ratify that proposal.

### [ART.] 32. [BIENNIAL MEETINGS, HOW WARNED, GOVERNED, AND CONDUCTED; RETURN OF VOTES, ETC.]

The meetings for the choice of governor, council and senators, shall be warned by warrant from the selectmen, and governed by a moderator, who shall, in the presence of the selectmen (whose duty it shall be to attend) in open meeting, receive the votes of all the inhabitants of such towns and wards present, and qualified to vote for senators; and shall, in said meetings, in presence of the said selectmen, and of the town or city clerk, in said meetings, sort and count the said votes, and make a public declaration thereof, with the name of every person voted for, and the number of votes for each person; and the town or city clerk shall make a fair record of the same at large, in the town book, and shall make out a fair attested copy thereof, to be by him sealed up and directed to the secretary of state, within five days following the election, with a superscription expressing the purport there of. *1784; amended 1792, 1889, 1958, 1974, and 1976.*

This article outlines the duties of the moderator and town clerk regarding the announcement and transmission of certain election results. The selectmen have the duty of "warning" or posting a warrant for elections for governor, councilor, and senator. The moderator must announce the results of votes cast by qualified voters in the presence of the selectmen "in open meeting." Requiring that the announcement be made in open meeting allows other interested parties present to object to an incorrect vote. Pursuant to this article, the town clerk must create an attested copy of the voting results declared by the moderator and transmit them to the secretary of state.

The 1784 version of this article, which followed a similar provision in the Massachusetts Constitution of 1780, required the selectmen to preside at meetings concerning the election of senators, and to sort and count the votes at the same meeting in the presence of the town clerk, who was responsible for recording the votes. The town clerk would transmit a copy of the record to the sheriff of the county, who would deliver it to the secretary of state within a certain time frame. Amendments in 1792 and 1889 reworded this article to comport with the change in time of the legislative session from June to January. Amendments in 1958, 1974, and 1976 related to references to parishes, city clerks, and the timing of the notification to the secretary of state.

In an 1891 case, the New Hampshire Supreme Court clarified that town clerks may be compelled by judicial process to perform the duty of making correct returns of votes declared by the moderator. *Bingham v. Jewett* (1891). A pair of 1873 cases concerned the election of representatives to the U.S. Congress. In *Bell v. Pike* (1873), the court held that town clerks lacked the authority to correct or change results of a vote announced by a moderator; a clerk had to make "a true record and return" of the election results given him by the moderator. In an advisory opinion, the court concluded that the obligation of the clerk to make "a fair record" referred to recording the moderator's public declaration. *Opinion of the Justices* (1873).

## [ART.] 33. [SECRETARY OF STATE TO COUNT VOTES FOR SENATORS AND NOTIFY PERSONS ELECTED.]

And that there may be a due meeting of senators and representatives on the first Wednesday of December, biennially, the secretary of state shall, as soon as may be, examine the returned copy of such records; and fourteen days before the first Wednesday of December, he shall issue his summons to such persons as appear to be chosen senators and representatives, by a plurality of votes, to attend and take their seats on that day. *1784; amended 1792, 1877, 1889, 1912, 1968, 1974, and 1976.*

This article requires the secretary of state to examine the official copies of voting records for senators and representatives as soon as possible after the November election, and to notify persons elected two weeks before the organizational meeting of the legislature on the first Wednesday of December. The framers of the 1784 version of this article followed a similar provision in the Massachusetts Constitution of 1780. The voters amended this article in 1877, 1889, and 1974 to conform to other changes in the constitution relating to the timing of elections and meeting of the legislature. A 1912 amendment changed the requirement of election by majority to election by plurality. The 1976 amendment transferred the responsibility for examination of the returns and notification of those elected from the governor and council to the secretary of state.

In an 1877 advisory opinion, the New Hampshire Supreme Court confirmed that the returns to be computed were the town clerk's official returns, and that the constitution required that the governor and council (who were at the time responsible for examining the returns under this article) had no authority to change voting results announced by the moderator and returned by the town clerk. The court concluded that the governor and council had the responsibility to ascertain not who had prevailed, but who, according to the returns filed by the town clerks, appeared to be chosen state senators. A statute required the governor and council to count votes for representative to Congress in the same manner that they counted votes for state senator. Accordingly, the governor and council had no authority to reject any votes for representative to Congress, but had to compute the votes that the returns showed the moderators had declared, in ascertaining who had been elected. See *Opinion of the Court* (1877).

### [ART.] 34. [VACANCIES IN SENATE, HOW FILLED.]

And in case there shall not appear to be a senator elected, by a plurality of votes, for any district, the deficiency shall be supplied in the following manner, viz. The members of the house of representatives, and such senators as shall be declared elected, shall take the names of the two persons having the highest number of votes in the district, and out of them shall elect, by joint ballot, the senator wanted for such district; and in this manner all such vacancies shall be filled up, in every district of the state and in case the person receiving a plurality of votes in any district is found by the Senate not to be qualified to be seated, a new election shall be held forthwith in said district. All vacancies in the senate arising by death, removal out of the state, or otherwise, except from failure to elect, shall be filled by a new election by the people of the district upon the requisition of the governor and council, as soon as may be after such vacancies shall happen. *1784; amended 1792, 1889, 1912, and 1968.*

This article sets forth how an election should be resolved if no candidate for the senate in a district receives a plurality of the votes; as well, if a person elected senator is not qualified, as determined by the senate, or if there is a vacancy in the office of senate, the governor and council must call a new election. The 1784 version of this article followed the corresponding provision in the Massachusetts Constitution of 1780, which provides for the resolution of senatorial elections in the event no senator received a majority of votes in a district.

An 1889 amendment provided for a new election in case of a vacancy in a senate seat. In 1912, the voters made a critical change, requiring the resolution of an election by the members of the house of representatives and senate only when no candidate received a plurality, rather than a majority, of votes in the district—in other words, such election need be resolved by the legislature only when there is a tie vote, for in all other circumstances there will be a candidate who received a plurality. The people adopted the 1968 amendment requiring a new election, if a person who was elected was found to be disqualified, after the senate in 1965 had found persons from two districts to be disqualified because they did not meet the constitutional residency requirements, and had proceeded to seat the persons with the next highest number of votes. See *Brown v. Lamprey* (1965).

### [ART.] 35. [SENATE, JUDGES OF THEIR OWN ELECTIONS.]

The senate shall be final judges of the elections, returns, and qualifications, of their own members, as pointed out in this constitution. *1784.*

This article corresponds to Part 2, Article 22, which grants the house of representatives the authority to be judge of the returns, elections, and qualifications of its members. The framers of this article followed the similar provision of the Massachusetts Constitution of 1780.

The New Hampshire Supreme Court in two cases addressed the 1875 election. The house and the senate each had sought an advisory opinion regarding the election, in which seats were contested in two districts. In the first case, the court concluded that there could be no appeal when the senate had examined the returns of votes for senators, determined who had received a majority, and seated the members summoned by the governor. *Opinion of the Justices* (1875). In the second case, the court declined to give an answer to the house's request for an opinion as to whether the governor had the authority to issue a summons to senators-elect from two senate districts, noting that the governor was discharging his constitutional duty under Article 33 and that only the senate, under Article 35, had the authority to revise an act of the governor regarding a senate election. *Opinion of the Justices* (1875).

In 1894, the court held that a determination by the senate regarding a senate election is a final determination of the facts. *Attorney General v. Sands* (1894). In *Petition of Dondero* (1947), the court held that decisions of the senate regarding the election of its members are final pursuant to this article. In 1965, the court addressed a challenge to a senate determination that persons in two senate districts were ineligible to be seated because they did not meet the constitutional residency requirement, following which the senate seated the persons with the next highest number of votes. See *Brown v. Lamprey* (1965). The court upheld these actions under the senate's authority to be the final judge of the election of its own members. The people in 1968 amended Article 34 to require a new election if the person receiving a plurality of the votes later was found to be unqualified, to prevent such a situation from recurring.

### [ART.] 36. [ADJOURNMENT.]

The senate shall have power to adjourn themselves, and whenever they shall sit on the trial of any impeachment, they may adjourn to such time and place as they may think proper although the legislature be not assembled on such day, or at such place. *1784; amended 1792, 1948, and 1966.*

This article authorizes the senate to adjourn itself. If conducting an impeachment trial, the senate may adjourn to another time and place, even if the legislature is not assembled there. Part 2, Article 19 grants the house of representatives the corresponding power to adjourn. The original 1784 version followed closely the similar provision in the Massachusetts Constitution of 1780. Both constitutions provided for a two-day limit on adjournments. A 1792 amendment added the proviso relating to impeachment, at the same time the voters added other provisions to the constitution regarding impeachment. A 1948 amendment increased the adjournment limit from two to five days, and a 1966 amendment eliminated any limitation on adjournment. The people adopted similar changes in those years regarding adjournment by the house.

The senate's power to adjourn itself under this article is independent of the power of the governor and council to adjourn the house and senate under Part 2, Article 50, when the two houses so desire. The adoption of the 1966 amendment allowing the senate to adjourn itself did not by implication limit the power of the governor and council under Part 2, Article 50 to call the general court into session, if the welfare of the state so requires. *Opinion of the Justices* (1975).

### [ART.] 37. [SENATE TO ELECT THEIR OWN OFFICERS; QUORUM.]

The senate shall appoint their president and other officers, and determine their own rules of proceedings: And not less than thirteen members of the senate shall make a quorum for doing business; and when less than sixteen senators shall be present, the assent of ten, at least, shall be necessary to render their acts and proceedings valid. *1784; amended 1792 and 1877.*

This article authorizes the senate to elect its own officers and determine its own rules. It also states the quorum requirements for the senate: a majority, or thirteen, is required for doing business, except that when fewer than sixteen senators (two-thirds of the total) are present, a supermajority of ten is required for the senate to take a valid action. This article resembles its counterpart in the Massachusetts Constitution of 1780. A 1792 amendment added the "president" to the officers to be appointed by the senate; the 1784 constitution had referred to the chief executive as the "president," and he presided over the senate. The voters eliminated that responsibility in 1792, at the same time changing the chief executive's title to "governor." When the people in 1877 acted to increase the size of the senate from twelve to twenty-four, they adopted corresponding changes to the quorum requirement.

The quorum requirement is mandatory. When in one case the senate journal showed less than a majority of the senate present for a vote on the third reading and final passage of a bill, the New Hampshire Supreme Court invalidated the act, even though it had been signed by the governor and engrossed as chapter 166 of the Laws of 1959. *Opinion of the Justices* (1959). In a 1973 case, *Bezio v. Neville* (1973), the court deemed a vote constitutionally defective and the particular actions of the senate a nullity when the journal did not indicate the number of members present for the vote. In *Bezio*, however, the court did not invalidate the act because the bill otherwise complied with the necessary procedure for enactment.

The senate has the authority to adopt its own "rules of proceedings." *Hughes v. Speaker of the House of Representatives* (2005) (quotation omitted). In *Bednar v. King* (1970), the court addressed a challenge to the validity of votes taken by the house and senate to place a proposed constitutional amendment on the ballot. The court held that the senate had the authority to determine the procedure by which the three-fifths vote was obtained, and that even violation of its own rules of procedure in the process of arriving at the constitutionally required three-fifths vote would not invalidate the result.

The president pro tem of the senate is one of the "other officers" mentioned in this article; unlike the senate president, he or she does not take on the constitutional duty of succeeding to the office of the governor when the governor is incapacitated or out of state. See *Opinion of the Justices* (1935).

## [ART.] 38. [SENATE TO TRY IMPEACHMENTS; MODE OF PROCEEDING.]

The senate shall be a court, with full power and authority to hear, try, and determine, all impeachments made by the house of representatives against any officer or officers of the state, for bribery, corruption, malpractice or maladministration, in office; with full power to issue summons, or compulsory process, for convening witnesses before them: But previous to the trial of any such impeachment, the members of the senate shall respectively be sworn truly and impartially to try and determine the charge in question, according to evidence. And every officer, impeached for bribery, corruption, malpractice or maladministration in office, shall be served with an attested copy of the impeachment, and order of the senate thereon with such citation as the senate may direct, setting forth the time and place of their sitting to try the impeachment; which service shall be made by the sheriff, or such other sworn officer as the senate may appoint, at least fourteen days previous to the time of trial; and such citation being duly served and returned, the senate may proceed in the hearing of the impeachment, giving the person impeached, if he shall appear, full liberty of producing witnesses and proofs, and of making his defense, by himself and counsel, and may also, upon his refusing or neglecting to appear hear the proofs in support of the impeachment, and render judgment thereon, his nonappearance notwithstanding; and such judgment shall have the same force and effect as if the person impeached had appeared and pleaded in the trial. *1784; amended 1792.*

Pursuant to this article, the senate acts as a court of impeachment, if the house of representative issues articles of impeachment against an officer of the state. The constitution does not specify who should be considered "officers of the state." The New Hampshire Supreme Court's broad description of the legislative power of impeachment arguably includes the discretion to determine who shall be eligible for impeachment. See *Horton v. McLaughlin* (2003) ("exclusive power to conduct impeachment proceedings necessarily carries with it the full authority to make, implement and interpret rules pertaining to impeachment"). The article spells out certain due process rights of an impeached person, including notice and an opportunity to defend himself or herself. The original version of this article closely resembled a similar provision in the Massachusetts Constitution of 1780; New Hampshire allowed impeachment for misconduct *or* maladministration, while Massachusetts required misconduct *and* maladministration. The 1792 amendment added bribery or corruption as bases for impeachment.

The senate held the first impeachment trial in New Hampshire history in 2000 following the impeachment by the house of New Hampshire Supreme Court Chief Justice David Brock under Part 2, Article 17. The senate acquitted him of all charges, and he continued to serve on the court. See *Horton, supra* (recounting facts of the 2000 impeachment and investigation). Notwithstanding the legislature's power of impeachment, the Supreme Court has the authority to impose alternative judicial remedies and disciplinary action, such as the suspension of a judge upon a showing of abuse or misconduct. *In re Mussman* (1972).

### [ART.] 39. [JUDGMENT ON IMPEACHMENT LIMITED.]

Their judgment, however, shall not extend further than removal from office, disqualification to hold or enjoy any place of honor, trust, or profit, under this state, but the party so convicted, shall nevertheless be liable to indictment, trial, judgment, and punishment, according to the laws of the land. *1784.*

This article limits the effect of a conviction following impeachment by the house of representatives: a person may be removed from office and disqualified from holding state office, but he or she cannot be fined or sentenced to imprisonment as a result of impeachment. This provision is identical to its counterpart in the Massachusetts Constitution of 1780. This provision has not been interpreted by the New Hampshire Supreme Court.

### [ART.] 40. [CHIEF JUSTICE TO PRESIDE ON IMPEACHMENT OF GOVERNOR.]

Whenever the governor shall be impeached, the chief justice of the supreme judicial court, shall, during the trial, preside in the senate, but have no vote therein. *1792.*

This article requires that the chief justice of the New Hampshire Supreme Court preside over the proceedings before the senate should the governor be impeached; but the chief justice cannot vote on the impeachment. The people added this article in 1792, at the same time they amended Article 38 to provide more details about how impeachment cases should proceed. Despite the chief justice's involvement, impeachment remains a strictly legislative process. *In re Mussman* (1972).

### [ART.] 41. [GOVERNOR, SUPREME EXECUTIVE MAGISTRATE.]

There shall be a supreme executive magistrate, who shall be styled the Governor of the State of New Hampshire, and whose title shall be His Excellency. The executive power of the state is vested in the governor. The governor shall be responsible for the faithful execution of the laws. He may, by appropriate court action or proceeding brought in the name of the state, enforce compliance with any constitutional or legislative mandate, or restrain violation of any constitutional or legislative power, duty, or right, by any officer, department or agency of the state. This authority shall not be construed to authorize any action or proceedings against the legislative or judicial branches. *1784; amended 1792 and 1966.*

This article establishes the position of governor, vests in that office the executive power of the state, and gives the governor broad authority to execute the laws. The 1784 version of this article, which consisted of the first sentence—referring to the chief executive as "President"—followed the model of the Massachusetts Constitution of 1780. In 1792, the people amended this provision to substitute the title "Governor" for "President." The 1966 amendment added all of the text after the first sentence. The people intended the 1966 amendment to vest in the governor strengthened executive power and responsibility, to be exercised within the dictates of the constitution and the lawful enactments of the legislative branch.

The New Hampshire Supreme Court has stated that Article 41 makes the governor "the supreme executive magistrate" and that this is "something more than a verbal adornment of the office." *Barry v. King* (1965). This authority "implies such power as will secure an efficient execution of the laws." *Opinion of the Justices* (2011) (quotation omitted). The people through the 1966 amendment sought to impose a duty upon the executive to carry out legislative mandates and to enforce constitutional requirements. See *Opinion of Justices* (1973). Thus in *New Hampshire Health Care Ass'n v. Governor* (2011), the court held valid the governor's actions taken pursuant to a law requiring that the executive ensure that a legislatively adopted balanced budget "remains balanced during the biennium." The 1966 amendment also provided the governor broader control over administrative action. See *State ex rel. Thomson v. State Board of Parole* (1975). In *Thomson,* for example, the court held that the governor had standing to challenge the legality of the parole board's decision to grant parole to certain individuals.

The court emphasized the broad scope of the governor's executive powers under the article in *Barry, supra*. In that case, the commissioner of health and welfare refused to answer questions concerning an investigation into his office without first seeing the questions in advance and in writing. Noting that this article, as implemented through Part 2, Article 62, makes the governor and council responsible for "ordering and directing the affairs of state," the court concluded the governor and council could demand the commissioner verbally respond to questions pursuant to an investigation into state departmental business.

The court has also viewed this article as providing the governor and council the inherent authority to direct and regulate the internal workings of the executive department. See *Opinion of the Justices* (1976). The governor's powers under this article also extend to the ability to create, by executive order and independent of the legislature, state agencies for the purpose of receiving federal funds. See *Opinion of the Justices* (1978). In addition, the governor has the authority under Article 41 to decide whether and how to prosecute alleged violations of the criminal law, and the responsibility for determining whether to initiate civil actions on behalf of New Hampshire. In light of this latter authority, the court concluded in *Opinion of the Justices* (2011), *supra*, that the legislature could not mandate that the attorney general join the state in a foreign case opposing a federal law.

The governor's authority under this article has some clear limits: he or she does not have the power to frustrate valid legislative enactments by issuing executive orders that contravene the general court's intent. Thus the court concluded in *O'Neil v. Thomson* (1974) that the governor could not issue executive orders in conflict with legislative appropriations regarding the hiring of new personnel and the purchase of automobiles. And it concluded in *Opinion of the Justices* (1973) that the governor could not access information beyond that authorized by a statute regulating the confidentiality of tax records. The court has also held that, while the governor and council can regulate appointment and employment within the executive branch, and exclude elected officials from the same, they cannot adopt a conflict of interest policy restricting the employment of legislators outside the executive branch. *Opinion of the Justices* (1976), *supra*.

### [ART.] 42. [ELECTION OF GOVERNOR, RETURN OF VOTES; ELECTORS; IF NO CHOICE, LEGISLATURE TO ELECT ONE OF TWO HIGHEST CANDIDATES; QUALIFICATIONS FOR GOVERNOR.]

The governor shall be chosen biennially in the month of November; and the votes for governor shall be received, sorted, counted, certified and returned, in the same manner as the votes for senators; and the secretary shall lay the same before the senate and house of representatives, on the first Wednesday following the first Tuesday of January to be by them examined, and in case of an election by a plurality of votes through the state, the choice shall be by them declared and published. And the qualifications of electors of the governor shall be the same as those for senators; and if no person shall have a plurality of votes, the senate and house of representatives shall, by joint ballot elect one of the two persons, having the highest number of votes, who shall be declared governor. And no person shall be eligible to this office, unless at the time of his election, he shall have been an inhabitant of this state for 7 years next preceding, and unless he shall be of the age of 30 years. *1784; amended 1792, 1852, 1877, 1889, 1912, and 1982.*

This article concerns matters related to the election of the governor: the governor's residency and age requirements, qualifications of voters for governor, the governor's term of office and time of election, and procedures to be followed in the event no candidate receives a plurality of the votes. The original 1784 provision resembled its counterpart in the Massachusetts Constitution of 1780: both contained residency, religious, and property requirements, and provided for the resolution by the house and representatives and senate of a gubernatorial election in which no candidate received a majority of votes. New Hampshire also included the requirement that the governor be at least thirty years old, and that the "president," as the governor was then called, preside over the senate.

The people have amended this article numerous times. A 1792 amendment deleted specific requirements for the handling of votes at town meeting and the requirement that the "president" preside over the senate. The people eliminated the requirement that the governor own property in the value of £500, one-half of which had to constitute a freehold, in 1852, at the same time they eliminated property requirements for representatives and senators. Amendments in 1877 replaced annual elections with biennial elections, changed the time of the election from March to November, and deleted the requirement that the governor be of the Protestant religion. An 1889 amendment changed the time at which the secretary of state presented the votes for governor before the house and senate from June to January, to comport with the change in time for the convening of the legislative session. A 1912 amendment changed the requirement that a candidate for governor, councilor, or senator be elected by a majority of the votes to a plurality. In the fifty years prior to that amendment, the legislature had resolved eight gubernatorial elections. Finally, a 1982 amendment changed the time at which the secretary of state presented the votes for governor before the house and senate to the Wednesday after the first Tuesday, to avoid the possibility of requiring the legislature to assemble on New Year's Day.

Though this provision has not been interpreted by the New Hampshire Supreme Court, the U.S. District Court for the District of New Hampshire in *Chimento v. Stark* (D.N.H. 1973) entertained a challenge to the residency requirement, rejecting the plaintiff's claim that the requirement violated equal protection under the Fourteenth Amendment to the U.S. Constitution.

### [ART.] 43. [IN CASES OF DISAGREEMENT GOVERNOR TO ADJOURN OR PROROGUE LEGISLATURE; IF CAUSES EXIST, MAY CONVENE THEM ELSEWHERE.]

In cases of disagreement between the two houses, with regard to the time or place of adjournment or prorogation, the governor, with advice of council, shall have a right to adjourn or prorogue the general court, not exceeding ninety days at any one time, as he may determine the public good may require, and he shall dissolve the same on the first Wednesday of December biennially. And, in cases whereby dangers may arise to the health or lives of the members from their attendance at the general court at any place, the governor may direct the session to be holden at some other the most convenient place within the state. *1784; amended 1792, 1889, 1974, and 1980.*

This article provides that the governor, with the advice of the council, may act to adjourn or prorogue (extend the adjournment of) the legislature for up to ninety days, if the two houses cannot agree; further, the governor may direct that the legislative session be held at another place in the event its regular meeting place poses a danger to the health or lives of members. The governor is required to dissolve the legislature on the first Wednesday of December every two years. This article should be read in conjunction with Part 2, Article 50, which also addressed the governor's authority of adjournment and prorogation. The framers based the 1784 article upon a similar provision of the Massachusetts Constitution of 1780. Subsequent amendments have served to make the article consistent with other changes updating the constitution. A 1792 amendment changes references to the chief executive from "president" to "governor," and added "place" of adjournment. In 1889, the people changed the time for dissolving the legislature from June to January to reflect a change in the time of the legislative session. A 1974 amendment provided that the legislature would be dissolved on the first Wednesday of December, so it would have time in which to accomplish its organizational actions before the January session. In 1980, the people removed an archaic reference to "infectious distemper" as a reason for the governor to convene the legislature at another place. This provision has not been interpreted by the New Hampshire Supreme Court.

### [ART.] 44. [VETO TO BILLS.]

Every bill which shall have passed both houses of the general court, shall, before it becomes a law, be presented to the governor, if he approves, he shall sign it, but if not, he shall return it, with his objections, to that house in which it shall have originated, who shall enter the objections at large on their journal, and proceed to reconsider it; if after such reconsideration, two-thirds of that house shall agree to pass the bill, it shall be sent, together with such objections, to the other house, by which it shall likewise be reconsidered, and, if approved by two-thirds of that house, it shall become a law. But in all such cases the votes of both houses shall be determined by yeas and nays, and the names of persons, voting for or against the bill, shall be entered on the journal of each house respectively. If any bill shall not be returned by the governor within five days (Sundays excepted) after it shall have been presented to him, the same shall be a law in like manner as if he had signed it unless the legislature, by their adjournment, prevent its return, in which case it shall not be a law. *1792.*

This article provides that a bill becomes a law after both houses of the legislature have passed it; it also describes the procedures for a gubernatorial veto and the manner in which the legislature may override such a veto. The chief executive of New Hampshire had no authority to veto a bill under the 1784 constitution. The people added this article in 1792; according to *Opinion of the Justices* (1950), the framers closely followed a provision of the Pennsylvania Constitution, though this article also resembles the veto provision in the Massachusetts Constitution of 1780. The people rejected proposals to give the governor an item veto in 1912, 1920, and 1930.

The process described in this article must be followed for a bill to become a law. The New Hampshire Supreme Court in *Opinion of the Justices* (1950), *supra,* advised the governor and council that a procedure outlined in a law for the enactment of a governmental reorganization plan inconsistent with the requirements of this article would be deemed unconstitutional. The court has held that, given the temporary absence of the governor from his or her office, the presentation of a bill to the governor's executive office—a practice reflecting settled usage—would qualify for presentation of the bill to the governor under this article. See *Opinion of the Justices* (1864). Further, the court concluded in *Opinion of the Justices* (1977) that the governor may waive at least some defects in the presentation of bills. In that case, the presentation to the governor of the wrong version of a bill three days before he was provided the correct version did not invalidate the presentation of the bill on the first occasion; in the event, the governor had filed a written statement with the secretary of state that he waived the presentation defect.

Though the constitution is silent as to the time at which the legislature must present a bill to the governor, see *Opinion of the Justices* (1965), this article requires a governor who wishes to veto a bill to return the bill to the house of origin "within five days (Sundays excepted)" after its presentation. The court has held that the day on which the bill is presented to the governor should be included when computing the five-day period within which the governor must act upon a bill, see *Opinion of the Justices* (1864), *supra,* and that legal holidays, such as the Fourth of July, as well as Sundays, should be excluded from the computation of the five-day period, see *Opinion of the Justices* (1961). The obligation to return a bill with objections is satisfied when the governor or another proper person returns the bill and objections to the house in which the bill originated and gives notice to that house; the house to which the governor brings the bill and message cannot refuse to receive them. See *Opinion of the Justices* (1864), *supra*. Further, adjournment other than final adjournment cannot prevent the return of a bill by the governor; the court deemed a bill effectively delivered to the office of the speaker of the house of representatives, even though the house had adjourned for the day. *Id.*

The last sentence of this article provides that a bill becomes a law if the governor does not return it within five days after its presentment to him, "unless the legislature, by their adjournment, prevent its return, in which case it shall not be a law." If a governor does not sign a bill during the five-day period, and during that period the legislature adjourns, the governor is said to have exercised a "pocket veto," and the bill does not become law. If a governor approves of and signs a bill, it does not matter if he or she does so after the legislature has adjourned. *Opinion of the Justices* (1961), *supra*.

In 1992, the court considered a case in which members of the house challenged the house's long-standing veto override procedure, which required two-thirds of the members present and voting to override a veto. The challengers contended that the constitution required a vote of two-thirds of the entire membership of each house to override a gubernatorial veto, as had been the practice in the senate since 1971. After examining evidence of the framers' intent and two centuries of veto-override cases, the court concluded that Article 44 required, for both the house and the senate, only a vote of two-thirds of the members present and voting to override a veto, assuming the presence of a quorum. See *Warburton v. Thomas* (1992).

## [ART.] 45. [RESOLVES TO BE TREATED LIKE BILLS.]

Every resolve shall be presented to the governor, and before the same shall take effect, shall be approved by him, or being disapproved by him, shall be repassed by the senate and house of representatives, according to the rules and limitations prescribed in the case of a bill. *1792.*

This article requires a "resolve" to be treated in the same manner as a bill in order to become law. In practice, this article applies only to joint resolutions of the house of representatives or senate, and not to simple or concurrent resolutions. Joint resolutions become law in the same manner as bills—that is, they must be passed by both houses and signed by the governor. Joint resolutions appear in the session laws of the state, and are assigned a chapter number in the same manner as a bill that becomes law. A "simple" resolution is the resolve of only one body, while a "concurrent" resolution is a resolve passed by both bodies; neither a simple nor a concurrent resolution has the effect of law, and neither is signed by the governor. This provision has not been interpreted by the New Hampshire Supreme Court.

## [ART.] 46. [NOMINATION AND APPOINTMENT OF OFFICERS.]

All judicial officers, the attorney general, and all officers of the navy, and general and field officers of the militia, shall be nominated and appointed by the governor and council; and every such nomination shall be made at least three days prior to such appointment; and no appointment shall take place, unless a majority of the council agree thereto. *1784; amended 1792, 1877, and 1976.*

This article describes the required procedures for the nomination and appointment, by the governor and council, of judicial officers, the attorney general, and certain military officers. Though New Hampshire does not have a navy, the reference to "officers of the navy" remains. The framers of the 1784 version of this article based it upon the similar provision in the Massachusetts Constitution of 1780. A 1792 amendment made minor modifications, including changing "solicitor-general" to "solicitors," and decreasing the minimum time for a nomination to precede an appointment from seven to three days. An 1877 amendment made solicitors and sheriffs elected officers under Part 2, Article 71, and removed them from this article. A 1976 amendment deleted coroners from this article. The constitutional convention meeting in 1974 proposed the 1976 amendment after the New Hampshire Supreme Court held unconstitutional a 1973 statute giving county commissioners the power to appoint medical referees (who were, effectively, coroners). *Opinion of the Justices* (1974).

The legislature cannot alter the selection process described in this article, though it has considerable latitude in determining the method of appointment of nonconstitutional officers. In *Opinion of the Justices* (1975), the court addressed the interaction between the authority of the legislature under Part 2, Article 5 to "provide by fixed laws for the naming... [of] all civil officers" except those otherwise provided for by the constitution, and the authority of governor and council to nominate and appoint officers under Part 2, Article 46. The court concluded that the authority of the governor and council did not restrict legislative authority under Article 5, and the legislature could delegate its authority to appoint a commissioner of health and welfare to the governor, place a sixty-day time limit on the appointment of that commissioner, and provide that the appointment be made by an advisory commission if the governor did not make an appointment within the prescribed time. Two years later, in *Opinion of the Justices* (1977), the court concluded the legislature could not enact a law creating a judicial selection commission that would screen judicial candidates and giving the governor authority to either appoint a person of his or her own choosing or make an appointment within sixty days from among the commission's candidates. The court reasoned that this kind of selection process encroached upon the governor's constitutional authority under this article.

Indeed, the court has held that judicial officers within the meaning of this article must be "nominated and appointed by the governor and council, and must be commissioned to hold office during good behavior." *Opinion of the*

*Justices* (1986). In a 2007 advisory opinion, the court concluded that, because marital masters—attorneys nominated and initially appointed by the governor and council—were not commissioned to hold office during good behavior, they could not be considered as judicial officers under this article, and they could not be authorized to make binding recommendations absent judicial approval. *Opinion of the Justices (Recommendations of Marital Masters)* (2007). The court has also concluded that a statute declaring the office of chief justice of the supreme court to be an administrative position violates this article and separation of powers, as the law encroached upon the authority of the executive branch and the independence of the judiciary. See *Petition of the Governor* (2004). The court has also concluded that members of the state board of claims should not be considered as judicial officers under this article, because at common law judicial power did not extend to actions against the state, and the members derived their jurisdiction from a statute that contained a limited waiver of the state's sovereign immunity. *Newell v. New Hampshire Division of Welfare* (1988).

### [ART.] 47. [GOVERNOR AND COUNCIL HAVE NEGATIVE ON EACH OTHER.]

The governor and council shall have a negative on each other, both in the nominations and appointments. Every nomination and appointment shall be signed by the governor and council, and every negative shall be also signed by the governor or council who made the same. *1792.*

This article describes the procedure for the making of appointments under Part 2, Article 46. Both governor and council must approve an appointment. The court has held that this article does not restrict the legislature from providing for the naming of civil officers under Part 2, Article 5, but refers only to the appointment of officers by the governor and council under Part 2, Article 46. In *Opinion of the Justices* (1975), the court concluded that the legislature could, consistent with this article, delegate its authority to appoint a commissioner of health and welfare to the governor, place a sixty-day time limit on the appointment of that commissioner, and provide that the appointment be made by an advisory commission if the governor did not make an appointment within the prescribed time.

### [ART.] 48. [FIELD OFFICERS TO RECOMMEND, AND GOVERNOR TO APPOINT, COMPANY OFFICERS.]

(Repealed in 1976)

This article, dating from 1784, addressed the nomination and appointment of company officers in the militia. It originally provided that the president (now governor) had to appoint the company officers (captains and subalterns) recommended by the field officers. The people amended the article in 1792 to allow field officers to recommend the company officers, but did not require the governor to appoint those so recommended. A 1902 amendment provided that the nominees had to be examined and qualified by an examining board.

### [ART.] 49. [PRESIDENT OF SENATE, ETC., TO ACT AS GOVERNOR WHEN OFFICE VACANT; SPEAKER OF HOUSE TO ACT WHEN OFFICE OF PRESIDENT OF SENATE IS ALSO VACANT.]

In the event of the death, resignation, removal from office, failure to qualify, physical or mental incapacity, absence from the state, or other incapacity of the governor, the president of the senate, for the time being, shall act as governor until the vacancy is filled or the incapacity is removed; and if the president of the senate, for any of the above-named causes, shall become incapable of performing the duties of governor, the same shall devolve upon the speaker of the house of representatives, for the time being, or in the case of the like incapacity of the speaker, upon the secretary of state, or in case of his like incapacity, upon the state treasurer, each of whom, in that order, shall act as governor, as hereinabove provided, until the vacancy is filled or the incapacity removed. Whenever a vacancy for the duration or remainder of the governor's term of office occurs before the commencement of the last year of such term, a special election for governor shall take place to fill the vacancy, as provided by law. Whenever the speaker of the house acts as governor, he shall act as such only until such time as the vacancy is filled or the incapacity removed in either the office of governor or of president of the senate, whichever occurs first. Whenever either the secretary of state or the treasurer acts as governor, he shall act as such only until such time as the vacancy is filled or the incapacity removed in the offices of governor, of president of the senate or of speaker of the house, whichever occurs first. While acting as governor under this article, the president of the senate, speaker of the house, secretary of state or state treasurer, as the case may be, shall be styled Acting Governor, shall not be required to take an additional oath of office, shall have and exercise all the powers, duties and authorities of, and receive compensation equal to that of the office of governor; and the capacity of each such officer to serve as president of the senate as well as senator, speaker of the house of representatives as well as representative, secretary of state, or state treasurer, as the case may be, or to receive the compensation of such office, shall be suspended only. While the governor or an acting governor is absent from the state on official business, he shall have the power and authority to transact such business.

*1784; amended 1792, 1889, 1968, 1956, and 1984.*

This article defines the circumstances in which the governor's office should be understood to be vacant, including the governor's death, resignation, removal from office, failure to qualify, physical or mental incapacity, absence from the state, or other incapacity. As well, this article spells out who may succeed the governor in such a situation: in order, the president of the senate, the speaker of the house, the secretary of state, and the state treasurer. The article provides for a new election should a vacancy occur in the office of governor before the beginning of the last year of his or her term. In addition, this article provides for an "acting governor," and clarifies that a person holding the office of acting governor may continue in the office only so long as the office is vacant or until the governor's incapacity is removed. During the time an officer serves as acting governor, the officer's capacity as senate president, senator, speaker of the house, member of the house, secretary of state, or state treasurer is suspended. Finally, this article provides that the governor or an acting governor has the authority to transact official business when absent from the state.

As originally written in 1784, this article required the senior senator to take over for the president (a 1792 amendment changed "president" to "governor") when the chair of the president was vacant due to death, absence from the state, or otherwise. The 1784 version followed the Massachusetts Constitution of 1780, except that the latter provided for a lieutenant governor to succeed the governor. The people amended this article in 1792 to provide that the senate president, when acting as governor, could not hold his office in the senate. An 1889 amendment added the speaker of the house to the line of gubernatorial succession, after the senate president; the people later added the secretary of state in 1889 and 1968, respectively. A 1956 amendment gave the governor the authority to transact official business when absent from the state. A 1984 amendment reworded the article and added language providing for succession if the governor were to suffer from a physical or mental incapacity (Article 49-a, also added in 1984, addressed incapacity) that would require a new election if a vacancy occurred before the last year of the governor's term; that amendment also required the compensation of the acting governor to be equal to that of the governor, and that the elected office of certain state officers when serving as acting governor would be suspended and not forfeited.

The New Hampshire Supreme Court first interpreted this article in *Attorney General v. Taggert* (1890), a case involving the attorney general's petition to require the senate president to exercise the powers and duties of the office of governor, because the governor had taken ill and notified the attorney general that he was unable to perform the duties of his office. The constitution at the time provided that the senate president could exercise the powers and duties of the governor when the chair of the governor was vacant by reason of the governor's death, absence from the state, "or otherwise" and the court held that "otherwise," as used in this article, included physical disability.

In 1935, when only the senate president and the speaker of the house stood in the line of succession, the former was ill and the senate had elected a president pro tem. The question arose as to whether the senate president pro tem or the speaker would fill the governor's chair when the governor was absent from the state. In *Opinion of the Justices* (1935), the court concluded that the disability of the senate president meant the chair of the senate president was vacant; therefore, the speaker, as next in line, would carry out the duties of governor when the governor was absent from the state. The court reasoned that, under

Article 49, the senate president pro tem was not a constitutional officer, and therefore lacked the authority to act as the president's substitute.

In a 1975 advisory opinion, the court concluded that this article prevents the senate president from occupying the constitutional office of senator as well as the office of senate president while acting as governor, except that, if the governor were temporarily or briefly absent from the state during the legislative session, the senate president could still exercise ceremonial, routine, signatory, proclamatory, ministerial, and similar functions of the gubernatorial office, without relinquishing his senatorial office. *Opinion of the Justices* (1975).

### [ART.] 49-a. [PROLONGED FAILURE TO QUALIFY; VACANCY IN OFFICE OF GOVERNOR DUE TO PHYSICAL OR MENTAL INCAPACITY, ETC.]

Whenever the governor transmits to the secretary of state and president of the senate his written declaration that he is unable to discharge the powers and duties of his office by reason of physical or mental incapacity and until he transmits to them a written declaration to the contrary, the president of the senate, for the time being, shall act as governor as provided in article 49, subject to the succession provisions therein set forth. Whenever it reasonably appears to the attorney general and a majority of the council that the governor is unable to discharge the powers and duties of his office by reason of physical or mental incapacity, but the governor is unwilling or unable to transmit his written declaration to such effect as above provided, the attorney general shall file a petition for declaratory judgment in the supreme court requesting a judicial determination of the ability of the governor to discharge the powers and duties of his office. After notice and hearing, the justices of the supreme court shall render such judgment as they find warranted by a preponderance of the evidence; and, if the court holds that the governor is unable to discharge the powers and duties of his office, the president of the senate, for the time being, shall act as governor as provided in article 49, subject to the succession provisions therein set forth, until such time as the disability of the governor is removed or a newly elected governor is inaugurated. Such disability, once determined by the supreme court, may be removed upon petition for declaratory judgment to the supreme court by the governor if the court finds, after notice and hearing, by a preponderance of the evidence that the governor is able to discharge the powers and duties of his office. Whenever such disability of the governor, as determined by his written declaration or by judgment of the supreme court, has continued for a period of 6 months, the general court may, by concurrent resolution adopted by both houses, declare the office of governor vacant. Whenever the governor-elect fails to qualify by reason of physical or mental incapacity or any cause other than death or resignation, for a period of 6 months following the inauguration date established by this constitution, the general court may, by concurrent resolution adopted by both houses, declare the office of governor vacant. The provisions of article 49 shall govern the filling of such vacancy, either by special election or continued service of an acting governor. If the general court is not in session when any such 6-month period expires, the acting governor, upon written request of at least 1/4 of the members of each house, shall convene the general court in special session for the sole purpose of considering and acting on the question whether to declare a vacancy in the office of governor under this article. *1984.*

This article details when and how the governor may be determined to suffer from a disability that prevents his or her functioning as governor, triggering the process of gubernatorial succession. Until the adoption of this article in 1984, no specific constitutional provisions addressed the procedures for dealing with a prolonged vacancy in the governor's office due to the governor's physical or mental incapacity. The 1983 legislature proposed this amendment, after a series of events in late 1982 brought the need for addressing gubernatorial disability. On November 20, 1982, Governor Hugh J. Gallen was confined to a Boston hospital; he died there in late December. John H. Sununu had been elected governor in November, but was not sworn in until January 6, 1983. Senate President Robert B. Monier had become acting governor when Gallen was hospitalized, but he ceased to be acting governor when all legislative terms expired at midnight on November 30. The succession briefly passed to the secretary of state until the new senate had organized and elected a president, Vesta M. Roy, who served as acting governor until Governor Sununu was sworn in. This provision has not been interpreted by the New Hampshire Supreme Court.

### [ART.] 50. [GOVERNOR TO PROROGUE OR ADJOURN LEGISLATURE, AND CALL EXTRA SESSIONS.]

The governor, with advice of council, shall have full power and authority, in the recess of the general court, to prorogue the same from time to time, not exceeding ninety days, in any one recess of said court; and during the sessions of said court, to adjourn or prorogue it to any time the two houses may desire, and to call it together sooner than the time to which it may be adjourned, or prorogued, if the welfare of the state should require the same. *1784; amended 1792.*

This article authorizes the governor and council to call a special legislative session; to extend the adjournment of the legislature when it is in recess, for up to ninety days; and, in accordance with the wishes of the general court, to adjourn or prorogue the legislature to another time. This article should be read in conjunction with Part 2, Article 43, which addresses the authority of the governor and council regarding adjournment and prorogation, should the two houses fail to agree. The 1784 version of this article followed the similar provision of the Massachusetts Constitution of 1780; a 1792 amendment changed "president" to "governor." The people twice rejected amendments eliminating the governor and council's authority to prorogue the legislature, in 1974 and 1984.

The New Hampshire Supreme Court has defined "recess," as the term is used in this article, to mean the time during which the general court is not assembled in either regular or special session. The authority of the governor and council to "prorogue" the legislature means that, if the general court has called itself back into session without the consent of governor and council, the governor and council may extend the reassembling of the legislature for up to ninety days. See *Opinion of the Justices* (1944). In a 1975 advisory opinion, the court addressed the governor's interest in calling a special session to consider issues related to group medical and hospital insurance. The adoption of amendments to Part 2, Articles 19 and 36, removing limitations on the ability of the house of representatives and senate to adjourn themselves, had called into question the authority of the governor and council to call a special session of the legislature when both houses had adjourned. The court concluded that the authority of the governor and council to adjourn the legislature under Article 50 was independent of the power of the house and senate to adjourn themselves under Articles 19 and 36; the 1966 amendments to the latter articles did not by implication undermine the power of the governor and council under this article to call the general court into session, should the welfare of the state require it. See *Opinion of the Justices* (1975).

## [ART.] 51. [POWERS AND DUTIES OF GOVERNOR AS COMMANDER-IN-CHIEF.]

The governor of this state for the time being, shall be commander-in-chief of all the military forces of the state; and shall have full power, by himself or by any chief commander, or other officer or officers, from time to time, to train, instruct, exercise and govern the militia; to call forth the militia and to put in warlike posture the inhabitants of the state; to execute the laws of the state and of the United States; to suppress insurrection and to repel invasion; and, in fine, the governor is hereby entrusted with all other powers incident to the office of commander-in-chief to be exercised agreeably to the rules and regulations of the constitution and the laws of the land. *1784; amended 1792 and 1968.*

This article defines the military powers of the governor as commander-in-chief of the militia, which includes the National Guard, the state guard, and the unorganized militia. The National Guard is highly regulated by federal law; the state guard and unorganized militia are regulated under New Hampshire law. The framers based the expansive language of the 1784 version of this article upon its counterpart in the Massachusetts Constitution of 1780. Both constitutions limited their chief executive's authority to remove inhabitants from the state without their free and voluntary consent, or the consent of the general court. A 1792 amendment changed "president" to "governor" and a 1968 amendment reworded and condensed the article. Before the latter amendment, this article gave the governor authority to assemble the state's inhabitants "in martial array" and lead them against any enemy "invading, conquering, or annoying" the state; the 1964 convention recommended eliminating obsolete references to the "navy" and grants of power contrary to federal law and the federal constitution. This provision has not been interpreted by the New Hampshire Supreme Court.

### [ART.] 52. [PARDONING POWER.]

The power of pardoning offenses, except such as persons may be convicted of before the senate, by impeachment of the house, shall be in the governor, by and with the advice of council: But no charter of pardon, granted by the governor, with advice of the council, before conviction, shall avail the party pleading the same, notwithstanding any general or particular expressions contained therein, descriptive of the offense or offenses intended to be pardoned. *1784; amended 1792.*

This article authorizes the governor and council the power to grant pardons to persons convicted of "offenses," which does not include impeachment following a trial before the senate. The 1784 version is virtually identical to a provision of the Massachusetts Constitution of 1780. The people amended this article in 1792 to change "president" to "governor." The New Hampshire Supreme Court has described a pardon under this article as an "act of executive grace completely eliminating all consequences of the conviction," but not removing the record of conviction. *Doe v. State* (1974). In *Doe*, the court upheld a statute granting the courts the power to annul the record of a conviction, concluding that the law did not unconstitutionally infringe upon the governor's powers under this article.

### [ART.] 53. [MILITIA OFFICERS, REMOVAL OF.]

(Repealed in 1976)

This article protected officers in the militia from being removed from office except by an address of both houses of the legislature to the governor, or by a "fair trial in court martial." The original article followed a similar provision of the Massachusetts Constitution of 1780. A 1792 amendment changed "president" to "governor." The people voted to repeal this article in 1976.

### [ART.] 54. [STAFF AND NON-COMMISSIONED OFFICERS, BY WHOM APPOINTED.]

(Repealed in 1976)

This article granted field officers the authority to appoint certain of their own higher-ranking subordinates. The original article followed a similar provision of the Massachusetts Constitution of 1780. The people voted to repeal this article in 1976.

### [ART.] 55. [DIVISION OF MILITIA INTO BRIGADES, REGIMENTS, AND COMPANIES.]

(Repealed in 1976)

This article provided that the divisions of the militia made under the militia laws then in force would remain in effect until changed by law. The original article followed a similar provision of the Massachusetts Constitution of 1780. The people voted to repeal this article in 1976.

### [ART.] 56. [DISBURSEMENTS FROM TREASURY.]

No moneys shall be issued out of the treasury of this state, and disposed of, (except such sums as may be appropriated for the redemption of bills of credit, or treasurer's notes, or for the payment of interest arising thereon) but by warrant under the hand of the governor for the time being, by and with the advice and consent of the council, for the necessary support and defense of this state, and for the necessary protection and preservation of the inhabitants thereof, agreeably to the acts and resolves of the general court. *1784; amended 1792.*

This article describes the required method and allowable purposes for expenditures of state money; similar warrant language appears in Part 2, Article 5. The original article followed a similar provision of the Massachusetts Constitution of 1780. A 1792 amendment changed "president" to "governor."

"The purpose of this article is to delegate to the Governor the power to insure that no payments be made from the public treasury execpt [*sic*] for public purposes and in accordance with the law." *Opinion of the Justices* (1976). The governor, with the consent of council, has the authority to issue a warrant for the payment of money from the state treasury only when the legislature has appropriated money for the purpose stated in the warrant; no payment can be made out of the state treasury except upon an appropriation or equivalent direction for payment by the legislature. See *Opinion of the Justices* (1910) (absent a specific appropriation, the governor and council could not issue a warrant for money to be used for the expenses of litigation to which the state might become a party).

The issuance of the governor's warrant is a prerequisite to payment by the state treasurer. The New Hampshire Supreme Court held in *State v. Kimball* (1950) that, absent a properly issued warrant, the state treasurer was personally liable for payments to a construction company in excess of the authorized appropriations, made in anticipation of the governor's warrant. It mattered not that the governor subsequently issued a warrant and that there was no bad faith: payment was made on the treasurer's authorization, and the state had no legal obligation to pay the excess amount.

This article also provides that the state cannot be sued or held liable for interest on its obligations absent its consent. In *Kaemmerling v. State* (1924), the court concluded that the state would have to make good on its obligation to pay an inheritance tax refund, but not the interest on the refund when no statute provided for the state to pay the same.

### [ART.] 57. [ACCOUNTS OF MILITARY STORES.]

(Repealed in 1950)

This article required various public officers to account every three months for all military stores and other public property in their care, along with the condition of forts and garrisons. The original article followed a similar provision of the Massachusetts Constitution of 1780. A 1792 amendment changed "president" to "governor." The people voted to repeal this article in 1950.

### [ART.] 58. [COMPENSATION OF GOVERNOR AND COUNCIL.]

The governor and council shall be compensated for their services, from time to time, by such grants as the general court shall think reasonable. *1784; amended 1792.*

[The text in the publication, *The New Hampshire Constitution of 1784, as Subsequently Amended and in Force January 2009*, contains a typographical error—"general courts" for "general court."]

This article requires the legislature to provide reasonable compensation for the governor and council. Based upon a similar provision of the Massachusetts Constitution of 1780, the original 1784 article required that compensation be "reasonable," while Massachusetts required that the governor have an "honorable stated salary" which was to be "amply sufficient." A 1792 amendment changed "president" to "governor." This provision has not been interpreted by the New Hampshire Supreme Court.

### [ART.] 59. [SALARIES OF JUDGES.]

Permanent and honorable salaries shall be established by law, for the justices of the superior court. *1784.*

This article requires the legislature to establish "permanent and honorable salaries" for judges of the "superior court"—at the time, the highest court in New Hampshire. The original article followed a similar provision of the Massachusetts Constitution of 1780. The framers sought by this provision to ensure the independence of the judiciary; as the New Hampshire Supreme Court has observed, this provision, along with the Part 2, Article 73, which establishes tenure for judges during good behavior, creates an "inducement for persons so to qualify themselves, as an encouragement to vigilance, and an antidote to bribery and corruption." *Opinion of Justices (Judicial Salary Suspension)* (1995). The court has held that, given its inherent authority to superintend the lower courts, it may suspend the salary of a judge upon a finding of abuse or misconduct; such a suspension does not violate the requirement that judges be provided permanent and reasonable salaries. *Id.*

### [ART.] 60. [COUNCILLORS; MODE OF ELECTION, ETC.]

There shall be biennially elected, by ballot, five councillors, for advising the governor in the executive part of government. The freeholders and other inhabitants in each county, qualified to vote for senators, shall some time in the month of November, give in their votes for one councillor; which votes shall be received, sorted, counted, certified, and returned to the secretary's office, in the same manner as the votes for senators, to be by the secretary laid before the senate and house of representatives on the first Wednesday following the first Tuesday of January. *1784; amended 1792, 1877, 1889, and 1984.*

This article provides for the election of five executive councilors; the councilor's role is to advise the governor "in the executive part of government." Other provisions of the constitution define the advisory role of the executive council in specific situations; for instance, the governor and council act together under Article 46 in the nomination and appointment of judges, the attorney general, and officers of the militia; exercise pardoning power under Article 52; and call special legislative sessions under Article 50. See *Opinion of the Justices* (1953). Statutes define other situations in which the council is to advise the governor. The provision's reference to the election of councilors by the "freeholders and other inhabitants in each county" is archaic; voters need not hold real property in fee simple to vote, and, since 1792, the legislature has had the authority to establish councilor districts. Under the 1784 constitution, "counsellors" were elected by joint ballot of the house of representatives and the senate, with two from the senate, and three from the house. The Massachusetts Constitution of 1780 also provided for a council to advise the governor, but specified that the nine councilors would come from the senate. A 1792 amendment to this article provided for the direct election of councilors, one from each of the five counties existing at that time, and changed "president" to "governor." Other amendments in 1877, 1889, and 1984 adjusted the time of the election and the time in which votes had to be returned to the secretary of state.

### [ART.] 61. [VACANCIES, HOW FILLED, IF NO CHOICE.]

And the person having a plurality of votes in any county, shall be considered as duly elected a councillor: But if no person shall have a plurality of votes in any county, the senate and house of representatives shall take the names of the two persons who have the highest number of votes in each county, and not elected, and out of those two shall elect by joint ballot, the councillor wanted for such county, and the qualifications for councillors shall be the same as for senator. *1792; amended 1912.*

This article provides for the election of councilors by a plurality and requires that the age and residency qualifications for councilors be the same as those for senators under Part 2, Article 29. As in Article 60, the reference to "county" is obsolete, as councilors now represent councilor districts. The voters ratified this article in 1792 and amended it in 1912 to provide for election by a plurality instead of a majority of votes. This provision has not been interpreted by the New Hampshire Supreme Court.

### [ART.] 62. [SUBSEQUENT VACANCIES; GOVERNOR TO CONVENE; DUTIES.]

If any person thus chosen a councillor, shall be elected governor or member of either branch of the legislature, and shall accept the trust; or if any person elected a councillor, shall refuse to accept the office, or in case of the death, resignation, or removal of any councillor out of the state, the governor may issue a precept for the election of a new councillor in that county where such vacancy shall happen and the choice shall be in the same manner as before directed. And the governor shall have full power and authority to convene the council, from time to time, at his discretion; and, with them, or the majority of them, may and shall, from time to time hold a council, for ordering and directing the affairs of the state, according to the laws of the land. *1792.*

Pursuant to this article, the governor must call for a new election in the event of a vacancy in the office of an executive councilor. The article authorizes the governor to convene the council at his discretion, and provides that the governor and a majority of the council are responsible for ordering and directing the affairs of the state. The people added this article to the constitution in 1792.

The New Hampshire Supreme Court has inferred from this article and Part 2, Article 46 that a majority of the council constitutes a quorum. See *Opinion of the Justices* (1977). Pursuant to their authority to order and direct the affairs of state, the governor and council may regulate the internal working of the executive branch. Accordingly, they could require that state officials resign their elected positions before taking a position in the executive branch, but could not adopt a procurement policy for services contracted with elected state officials or regulate the employment of members of the legislative branch. *Opinion of the Justices* (1976).

### [ART.] 63. [IMPEACHMENT OF COUNCILLORS.]

The members of the council may be impeached by the house, and tried by the senate for bribery, corruption, malpractice, or maladministration. *1784; amended 1792.*

Under this article, members of the executive council may be impeached and tried for "bribery, corruption, malpractice, or maladministration." This is the same impeachment procedure used for state officers under Part 2,

Articles 17 and 38. In the original 1784 version, members of the council could be impeached for "mal-conduct"; the people changed the wording in 1792. This provision has not been interpreted by the New Hampshire Supreme Court.

### [ART.] 64. [SECRETARY TO RECORD PROCEEDINGS OF COUNCIL.]

The resolutions and advice of the council shall be recorded by the secretary, in a register, and signed by all members present agreeing thereto; and this record may be called for at any time, by either house of the legislature; and any member of the council may enter his opinion contrary to the resolutions of the majority, with the reasons for such opinion. *1784; amended 1792.*

This article provides that the secretary of state shall record the "resolutions and advice" of the executive council. Councilors must sign the register to attest to their votes, and a dissenting member of the council may enter his reasons for dissenting in the register. The register is available to both houses of the legislature. The 1784 version covered the main points of this article, and the 1792 amendment specified that the secretary would be the recording officer, provided that members "agreeing thereto" had to sign the register, and provided that a dissenting member could enter an opinion "with the reasons for such opinion." The New Hampshire Supreme Court concluded in *Opinion of the Justices* (1919), that the members of the council by their signatures attest to the verity of the council's records, notwithstanding that the secretary of state is the recording officer.

### [ART.] 65. [COUNCILLOR DISTRICTS PROVIDED FOR.]

The legislature may, if the public good shall hereafter require it, divide the state into five districts, as nearly equal as may be, governing themselves by the number of population, each district to elect a councillor: And, in case of such division, the manner of the choice shall be conformable to the present mode of election in counties. *1792; amended 1912.*

This article authorizes the legislature to divide the state into five executive councilor districts, based upon population. Under the 1784 constitution, one councilor was elected from each of the state's five counties (Rockingham, Strafford, Hillsborough, Cheshire, and Grafton). This article, added in 1792, allowed the legislature to create executive council districts based upon rateable polls and proportion of public taxes paid. After the legislature in 1829 increased the number of counties from five to eight (adding Coos, Merrimack, and Sullivan), it divided the state into five districts (not organized on county lines) for the election of councilors. A 1912 amendment changed the basis for these districts from rateable polls and public taxes to population. This provision has not been interpreted by the New Hampshire Supreme Court.

### [ART.] 66. [ELECTIONS BY LEGISLATURE MAY BE ADJOURNED FROM DAY TO DAY; ORDER THEREOF.]

And, whereas the elections, appointed to be made by this constitution on the first Wednesday of January biennially, by the two houses of the legislature, may not be completed on that day, the said elections may be adjourned from day to day, until the same be completed; and the order of the elections shall be as follows—the vacancies in the senate, if any, shall be first filled up: The governor shall then be elected, provided there shall be no choice of him by the people: And afterwards, the two houses shall proceed to fill up the vacancy, if any, in the council. *1784; amended 1792, 1877, and 1889.*

This article provides that the legislature may adjourn from day to day if it does not complete elections required because no person received a plurality of the votes for senator (Article 34), governor (Article 42), or member of the council (Article 61). The original article followed a similar provision of the Massachusetts Constitution of 1780. A 1792 amendment changed "president" to "governor" and required an election of the council only in the event of a vacancy. Amendments in 1877 and 1889 changed references from annual to biennial elections and the time of the convening of the legislature from June to January. After the people voted to amend Articles 34, 42, and 61 in 1912 to require that senators, the governor, and members of the council be elected by a plurality of votes instead of a majority, Article 66 would be relevant only in the unlikely event that no candidate received more votes than another. The reference to the elections to be made on the "first Wednesday of January" is outdated; amendments in 1982 and 1984, respectively, to Articles 42 and 60 changed the date of the laying of the returns by the secretary of state before the legislature from the "first Wednesday of January" to the "first Wednesday following the first Tuesday in January." This provision has not been interpreted by the New Hampshire Supreme Court.

### [ART.] 67. [ELECTION OF SECRETARY AND TREASURER.]

The secretary and treasurer shall be chosen by joint ballot of the senators and representatives assembled in one room. *1784; amended 1950.*

This article requires that the secretary of state and the state treasurer be elected by the legislature. Aside from the requirement that the legislature vote by joint ballot to decide elections under Articles 34, 42, and 61 (see the discussion under Article 66), which would be a most unlikely occurrence, Article 67 contains the only constitutional requirement for the legislature to meet in joint session and vote by joint ballot. The 1784 article followed a similar provision of the Massachusetts Constitution of 1780 and included the election of the commissary-general in the same manner. A 1950 amendment eliminated the obsolete reference to the commissary-general. The New Hampshire Supreme Court has noted that, though the legislature elects the secretary of state under this article, the secretary's duties, as described in Article 68, are executive as well as legislative, and continue after the adjournment of the legislature. *Opinion of the Justices* (1965).

### [ART.] 68. [STATE RECORDS, WHERE KEPT; DUTY OF SECRETARY.]

The records of the state shall be kept in the office of the secretary, and he shall attend the governor and council, the senate and representatives, in person, or by deputy, as they may require. *1784; amended 1792.*

This article requires the records of the state be kept in the office of the secretary of state and that the secretary attend the governor, council, and members of the legislature as they may require. The original article followed a similar provision of the Massachusetts Constitution of 1780. A 1792 amendment changed "president" to "governor" and moved material concerning the appointment of the deputy secretary of state to what is now Article 69. The New Hampshire Supreme Court case has made clear that records of the state include the journals of each house of the legislature. *Opinion of the Justices* (1857).

### [ART.] 69. [DEPUTY SECRETARY.]

The secretary of the state shall, at all times, have a deputy, to be by him appointed; for whose conduct in office he shall be responsible: And, in case of the death, removal, or inability of the secretary, his deputy shall exercise all the duties of the office of secretary of this state, until another shall be appointed. *1784; amended 1792.*

This article requires the secretary of state to appoint a deputy secretary who will assume his or her duties if the secretary is unable to carry them out, until a new secretary is chosen pursuant to Article 67. The 1784 article referred to the appointment of "his deputies" by the secretary of state, for whose conduct the secretary would be responsible. The 1792 amendment required the secretary to appoint "a deputy," and added the second sentence, describing the circumstances in which the deputy would be required to exercise the duties of the secretary. This provision has not been interpreted by the New Hampshire Supreme Court.

### [ART.] 70. [SECRETARY TO GIVE BOND.]

The secretary, before he enters upon the business of his office, shall give bond, with sufficient sureties, in a reasonable sum, for the use of the state, for the punctual performance of his trust. *1792.*

This article requires the secretary of state to give a bond to secure the performance of his or her duties as secretary. The legislature sets the amount of the bond by statute. This provision has not been interpreted by the New Hampshire Supreme Court.

## [ART.] 71. [COUNTY TREASURERS, REGISTERS OF PROBATE, COUNTY ATTORNEYS, SHERIFFS, AND REGISTERS OF DEEDS ELECTED.]

The county treasurers, registers of probate, county attorneys, sheriffs and registers of deeds, shall be elected by the inhabitants of the several towns, in the several counties in the state, according to the method now practiced, and the laws of the state, Provided nevertheless the legislature shall have authority to alter the manner of certifying the votes, and the mode of electing those officers; but not so as to deprive the people of the right they now have of electing them. *1784; amended 1792, 1877, and 1958.*

This article requires the election of county treasurers, registers of probate, county attorneys, sheriffs, and registers of deeds by the citizens of the appropriate town or county. The legislature may change certain features of the manner of election, but not the right of the people to elect these officers. The original 1784 provision referred only to the county treasurers and registers of deeds. A 1792 amendment authorizes the legislature to alter the manner of certifying the votes and the mode of electing the officers and moved material regarding the oath and bond of these officers to what is now Article 72. An 1877 amendment added registers of probate, county solicitors, and sheriffs. A 1958 amendment changed "county solicitors" to "county attorneys."

The article requires that the elections must be "according to the method now practiced." The method practiced in 1784 for county treasurers and registers of deeds was election by the people in the county. The New Hampshire Supreme Court reviewed the history of the early laws and the 1776 constitution regulating the selection of these county officers in *Opinion of the Justices* (1835). Provincial law in 1771 allowed the governor, council, and assembly to appoint these officers; the 1776 constitution changed this to election by the people of the county, a practice continued in the 1784 constitution.

Except for the restrictions in the constitution regarding the election of these officers and the provisions of Article 72 regarding registers of deeds, the legislature may regulate all other aspects of these offices. See, e.g., *Linehan v. Rockingham County Com'rs* (2004) (the sheriff's duties and responsibilities, except when expressed by state constitution, are subject to legislative alteration and control). The court concluded in 1835, for example, that the legislature would not violate this article if it changed the place of registration of deeds from the county office to the office of the town clerk in the town where the real estate was located; it would in that case continue to exist and the register would continue to be elected pursuant to the constitution. *Opinion of the Justices, supra.* In *Opinion of the Justices* (1905), the court again affirmed this broad power, concluding that this article, and other articles relating to elections, would not be violated should the legislature choose to divide towns into voting precincts and authorize voting in such precincts instead of at town meetings.

### [ART.] 72. [COUNTIES MAY BE DIVIDED INTO DISTRICTS FOR REGISTERING DEEDS.]

And the legislature, on the application of the major part of the inhabitants of any county, shall have authority to divide the same into two districts for registering deeds, if to them it shall appear necessary; each district to elect a register of deeds: And before they enter upon the business of their offices, shall be respectively sworn faithfully to discharge the duties thereof, and shall severally give bond, with sufficient sureties, in a reasonable sum, for the use of the county for the punctual performance of their respective trusts. *1784; amended 1792.*

This article allows a county to be divided into two districts with two registers of deeds, for the purpose of registering deeds, if the majority of the county voters so request. Registers must take an oath and post a bond. The 1784 version required the oath and bond; the 1792 amendment added the legislative authority to divide counties into districts. Reviewing this article in 1835 in conjunction with Article 71, the New Hampshire Supreme Court addressed a proposal to change the place of registration of deeds from the county registry office to the office of the town clerk in the town where the real estate was located. The court held the constitution would not be violated by such action. The court declined to infer that Article 72 restricted the authority of the legislature to divide a county into more than two districts for registering deeds when the legislature could, consistent with the constitution, divide the state into as many counties as it wished, even to the point of making each town a district for registering deeds. See *Opinion of the Justices* (1835).

### [ART.] 72-a. [SUPREME AND SUPERIOR COURTS.]

The judicial power of the state shall be vested in the supreme court, a trial court of general jurisdiction known as the superior court, and such lower courts as the legislature may establish under Article 4th of Part 2. *1966.*

This article establishes the supreme court and the superior court and vests the judicial power of the state in the those and other courts as may be established by the legislature. The supreme court is the highest in New Hampshire, and the superior court is a trial court of general jurisdiction. The legislature has the authority to determine the size and jurisdiction of each court and to establish lower courts under Part 2, Article 4. The Commission to Study the State Constitution, created by the legislature to make recommendations to the 1964 constitutional convention, recommended that the supreme and superior courts be given constitutional status to protect them from political assaults and change at the whim of the legislature. The general court five times in the nineteenth century acted to legislate courts out of existence so that the newly dominant political party could appoint its own judges.[6] Supporters of this article favored its adoption to prevent instability in the judiciary and to ensure its integrity consistent with the doctrine of separation of powers.

The court generally assumes that the judicial branch possesses all the authority necessary to perform its functions; otherwise, the power vested in the court under this article would be hollow. See *In re Tocci* (1997) (court has the power to regulate the state bar). Further, while there are instances in which the legislature and the judiciary share authority to regulate court procedure, "[t]he legislature may not, for example, enact procedural statutes that compromise the core adjudicatory functions of the judiciary to resolve cases fairly and impartially and to protect the constitutional rights of all persons who come before the courts." *In re Southern New Hampshire Medical Center* (2012).

### [ART.] 73. [TENURE OF OFFICE TO BE EXPRESSED IN COMMISSIONS; JUDGES TO HOLD OFFICE DURING GOOD BEHAVIOR, ETC.; REMOVAL.]

The tenure that all commissioned officers shall have by law in their offices shall be expressed in their respective commissions, and all judicial officers duly appointed, commissioned and sworn, shall hold their offices during good behavior except those for whom a different provision is made in this constitution. The governor with consent of the council may remove any commissioned officer for reasonable cause upon the address of both houses of the legislature, provided nevertheless that the cause for removal shall be stated fully and substantially in the address and shall not be a cause which is a sufficient ground for impeachment, and provided further that no officer shall be so removed unless he shall have had an opportunity to be heard in his defense by a joint committee of both houses of the legislature. *1784; amended 1792 and 1966.*

This article provides that the tenure of office for commissioned officers be expressed in their commissions and that judges shall hold office during good behavior. Officers and judges may be removed by the governor and council upon address by the legislature. Before a person may be removed by address, he or she must be informed of the reasons for removal and has the right to be heard. The cause for a removal based upon address cannot rise to the level of a cause sufficient to justify impeachment. The original article followed a similar provision of the Massachusetts Constitution of 1780. A 1792 amendment changed "president" to "governor." A 1966 amendment added the procedures for removal by address, providing for basic process to protect individuals from arbitrary or unjust removal by the legislature and governor. The voters failed to ratify similar amendments in 1877 and 1903.

---

[6] For a detailed account of this period, see Richard F. Upton, "The Independence of the Judiciary in New Hampshire," *New Hampshire Bar Journal* 1 (1959): 28.

The power of the governor and council to remove a state officer "for reasonable cause upon the address of both houses of the legislature" is an executive and legislative proceeding. The judiciary does not have the power to remove judges in this way, but it may exercise disciplinary authority short of removal. *In re Mussman* (1972). The New Hampshire Supreme Court has concluded that its suspension of a judge's pay as a matter of internal discipline did not violate this article or Part 1, Article 35. *Opinion of the Justices (Judicial Salary Suspension)* (1995).

In *Blake v. State* (1975), the court addressed the requirement that the tenure of a commissioned officer be expressed in his commission at the time of appointment. In that case, a statute that provided that the director of business profits tax served at the pleasure of the commissioner of revenue administration. After being terminated, the director argued that he was removed from office without cause in violation of his commission. The court held the state had failed to adhere to this article's requirement that tenure be stated in the director's commission at the time of his appointment, and he was entitled to protection commensurate with his reliance on the express terms of his commission.

### [ART.] 73-a. [SUPREME COURT, ADMINISTRATION.]

The chief justice of the supreme court shall be the administrative head of all the courts. He shall, with the concurrence of a majority of the supreme court justices, make rules governing the administration of all courts in the state and the practice and procedure to be followed in all such courts. The rules so promulgated shall have the force and effect of law. *1978.*

This article grants the chief justice of the supreme court superintendence power over all the courts. The chief justice must adopt rules to govern the courts, with a concurrence of a majority of the justices of the supreme court. The supreme court's supervisory and rulemaking authority derives primarily from this article and from the common law. *In re Proposed N.H. Rules of Civil Procedure* (1995). The rulemaking authority under this article lies only with the supreme court. See *Cotter v. Wright* (2000) (superior court could not issue an order unilaterally amending superior court administrative rule).

The supreme court's superintending authority over the courts is broad and includes the inherent authority to discipline the legal profession. See *Petition of Grimm* (1993). The court may discipline judges for misconduct, suspend a sitting judge, assign another judge to a case, and review a judge's refusal to grant a motion to recuse. See *Douglas v. Douglas* (1999). The court has used its authority to order a particular method of jury selection, see *State v. Elbert* (1981); suggest a model trial court instruction relative to reasonable doubt, see *State v. Wentworth* (1978); and establish a committee to regulate attorney conduct, see *Rousseau v. Eshleman* (1986). In a 1995 advisory opinion, the court concluded that a proposed bill mandating the suspension of the salary and benefits of every judge suspended for misconduct interfered with the court's superintendence power. See *Opinion of the Justices (Judicial Salary Suspension)* (1995).

### [ART.] 74. [JUDGES TO GIVE OPINIONS, WHEN.]

Each branch of the legislature as well as the governor and council shall have authority to require the opinions of the justices of the supreme court upon important questions of law and upon solemn occasions. *1784; amended 1792 and 1958.*

This article allows either house of the legislature, as well as the governor and council, to request an opinion of the court on important legal questions arising in the course of their official duties. The 1784 article followed the similar provision of the Massachusetts Constitution of 1780. A 1792 amendment changed "president" to "governor," and another in 1958 changed "superior court" to "supreme court." The earliest formally reported opinions issued pursuant to this article date from 1816, although they were not printed in the *New Hampshire Reports* until 1889 (the opinions share the same citation: *Opinion of the Court* (1816)).

Pursuant to this article, the justices of the supreme court may "render advisory opinions, outside the context of concrete, fully-developed factual situations and without the benefit of adversary legal presentations, only in carefully circumscribed situations." *Opinion of the Justices* (1998). When the justices render such opinions, they act "not as a court, but as individual constitutional advisers to the legislative or executive branches." *Id.* The court's power to issue an advisory opinion represents an exception to the general constitutional principle that courts cannot give opinions without first providing an opportunity for notice and hearing to parties involved. See *Faulkner v. Keene* (1931). The cases interpreting this article have clarified who may request an advisory opinion, who may issue an advisory opinion, when advice may be requested and given, and the restrictions on a question.

## Who May Request an Advisory Opinion, Who May Issue an Advisory Opinion

Either house of the legislature, or the governor and council, may pose a question to the court under this article. Neither a mayor and board of aldermen, see *Opinion of the Justices* (1877), *supra*, nor a private citizen, see *State v. Harvey* (1965), nor the tax commission, see *Petition of Turner* (1952), may request an advisory opinion under this article. The obligation of the justices to answer a question does not depend upon the consent or approval of both branches of the legislature; when the senate requested the court address whether a bill qualified as a "money bill" under Part 2, Article 18, the court disregarded the plea from the house of representatives that the court not respond. See *Opinion of the Justices* (1959). If a legislative body withdraws its request, the court has no authority to render an advisory opinion. *Opinion of the Justices* (1969). Only the supreme court may issue an advisory opinion. See *Piper v. Town of Meredith* (1969) (superior court lacked jurisdiction to give advisory opinion regarding town ordinance).

## When Advice May Be Requested and Given

The court will furnish an advisory opinion upon a legal question pending in, and awaiting consideration and action by, the body entitled to seek the court's advice. Accordingly, the court will not issue an advisory opinion regarding pending legislation after the general court has adjourned, unless an exception applies, see *Opinion of the Justices* (1939), or when a bill is no longer in the possession of the body requesting the opinion, see *Opinion of the Justices* (1975). The court has also declined to respond to a question received from the governor and council on the same day that their terms expired, because it could not return a timely answer. *Opinion of the Justices* (1901).

The court has recognized an exception to these protocols when the opinion has been requested for the guidance of the legislature at a possible special session or at the next regular one, see *Opinion of the Justices* (1963), or, more particularly, when the body requesting the opinion requested the advice during a regular legislative session and, for good cause, intended to consider and act on the question during an expected special session, see *Opinion of the Justices* (1969). The court also responded to a request for advice from the house meeting in special session that related to the authority of the general court to call itself back into session; the court reasoned that the opinion might be of use to the legislature if it had to convene for a wartime emergency. *Opinion of the Justices* (1944).

## Restrictions on the Questions That May Be Asked

This article "permits the justices of the supreme court to render advisory opinions only 'upon important questions of law and upon solemn occasions.'" *Opinion of the Justices (Appointment of Chief Justice of the Supreme Court)* (2003). Both the governor and council, see *Opinion of the Justices* (1959), and either branch of the legislature, see *Opinion of the Court* (1881), may seek an opinion on matters involving their duties. Most often, requests from the legislature are related to the constitutionality of proposed legislation. The court has placed limits on those questions of law and occasions that should be deemed "important" and "solemn," respectively.

The court has no authority under this article to issue advisory opinions regarding existing legislation. *Opinion of the Justices* (1981). The court cannot give opinions on questions which involve the resolution of questions of fact, see *Opinion of the Justices* (1976), or questions that involve any matter which might come before the court for decision, see *Opinion of the Justices* (1892). The court will make an exception when the question concerns doubts about the official powers or duties of the legislature or governor and council. *Id.* The court has long declined to answer questions that ask whether proposed legislation violates any constitutional provision because of the generality of the question. See *Opinion of Justices (School Financing)* (1998).

The court has declined to answer questions in numerous instances. In *Opinion of the Justices* (1981), for example, the court rejected the request of the house of representatives for an advisory opinion relating to the greyhound racing commission on the grounds that the request concerned the meaning and constitutionality of existing, rather than proposed, laws, and touched on the authority of the commission, rather than the house itself. See also *Opinion of the Justices* (1959) (rejecting question relating to the meaning of existing law); *Opinion of the Justices* (1955) (rejecting question relating to constitutionality of existing law); and *Opinion of the Justices* (1949) (rejecting questions affecting private rights, upon which interested persons were entitled to be heard).

### [ART.] 75. [JUSTICES OF PEACE COMMISSIONED FOR FIVE YEARS.]

In order that the people may not suffer from the long continuance in place of any justice of the peace who shall fail in discharging the important duties of his office with ability and fidelity, all commissions of justice of the peace shall become void at the expiration of five years from their respective dates, and upon the expiration of any commission, the same may if necessary be renewed or another person appointed as shall most conduce to the well being of the state. *1784.*

This article restricts the term of a commission for a justice of the peace to five years, after which it may be renewed. The original 1784 article resembles its counterpart in the Massachusetts Constitution of 1780, except that commissions in Massachusetts expired after seven years rather than five. The New Hampshire Supreme Court has held that the constitutional age limitation of seventy for judges under Part 2, Article 78 does not apply to justices of the peace, in part because this article provides for a five-year term and does not state when the commission would expire or not be renewed because a justice of the peace had attained the age of seventy. See *Keniston v. State* (1884).

### [ART.] 76. [DIVORCE AND PROBATE APPEALS, WHERE TRIED.]

All causes of marriage, divorce and alimony; and all appeals from the respective judges of probate shall be heard and tried by the superior court until the legislature shall by law make other provision. *1784.*

This article grants jurisdiction in marital matters and appeals from the judges of probate to the superior court (in 1784 the state's highest court), unless the legislature provides otherwise. This article resembles a provision of the Massachusetts Constitution of 1780, with the exception that in Massachusetts the governor and council would hear appeals. This article has not been amended.

The framers included this article in the 1784 constitution to invest the judicial branch with jurisdiction over separation and divorce. See *Opinion of the Justices* (1986). Prior to the American Revolution, ecclesiastical courts exercised jurisdiction over the validity of marriage, separation, and support in the case of a separation, while divorces could be granted only by act of Parliament. *Clough v. Clough* (1922). During New Hampshire's Provincial and Revolutionary periods, prior to the adoption of the 1784 constitution, the legislature had the authority to grant divorces. *Clark v. Clark* (1839).

Jurisdiction over marriage, divorce, and alimony also includes nullity proceedings. See *Heath v. Heath* (1932). Because this article grants the judiciary jurisdiction over marital cases, only judicial officers may exercise that jurisdiction, though the legislature may determine which judicial officers should do so. See *Opinion of the Justices* (1986), *supra*. Indeed, jurisdiction over marriage, divorce, and alimony is vested in the superior court "until the legislature shall by law make other provision," and the court's authority in respect to marital matters has been considered to be entirely statutory. See *Veino v. Veino* (1951). The legislature has given the judiciary wide discretion to hear cases of divorce and alimony, but that discretion is subject to revision by the legislature. *Kennard v. Kennard* (1925).

## [ART.] 77. [JURISDICTION OF JUSTICES IN CIVIL CAUSES.]

The general court are empowered to give to justices of the peace jurisdiction in civil causes, when the damages demanded shall not exceed one hundred dollars and title of real estate is not concerned; but with right of appeal, to either party, to some other court. And the general court are further empowered to give to police courts original jurisdiction to try and determine, subject to right of appeal and trial by jury, all criminal causes wherein the punishment is less than imprisonment in the state prison. *1792; amended 1877 and 1912.*

This article authorizes the legislature to grant jurisdiction to justices of the peace in certain civil cases, and to grant jurisdiction to police courts to try misdemeanor criminal cases, both subject to the right of appeal. As originally adopted in 1792, this article concerned only justices of the peace and set a jurisdictional limit of £4. An 1877 amendment increased that amount to $100. The people amended this article in 1912 to allow the legislature to give police courts jurisdiction in criminal cases punishable by less than imprisonment in the state prison. Police courts, which no longer exist as such, had been created in 1852 to assume some of the jurisdiction of justices of the peace. See *Smith v. Tallman* (1934). In time, municipal and, later, district courts would assume the functions of the police courts. The 1912 amendment aimed to relieve the superior courts of the burden of trying many minor criminal offenses, while preserving the right to a jury trial if the defendant sought to appeal the police court's decision.

This article is one of two devoted to justices of the peace (Article 75 is the other). The office of justice of the peace was once of great importance; prior to 1784, justices of the peace had long exercised both civil and criminal jurisdiction. See *State v. Jackson* (1898). At the time the people adopted the 1784 constitution, justices of the peace had jurisdiction over criminal offenses punishable by a fine not exceeding forty shillings, by whipping, or by setting in the stocks. See *State v. Gerry* (1896). When the people adopted this article, in 1792, it addressed only the civil jurisdiction of justices of the peace; the amendment ratified in 1912 clarified the criminal jurisdiction of justices of the peace and police courts and empowered the legislature to grant them jurisdiction over criminal cases that would not result in imprisonment exceeding one year. The criminal jurisdiction of justices of the peace and police courts had been in contention in the courts for several years prior to the 1912 amendment. Justice courts eventually fell into disuse and were abolished in 1951.[7]

The "civil causes" to which this article refers are actions in which a plaintiff demands specific damages. The court held in *Hayes v. Bennett* (1822) that a statute allowing justices of the peace to render judgment on the report of referees, whenever the subject of controversy was less than $200, did not violate the jurisdictional limitations of this article. The parties in that case voluntarily agreed to proceedings according to the statute, and this was not a case in which one party had forced another into litigation.

This article provides the basis for New Hampshire's two-tiered system in which a person charged with a misdemeanor will be tried in district court, without a jury, and may appeal a verdict of guilty to the superior court with a trial de novo by jury. The New Hampshire Supreme Court upheld the system as constitutional in *State v. Handfield* (1975).

The article has been applied by the court to prohibit the imposition of enhanced penalties by the district court that would have exceeded the police (district) court's authority to address criminal offenses with punishment "less than imprisonment in the state prison." Maximum sentences of more than one year are served in the state prison, while sentences of a year or less are served

---

[7] See Charles G. Douglas, III, *Manual for Notaries Public and Justices of the Peace* (Orford, NH: Equity Publishing Corp., 1991), 26.

in a county correctional facility. The court held that district courts could only sentence a convicted criminal defendant to a year or less to a county correctional facility. See *Kulik v. Potter* (1990).

### [ART.] 78. [JUDGES AND SHERIFFS, WHEN DISQUALIFIED BY AGE.]

No person shall hold the office of judge of any court, or judge of probate, or sheriff of any county, after he has attained the age of seventy years. *1792.*

This article mandates retirement at the age of seventy for any person holding the office of judge or county sheriff. The mandatory retirement age does not apply to justices of the peace because the office of a justice of the peace is not included in the "office of judge of any court." *Keniston v. State* (1884). The distinction in Article 79 between "judge of any court" and "justice of the peace" shows they are separate offices, and that justices of the peace are not judges of a court.

A district court judge required to retire pursuant to this provision raised a federal constitutional challenge in *Grinnell v. State* (1981), asserting violations of due process and equal protection under the Fourteenth Amendment. The New Hampshire Supreme Court examined the history of the adoption of Article 78 in *Grinnell*: under the constitution of 1776, all power was concentrated in the legislative branch. The 1784 constitution, by contrast, mandated the separation of powers. To foster an independent judiciary, the people granted judges the right to permanent and honorable salaries (Part 1, Article 35 and Part 2, Article 58), and tenure during good behavior (Part 1, Article 35), and prohibited them from holding certain other offices (Part 2, Article 95). The seventy-year age cap, the court reasoned, had placed a neutral outside limit on tenure, a cap that was not arbitrary or capricious and therefore survived rational basis scrutiny.

The court has interpreted the article as not prohibiting the appointment of a retired judge over the age of seventy to sit temporarily. The legislature has the power under Part 2, Article 4 to authorize the assignment of a retired justice on a temporary basis to ensure the adequate and orderly administration of justice. In *Claremont School District v. Governor* (1998), the court concluded that the temporary assignment of a retired New Hampshire Supreme Court justice pursuant to the statute did not and could not prolong the justice's term, but simply enabled him to exercise his power as a judicial officer in a specific matter.

### [ART.] 79. [JUDGES AND JUSTICES NOT TO ACT AS COUNSEL.]

No judge of any court, or justice of the peace, shall act as attorney, or be of counsel, to any party, or originate any civil suit, in matters which shall come or be brought before him as judge, or justice of the peace. *1792.*

This article prohibits any judge or justice of the peace from acting as attorney or being of counsel in any matter which could come before him or her for decision. Its framers intended this article to protect the integrity of the judicial process by prohibiting certain conflicts of interest for judges and justices of the peace. The New Hampshire Supreme Court has reasoned that a judge hearing a matter in which he acted as counsel would be inconsistent with the inherent impartiality of his office. *In re School-Law Manual* (1885). The court has cited to Articles 79 and 81 as authority for prohibiting a judge of probate from proving a will he had written for the testator. See *Moses v. Julian* (1863). Further, the court has stated that the actions of a probate judge who acted as counsel to one of the parties are not void, but voidable. See *Stearns v. Wright* (1872).

### [ART.] 80. [JURISDICTION AND TERM OF PROBATE COURTS.]

All matters relating to the probate of wills, and granting letters of administration, shall be exercised by the judges of probate, in such manner as the legislature have directed, or may hereafter direct: And the judges of probate shall hold their courts at such place or places, on such fixed days, as the conveniency of the people may require; and the legislature from time to time appoint. *1784; amended 1792.*

The original article in the 1784 constitution provided that the "judges of probate of wills, and for granting letters of administration" would set the dates when the probate courts would sit, until the legislature provided otherwise. The 1792 amendment reworded the article to give the probate courts exclusive jurisdiction over matters relating to the probate of wills and granting letters of administration, and the legislature the responsibility of setting the times at which the probate court would meet. This article grants the probate court exclusive, original jurisdiction over the probate of wills and the settlement and distribution of the estates of deceased persons. See *Knight v. Hollings* (1906).

The exclusive jurisdiction of the court has been confirmed in several cases. For example, in *Heath v. Seymour* (1970), the New Hampshire Supreme Court held that, because the superior court had no jurisdiction over the estate of a deceased minor child, it could not, in a divorce decree approving the settlement of tort actions resulting from an automobile accident, regulate the transfer of the proceeds of a settlement made to benefit the minor child while the child still lived. In *Lisbon Savings Bank & Trust Co. v. Moulton's Estate* (1941), the court concluded that an accounting to determine an administrator's liability had to first be rendered in the probate court. And in *Glover v. Baker* (1912), the court held that the superior court had no power to require an administrator of an estate to account for his administration upon a bill in equity or to revise proceedings in the probate court, except upon appeal.

Though the probate court has exclusive jurisdiction, still it possesses only the powers given it by the legislature, and the legislature defines how the court must exercise such powers. See *Robinson v. Carroll* (1934). The probate court's special jurisdiction, unless enlarged by statute, is limited to the probate of wills, the administration and settlement of estates, the distribution of estates, and other like administrative and ministerial acts. See *In re Estate of O'Dwyer* (1992). The court held a statutory action brought by one co-executor against another not exclusively within the jurisdiction of the probate court, because the plaintiff filed suit not to settle the estate but as an incident to the business of conducting the administration of the estate. *Patton v. Patton* (1920).

### [ART.] 81. [JUDGES AND REGISTERS OF PROBATE NOT TO ACT AS COUNSEL.]

No judge, or register of probate, shall be of counsel, act as advocate, or receive any fees as advocate or counsel, in any probate business which is pending, or may be brought into any court of probate in the county of which he is judge or register. *1792.*

This article prohibits judges of probate and registers of probate from acting or receiving fees as counsel or advocate in any probate business coming before the probate court in the county in which the person is judge or register. The New Hampshire Supreme Court has interpreted this article as prohibiting a judge of probate from proving a will he had written for the testator, see *Moses v. Julian* (1863), and to void the acts of a judge of probate in the settlement of an estate in which th judge has an interest, see *Bedell v. Bailey*, 58 N.H. 62 (1876). The actions of a probate judge who acted as counsel to one of the parties are not void, but voidable. *Stearns v. Wright* (1872).

### [ART.] 82. [CLERKS OF COURTS, BY WHOM APPOINTED.]

The judges of the courts (those of probate excepted) shall appoint their respective clerks to hold their office during pleasure: And no such clerk shall act as an attorney or be of counsel in any cause in the court of which he is clerk, nor shall he draw any writ originating a civil action. *1784; amended 1792.*

This article authorizes the judges of all the courts, except the probate court, to appoint their clerks, who serve at the pleasure of the judges. The article also prohibits a court clerk from acting as an attorney or bringing a civil action in the court in which the clerk serves. The original 1784 article referred to the appointment of clerks by judges in certain specific courts—the superior court of judicature, inferior courts of common pleas, and general sessions of the peace. The people in 1792 amended the article to remove the references to the specific courts and create an exception for the register of probate. Another amendment in 1792 provided for the election of registers of probate. The New Hampshire Supreme Court has made clear that the superior court, acting as a body, and not the county, exercises control over the hiring and firing of a superior court clerk. *Samaha v. Grafton County* (1985).

The court addressed the final clause of the article in *Carlisle v. Dodge* (1831). The court held a clerk was prohibited from making a writ for a civil action only in the court in which he or she served as the clerk. The court reasoned that the constitution prohibits a clerk from acting as attorney or counsel only in cases in the court in which he or she is clerk, and that, if the clerk could act as attorney in other courts, he or she should not be prohibited from initiating an action in another court.

### [ART.] 83. [ENCOURAGEMENT OF LITERATURE, ETC.; CONTROL OF CORPORATIONS, MONOPOLIES, ETC.]

Knowledge and learning, generally diffused through a community, being essential to the preservation of a free government; and spreading the opportunities and advantages of education through the various parts of the country, being highly conducive to promote this end; it shall be the duty of the legislators and magistrates, in all future periods of this government, to cherish the interest of literature and the sciences, and all seminaries and public schools, to encourage private and public institutions, rewards, and immunities for the promotion of agriculture, arts, sciences, commerce, trades, manufactures, and natural history of the country; to countenance and inculcate the principles of humanity and general benevolence, public and private charity, industry and economy, honesty and punctuality, sincerity, sobriety, and all social affections, and generous sentiments, among the people: Provided, nevertheless, that no money raised by taxation shall ever be granted or applied for the use of the schools or institutions of any religious sect or denomination. Free and fair competition in the trades and industries is an inherent and essential right of the people and should be protected against all monopolies and conspiracies which tend to hinder or destroy it. The size and functions of all corporations should be so limited and regulated as to prohibit fictitious capitalization and provision should be made for the supervision and government thereof. Therefore, all just power possessed by the state is hereby granted to the general court to enact laws to prevent the operations within the state of all persons and associations, and all trusts and corporations, foreign or domestic, and the officers thereof, who endeavor to raise the price of any article of commerce or to destroy free and fair competition in the trades and industries through combination, conspiracy, monopoly, or any other unfair means; to control and regulate the acts of all such persons, associations, corporations, trusts, and officials doing business within the state; to prevent fictitious capitalization; and to authorize civil and criminal proceedings in respect to all the wrongs herein declared against. *1784; amended 1877 and 1903.*

[The text in the publication, *The New Hampshire Constitution of 1784, as Subsequently Amended and in Force January 2009*, contains a typographical error—"schools of institutions" for "schools or institutions."]

This article imposes a duty upon the legislators and magistrates of the state to "cherish" education, prohibits public tax money from being used to support sectarian schools, and grants the legislature the power to enact laws to prevent restraint of trade by trusts and monopolies. The 1784 version of this article closely followed its counterpart in the Massachusetts Constitution of 1780 and consisted of the first part of the article, addressing the promotion of education. An 1877 amendment prohibited tax money from being used for schools of any religious sect or denomination, and a 1903 amendment authorized the general court to enact laws to prevent unfair competition caused by trusts or monopolies. The New Hampshire Supreme Court has concluded that "seminaries," as used in the article, includes colleges and universities, as well as schools of the preparatory grades and academies. See *Sisters of Mercy v. Town of Hooksett* (1945).

## The Promotion of Education

As early as 1871, the court acknowledged the importance of education, as recognized by this article. In *Farnum's Petition* (1871), the court stated that "the clause . . . in regard to the encouragement of literature" demonstrated that "the framers of the constitution, as well as their contemporaries in the legislature, regarded the subject of education as one of public concern, to be cherished, regulated, and controlled by the State" and that "the constitution enjoins the duty, in very general and comprehensive terms, on magistrates and legislators as one of paramount public importance." Forty years later, in *Fogg v. Board of Education of Littleton* (1912), the court observed that public schools, maintained by the government, serve to protect the state from the consequences of an "ignorant and incompetent citizenship."

The court gave the encouragement clause its most exhaustive and decisive reading in *Claremont School District v. Governor* (1993). In that case, the court held that Article 83 imposes a duty on the state to provide a constitutionally adequate education to every educable child in the public schools and to guarantee the funding necessary to provide that education. Examining the historical record, the court concluded that the words "shall be the duty . . . to cherish" constituted an affirmative command, and not merely an aspiration. Though the state could delegate some of the implementation of its duty to local government, it could not abdicate its central obligation; the duty to support schools lies with the "legislators and magistrates," and the legislature and governor, therefore, must define the specific and appropriate means of meeting the constitutional obligation.

In 1997, the court held the system of financing public education then in effect unconstitutionally disproportionate and unreasonable under Part 2, Article 5; in addition, the court declared the right to a state-funded constitutionally adequate public elementary and secondary education under Article 83 to be fundamental. *Claremont School District v. Governor* (1997). In another iteration of *Claremont*, in 2002, the court concluded that standards of accountability "are an essential component of the State's duty to provide a constitutionally adequate education." *Claremont School District v. Governor* (2002). In a later case, *Londonderry School District v. State* (2006), the court reiterated that "[a]ny definition of constitutional adequacy [in respect to public education] crafted by the political branches must be sufficiently clear to permit common understanding and allow for an objective determination of costs. Whatever the State identifies as comprising constitutional adequacy it must pay for."

In other cases the court has considered various issues related to education in light of Article 83, including the legislative power to grant tax exemptions, mandatory school attendance, and hiring of teachers. The court held in *Trustees of Phillips Exeter Academy v. Exeter* (1940) that the legislature could grant tax exemptions to educational institutions. In *Town of New London v. Colby Academy* (1898), the court ruled that the state's obligation to "cherish" education did not extend to exempting all the property of seminaries and public school from taxation, just that property to be used for school purposes. In *State v. Jackson* (1902), the court held mandatory school attendance constitutional pursuant to this article.

The court has also held that, notwithstanding the importance this article places on public education, it does not restrict the legislature's authority to determine how teachers should be hired and dismissed. See *Coleman v. School District of Rochester* (1936). And, despite the language of Article 83 that requires legislators and magistrates to "inculcate the principles of humanity... [and] sobriety... among the people," this article does not require that the sale of alcohol be prohibited. See *State v. Roberts* (1908).

## Public Money and Sectarian Schools

The court has interpreted the clause of Article 83 prohibiting the use of money raised by taxation for religious schools or institutions serves to prevent the support of any particular sect or denomination at taxpayer expense, but not to deprive members of a denomination from receiving public benefits because of their beliefs. *Opinion of the Justices* (1955). Thus the court concluded that provision of public funds for nursing scholarships and grants in aid to hospitals offering nursing training did not violate this article, even though many of the hospitals were operated under the auspices of certain religious denominations. The court reasoned that the legislature intended to further the teaching of nursing, a legitimate public health purpose, and not to aid any sects or denominations. The court deemed immaterial the fact that some denominations would derive an incidental benefit through the funds.

The court has also found no Article 83 violation in proposals to authorize school boards to furnish pupils in both public and nonpublic school with certain child benefit services, including medical and school guidance services, or to require school boards to purchase secular textbooks for use in public schools and loan them free of charge or sell them at cost to pupils enrolled in nonpublic schools. See *Opinion of the Justices* (1969). The court did conclude, however, that allowing a real estate tax exemption of $50 to persons with one or more children attending a nonpublic school, and authorizing school boards to furnish transportation for pupils attending nonpublic school outside the district, would violate this article. Further, the court concluded that requiring districts to pay up to 75 percent of the tuition to an alternative school, which could include a sectarian school chosen by a parent or guardian, would violate this article. See *Opinion of the Justices (Choice in Education)* (1992).

## Control of Trusts and Monopolies

The last part of Article 83 declares that New Hampshire favors free enterprise. The court has stated that "limitations on the right of the people to 'free and far competition' must be construed narrowly, with all doubts resolved against the establishment or perpetuation of monopolies." *Appeal of Public Service Co. of N.H.* (1996). The legislature has broad authority to enact legislation to promote the goal of free competition. *Appeal of Omni Communications, Inc.* (1982). Several cases implicating this article have involved the public utilities commission; that agency has the statutory responsibility to oversee and regulate necessary monopolies so as to disrupt free trade and private enterprise as little as possible. In *Appeal of Omni Communications, Inc., supra,* for example, the court concluded that, consistent with the constitution, the legislature did not intend for the commission to regulate all companies and businesses somehow related to the utilities it did regulate, as such regulation could interfere and disrupt free market enterprise.

The court has concluded that a proposed prohibition on petroleum suppliers, as a class, from operating retail gasoline stations, would not offend this article, because the prohibition served the end of preventing monopolistic control of the retail gasoline market. See *Opinion of the Justices* (1977). A restriction on certain businesses in this instance, in other words, worked to promote free competition. Other examples of cases in which the court concluded that regulation did not offend this article include: *Anderson v. McCann* (1983) (upholding law which allowed state housing authority to contract with developers to develop state projects); *Corning Glass Works v. Max Dichter Co.* (1960) (upholding Fair Trade Law, which removed the bar on contracts establishing minimum resale prices of trademarked products, to be constitutional); and *McIntire v. Borofsky* (1948) (upholding the Unfair Sales Act, which prohibited retailers from selling merchandise below cost).

### [ART.] 84. [OATH OF CIVIL OFFICERS.]

Any person chosen governor, councillor, senator, or representative, military or civil officer, (town officers excepted) accepting the trust, shall, before he proceeds to execute the duties of his office, make and subscribe the following declaration, viz. -

I, A.B. do solemnly swear, that I will bear faith and true allegiance to the United States of America and the state of New Hampshire, and will support the constitutions thereof. So help me God.

I, A.B. do solemnly and sincerely swear and affirm that I will faithfully and impartially discharge and perform all duties incumbent on me as......... according to the best of my abilities, agreeably to the rules and regulations of this constitution and laws of the state of New Hampshire. So help me God.*

Any person having taken and subscribed the oath of allegiance, and the same being filed in the secretary's office, he shall not be obliged to take said oath again.

Provided always, when any person chosen or appointed as aforesaid shall be of the denomination called Quakers, or shall be scrupulous of swearing, and shall decline taking the said oaths, such person shall take and subscribe them, omitting the word "swear," and likewise the words "So help me God," subjoining instead thereof, "This I do under the pains and penalties of perjury."

*1784; amended 1792 and 1970.*

This article requires two oaths for various state officers: an oath of allegiance to the state of New Hampshire and the United States, and an oath of office requiring faithful and impartial performance of the duties of the office to which the person was appointed or elected. The article expressly exempts town officers from its requirements, but they are required to take the oaths by statute (RSA 42:1 and RSA 669:9, at this writing). The 1784 version of this article resembled a condensed version of a similar provision of the Massachusetts Constitution of 1780, and contained a promise to defend against "all treacherous conspiracies and hostile attempts." A 1792 amendment changed "president" to "governor," shortened the oath of allegiance, and added the provision dispensing with the need to retake the oath once it had been taken. A 1970 amendment added the oath of allegiance to the United States of America.

Any person required by this article to take the oath of allegiance and the oath of office must do so before assuming the duties of office. A person objecting to an action taken by an official because he or she failed to take one or both of the oaths must do so in timely fashion. In *Goodwin v. Milton* (1852), a specially appointed commissioner had failed to take the oath of allegiance, but the New Hampshire Supreme Court held that, once he had taken an official act, an objection came too late when the challenger knew or should have known the oath had not been taken. See *Wentworth v. Farmington* (1871) (same).

All the officers required to take the oath under Article 84 commit to "support the constitutions" of the United States and New Hampshire. In *Claremont School District v. Governor* (1998), the court denied the state's motion for a two-year extension of the time within which to remedy the unconstitutional education funding system, explaining that support of the state constitution required the governor and legislature to satisfy their responsibilities by remedying without further delay the constitutional defects noted by the court in *Claremont School District v. Governor* (1997).

### [ART.] 85. [BEFORE WHOM TAKEN.]

The oaths or affirmations shall be taken and subscribed by the governor before a justice of a New Hampshire court, in the presence of both houses of the legislature, by the senators and representatives before the governor and council for the time being, and by all other officers before such persons and in such manner as the general court shall from time to time appoint. *1784; amended 1792, 1968, and 1984.*

The original article followed a similar provision of the Massachusetts Constitution of 1780. A 1792 amendment reworded the provision and updated terminology. In 1968, the people voted to repeal an obsolete portion dealing with the taking of the oath by those first elected. A 1984 amendment required that the governor's oath be taken before a justice of the New Hampshire Supreme Court rather than the president of the senate. This provision has not been interpreted by the New Hampshire Supreme Court.

### [ART.] 86. [FORM OF COMMISSIONS.]

All commissions shall be in the name of the state of New Hampshire, signed by the governor, and attested by the secretary, or his deputy, and shall have the great seal of the state affixed thereto. *1784; amended 1792.*

This article states the formal requirements for commissions issued by the governor. The original article followed a similar provision of the Massachusetts Constitution of 1780. A 1792 amendment changed "president" to "governor." This provision has not been interpreted by the New Hampshire Supreme Court.

### [ART.] 87. [FORM OF WRITS.]

All writs issuing out of the clerk's office in any of the courts of law, shall be in the name of the state of New Hampshire; shall be under the seal of the court whence they issue, and bear test of the chief, first, or senior justice of the court; but when such justice shall be interested, then the writ shall bear test of some other justice of the court, to which the same shall be returnable; and be signed by the clerk of such court. *1784.*

This article states the formal requirements for writs: they must be in the name of the state, be under seal of the court, bear "test" (teste or formal attestation) of the justice, and be signed by the clerk of the court. This article resembles its counterpart in the Massachusetts Constitution of 1780. The New Hampshire Supreme Court has declared that the requirements of this article are "largely a matter of form." *Opinion of the Justices* (1979). Before the Revolution, writs in the province of New Hampshire were issued in the king's name; the framers of this article sought to avoid even the appearance of recognizing royal authority. See *Parsons v. Swett* (1855).

The "writs" to which this article refers include "writs of mesne process by which civil actions are commenced, and writs of execution by which the judgments of the court are executed." *Smith v. Tallman* (1934). Such writs did not include writs of venire, used by the court to direct town clerks to select the requisite number of persons to serve as jurors, see *State v. Bradford* (1876); or a mittimus (warrant of commitment) issued by a court for the detention of a person who had violated a condition of his suspended sentence, see *Carpenter v. Berry* (1948). The signature of the clerk or the seal of the court served to identify the process as issuing from the proper court. See *Reynolds v. Damrell* (1849). In *Reynolds,* the court held that the defect of the lack of teste of a writ was merely formal, unlike the requirement for the signature of the clerk or the seal of the court. Nonetheless, in a municipal court that had no clerk, no clerk's signature would be required; the signature of the justice would be sufficient.

The court has refused to hold certain writs invalid because they did not comply with the formal requirements of this article. In *Parsons, supra,* for example, the court upheld a writ issued over the printed signature of a former chief justice of the superior court. The court has also upheld writs issued by police courts (predecessors of the district courts) that had no clerks even though they contained only the seal of the court and the signature of the justice. See *Smith, supra.* The court cited to *Parsons* and *Smith* in *Opinion of the Justices* (1979), to uphold as constitutional a bill providing for the use of a universal writ in the district and municipal courts. But in the early case of *Hutchins v. Edson* (1817), the court ruled void a writ of execution issued without the required seal.

### [ART.] 88. [FORM OF INDICTMENTS, ETC.]

All indictments, presentments, and informations, shall conclude, "against the peace and dignity of the state." *1784.*

This article states the required form for the conclusion of indictments, presentments, and informations, all different forms of criminal complaints. This provision has not been interpreted by the New Hampshire Supreme Court.

### [ART.] 89. [SUICIDES AND DEODANDS.]

The estates of such persons as may destroy their own lives, shall not for that offense be forfeited, but descend or ascend in the same manner, as if such persons had died in a natural way. Nor shall any article, which shall accidentally occasion the death of any person, be henceforth deemed a deodand, or in any wise forfeited on account of such misfortune. *1784.*

This article expressly rejects two common law concepts relating to forfeiture of property. Under common law, any instrument by which a person was killed—that is, a deodand—or its value, would be subject to forfeiture. As well, the common law prohibited suicide and, as a penalty, the suicide's estate was subject to forfeiture. This provision has not been interpreted by the New Hampshire Supreme Court.

### [ART.] 90. [EXISTING LAWS CONTINUED IF NOT REPUGNANT.]

All the laws which have heretofore been adopted, used, and approved, in the province, colony, or state of New Hampshire, and usually practiced on in the courts of law, shall remain and be in full force, until altered and repealed by the legislature; such parts thereof only excepted, as are repugnant to the rights and liberties contained in this constitution: Provided that nothing herein contained, when compared with the twenty-third article in the bill of rights, shall be construed to affect the laws already made respecting the persons, or estates of absentees. *1784.*

This article provides for the continuation of the common law, and statutes amending it, in existence at the time of the adoption of the 1784 constitution, until amended or repealed by the legislature, except those laws in conflict with the constitution. The first part of this article resembles a similar provision of the Massachusetts Constitution of 1780. The New Hampshire version added the caveat relating to Part 1, Article 23, which prohibits retrospective laws. The "estates of absentees" refers to the estates of Tories who had fled the state during the Revolution.

The laws "heretofore... adopted, used, and approved" refers to the body of English common law and the statutes amending it in effect at the time of the adoption of the 1784 constitution. The New Hampshire Supreme Court clarified in *State v. Rollins* (1837) that the common law continued by Article 90 included law that had not necessarily been applied by the courts in New Hampshire. In *Rollins,* the defendant, charged with kidnapping a six-year-old boy, argued that no statute recognized the crime of kidnapping, and that the common law on kidnapping did not apply because it had never been the subject of actual and usual practice in the state. The court concluded that Article 90 continued in New Hampshire the body of English common law and the statutes amending it, so far as they were consistent with the constitution; Article 90 represented a continuation of a law passed by the legislature in April 1777 reestablishing the general system of laws then in force, except such parts that conflicted with the new form of government established in 1776.

In *State v. Martineau* (2002), the court addressed the question of which criminal actions may be instituted and prosecuted by citizens "without authorization from a prosecuting authority." The court noted that private prosecutions continue to exist as a matter of New Hampshire law so long as they are not "repugnant to the rights and liberties" embraced by the constitution. After reviewing the case law, the court concluded that "the common law does not authorize private prosecutions of criminal offenses which may be punished by imprisonment," and the plaintiff therefore could not prosecute a complaint charging the defendant with a misdemeanor that carried with it a potential prison term.

The court in several cases has concluded that common law applies. See, e.g., *Currier v. Perley* (1851) (common law in relation to tenancies at will from year to year and from month to month in force, except when modified by statute); *Dennett v. Dennett* (1862) (common law rule in *Shelley's Case* a part of law of New Hampshire in 1818 when will was written). In *Cole v. Lake Company* (1874), the court rejected a feudal rule that a fee could never pass by deed without the word "heirs."

### [ART.] 91. [HABEAS CORPUS.]

The privilege and benefit of the habeas corpus, shall be enjoyed in this state, in the most free, easy, cheap, expeditious, and ample manner, and shall not be suspended by the legislature, except upon most urgent and pressing occasions, and for a time not exceeding three months. *1784.*

This article guarantees the remedy of habeas corpus, but allows its suspension by the legislature on "most urgent and pressing occasions" for up to three months. This article resembles its counterpart in the Massachusetts Constitution of 1780, except that the New Hampshire provision allows suspension for no more than three months as opposed to twelve in Massachusetts. The right to habeas corpus dates back at least to *Magna Charta,* and is also protected by Article I, Section 9 of the U.S. Constitution. The writ requires a person detaining an individual to produce the individual in court and explain the reason for the detention. Though the New Hampshire Supreme Court has heard numerous cases addressing habeas issues, it has not had occasion to directly interpret this article.

### [ART.] 92. [ENACTING STYLE OF STATUTES.]

The enacting style in making and passing acts, statutes, and laws, shall be, Be it enacted by the Senate and House of Representatives in General Court convened. *1784*

This article states the official wording to be used by the legislature as the enacting clause in a bill or as the resolving clause in a joint resolution. It resembles a similar provision of the Massachusetts Constitution of 1780. The New Hampshire Supreme Court noted failure to adhere to this article among the reasons given in *In re School-Law Manual* (1885) for invalidating a joint resolution purporting to give authority to an appointed commissioner to compile the statutes relating to schools and to form rules and proceedings in towns.

### [ART.] 93. [GOVERNOR AND JUDGES PROHIBITED FROM HOLDING OTHER OFFICES.]

No governor, or judge of the supreme judicial court, shall hold any office or place under the authority of this state, except such as by this constitution they are admitted to hold, saving that the judges of the said court may hold the offices of justice of the peace throughout the state; nor shall they hold any place or office, or receive any pension or salary, from any other state, government, or power, whatever. *1784; amended 1792.*

This article prohibits the governor and judges from holding other state offices, except that judges may also be justices of the peace. The article also prohibits the governor and judges from holding an office or receiving a pension or salary from any other state or government. The original 1784 article followed its Massachusetts counterpart; the framers included it to curtail the practice of plural office holding in and around the time of the Revolution. A 1792 amendment changed "president" to "governor." The engrossed parchment copy of the constitution as amended in 1792 also reflected the unauthorized change of "superior court" to "supreme judicial court," which change has become accepted. This provision has not been interpreted by the New Hampshire Supreme Court.

### [ART.] 94. [INCOMPATIBILITY OF OFFICES; ONLY TWO OFFICES OF PROFIT TO BE HOLDEN AT SAME TIME.]

No person shall be capable of exercising, at the same time more than one of the following offices within this state, viz. judge of probate, sheriff, register of deeds; and never more than two offices of profit, which may be held by appointment of the governor, or governor and council, or senate and house of representatives, or superior or inferior courts; military offices, and offices of justice of the peace excepted. *1784; amended 1792.*

This article specifies that a person cannot, at the same time, hold more than one of the offices of judge of probate, sheriff, and register of deeds. The article also prohibits the holding of two offices of profit, resulting from appointment by various appointing authorities. Closely based upon a similar provision of the Massachusetts Constitution of 1780, the New Hampshire article also included the "superior or inferior court" as appointing powers for offices of profit to which the constitutional limitation applied. A 1792 amendment changed "president" to "governor." This provision has not been interpreted by the New Hampshire Supreme Court.

### [ART.] 95. [INCOMPATIBILITY OF CERTAIN OFFICES.]

No person holding the office of judge of any court, (except special judges) secretary, treasurer of the state, attorney-general, register of deeds, sheriff, collectors of state and federal taxes, members of Congress or any person holding any office under the United States, including any person in active military service, shall at the same time hold the office of governor, or have a seat in the senate, or house of representatives, or council; but his being chosen and appointed to, and accepting the same, shall operate as a resignation of his seat in the chair, senate, or house of representatives, or council; and the place so vacated shall be filled up. No member of the council shall have a seat in the senate or house of representatives. *1784; amended 1792, 1950, 1958, and 1980.*

This article defines certain offices, the holding of which is incompatible with holding the office of governor, legislator, or member of the executive council, and makes the acceptance of an incompatible office an automatic resignation of the person's seat in the legislature or council or as governor. The article originally resembled a similar provision in the Massachusetts Constitution of 1780; a 1792 amendment substituted "judge of any court" for references to specific courts, added collectors of excise and state and continental taxes, members of Congress or any person holding any office under the United States, and eliminated "president, professor or instructor of any college." The same amendment also added the final sentence prohibiting an executive councilor from holding a seat in the legislature. A 1950 amendment eliminated the commissary-general. A 1958 amendment substituted the general term "collectors of state and federal taxes" for the reference to collectors of excise, state, and continental taxes and changed the obsolete reference to military officers receiving pay from the "Continent" to pay from the "United States." A 1980 amendment revised the reference to military officers receiving pay from the state or the United States, excepting officers of the militia called up in an emergency, to refer only to persons in active military service. This provision has not been interpreted by the New Hampshire Supreme Court.

### [ART.] 96. [BRIBERY AND CORRUPTION DISQUALIFY FOR OFFICE.]

No person shall ever be admitted to hold a seat in the legislature or any office of trust or importance under this government, who, in the due course of law, has been convicted of bribery or corruption, in obtaining an election or appointment. *1784.*

This article prohibits persons who have been convicted of bribery or corruption from obtaining or holding certain government offices or a seat in the legislature. This article resembles a similar provision of the Massachusetts Constitution of 1780. This provision has not been interpreted by the New Hampshire Supreme Court.

### [ART.] 97. [VALUE OF MONEY, HOW COMPUTED.]

(Repealed in 1950)

Originally a part of the 1784 constitution, this article resembled a similar provision of the Massachusetts Constitution of 1780, and stated a fixed value (6 shillings, 8 pence) per ounce of silver, to be used when computing the value of sums of money mentioned in the constitution. The property requirements for governor, senator, and representative all referenced sums of money; an 1852 amendment removed all such requirements. The people voted to repeal this article in 1950.

### [ART.] 98. [CONSTITUTION, WHEN TO TAKE EFFECT.]

To the end that there may be no failure of justice, or danger to the state, by the alterations and amendments made in the constitution, the general court is hereby fully authorized and directed to fix the time when the alterations and amendments shall take effect, and make the necessary arrangements accordingly. *1792.*

This article authorizes the legislature to set the effective date for amendments to the constitution. The convention that proposed the constitution of 1784 set that constitution's effective date as the first Wednesday of June 1784. The 1792 amendments included this one, to provide for the time at which amendments would take effect. The legislature set effective dates in 1793 for the amendments ratified by the voters in 1792. It then became the practice of the legislature to delegate to conventions its power to set the effective date for amendments, and that power has been exercised by conventions since 1850, requiring that amendments take effect when the governor proclaims their adoption.

In an 1889 advisory opinion, the New Hampshire Supreme Court concluded that, under this article, the legislature had no power to change the effective time of an amendment following a delegation of its authority to do so to a convention, and after the convention had exercised that power. See *Opinion of the Justices* (1889). The court decided two more cases consistent with this conclusion in 1961. In *Opinion of the Justices* (1961), the court ruled that the legislature could not postpone the effective dates of amendments after the governor declared them as having been adopted on November 30, 1960. The other case—*Rix v. Asadoorian* (1961)—concerned the right of a litigant to a jury trial in a case worth $260, which depended upon the effective date of an amendment to Part 1, Article 20, increasing the required minimum amount in controversy for such a trial from $100 to $500. The voters had ratified the amendment on November 8, 1960, and the governor proclaimed it adopted on November 30, 1960. The defendant requested a jury trial in October 1959 and the plaintiff moved to have the action tried by the court on November 28, 1960. The court held the defendant entitled to a jury trial because the amendment increasing the minimum amount in controversy did not go into effect until November 30, 1960, and the amendment was not retroactive in its application.

### [ART.] 99. [REVISION OF CONSTITUTION PROVIDED FOR.]

(Repealed in 1980)

This article, original to the 1784 constitution, required the legislature to call elections for a constitutional convention after seven years from the time the constitution took effect; that delegates would be elected in the same manner as representatives to the house; and that amendments proposed by the convention would take effect if approved by two-thirds of the qualified voters present and voting. A 1792 amendment established detailed procedures for the calling of conventions, required that the question of calling a convention to revise the constitution be submitted to the people after seven years, and specified that a convention would be held if a majority of the people voted in favor of one. At the time the people voted to repeal this article in 1980, Article 100 covered these matters. This article resembled a similar provision in the Massachusetts Constitution of 1780, though in Massachusetts the voters were given the option of holding a convention in 1795, while the New Hampshire Constitution required elections for a convention to be held in 1791. Cases decided under this article established that convention delegates could be elected by nonpartisan ballot, see *Opinion of the Justices* (1973), and that the legislature could choose the time of the election of delegates, see *Opinion of the Justices* (1911); these are also matters now covered under Article 100.

### [ART.] 100. [ALTERNATE METHODS OF PROPOSING AMENDMENTS.]

Amendments to this constitution may be proposed by the general court or by a constitutional convention selected as herein provided.

(a) The senate and house of representatives, voting separately, may propose amendments by a three-fifths vote of the entire membership of each house at any session.

(b) The general court, by an affirmative vote of a majority of all members of both houses voting separately, may at any time submit the question "Shall there be a convention to amend or revise the constitution?" to the qualified voters of the state. If the question of holding a convention is not submitted to the people at some time during any period of ten years, it shall be submitted by the secretary of state at the general election in the tenth year following the last submission. If a majority of the qualified voters voting on the question of holding a convention approves it, delegates shall be chosen at the next regular general election, or at such earlier time as the legislature may provide, in the same manner and proportion as the representatives to the general court are chosen. The delegates so chosen shall convene at such time as the legislature may direct and may recess from time to time and make such rules for the conduct of their convention as they may determine.

(c) The constitutional convention may propose amendments by a three-fifths vote of the entire membership of the convention.

Each constitutional amendment proposed by the general court or by a constitutional convention shall be submitted to the voters by written ballot at the next biennial November election and shall become a part of the Constitution only after approval by two-thirds of the qualified voters present and voting on the subject in the towns, wards, and unincorporated places. *1792; amended 1964 and 1980.*

This article provides that (1) either a constitutional convention or the legislature may propose amendments to the constitution by a three-fifths vote of the entire membership of the convention or of each house of the legislature, (2) proposed questions must be submitted to the voters at the next biennial November election, and (3) proposed amendments take effect if approved by two-thirds of the qualified voters present and voting. The article also requires that the question of holding a convention to revise the constitution must be submitted to the voters at least once every ten years, that a convention will be held if approved by a majority of the qualified voters present and voting, and that delegates to a convention must be elected in the same manner as representatives.

The people added this provision to the constitution in 1792 and at that time required that the question whether to hold a convention be submitted to the voters every seven years. A 1964 amendment authorized the legislature to propose amendments by a three-fifths vote of the entire membership of each body and to require that the question whether to hold a convention be submitted to the voters at least once in ten years, instead of every seven. The 1964 amendment also included language from Article 99 regarding the election of delegates and the approval of the calling of a convention by a majority of the voters. A 1980 amendment required a three-fifths vote of the entire membership of a constitutional convention, rather than a majority, to propose an amendment to the constitution (thus equalizing the voting requirement for conventions and the legislature) and required that all proposed amendments be submitted at the next biennial November election. The 1980 amendments also incorporated provisions from repealed Article 99 relating to the two-thirds majority approval for ratification of amendments.

Until the people amended this article in 1964 to allow both the legislature and a specially elected convention to propose amendments, New Hampshire was the only state that did not allow its legislature to propose constitutional amendments. The issue had been debated at earlier conventions, but only appeared on the ballot for ratification twice before 1964, both times as a result of proposals by the 1850 convention.

The constitutional requirement of "a three-fifths vote of the entire membership of each house at any session" under paragraph (a) is mandatory, but the procedure by which the vote is obtained in the legislature is to be determined by each house's own rules of proceedings. In *Bednar v. King* (1970), the New Hampshire Supreme Court concluded that, despite various irregularities in the proceedings in the house of representatives and the senate, it would not invalidate the adoption of a concurrent resolution that contained a proposed amendment to the constitution. Cases decided under former Article 99 relating to provisions now in Article 100 established that convention delegates could be elected by nonpartisan ballot, see *Opinion of the Justices* (1973), and that the legislature could choose the time of the election of delegates, see *Opinion of the Justices* (1911).

The final paragraph of Article 100 requires that all questions proposed either by the legislature or a convention be submitted to the voters by written ballot at the next biennial November election. The legislature may prescribe matters of form as to the ballot, but any proposed amendments must appear on a written ballot at the biennial November election following the vote to propose the amendment.

### [ART.] 101. [ENROLLMENT OF CONSTITUTION.]

This form of government shall be enrolled on parchment, and deposited in the secretary's office, and be a part of the laws of the land and printed copies thereof shall be prefixed to the books containing the laws of this state, in all future editions thereof. *1784.*

This article provides for the enrollment on parchment of the constitution of 1784 and requires that the constitution be printed in the books containing the state laws; it is virtually the same as its counterpart in the Massachusetts Constitution of 1780. Unfortunately—and ironically—there is no known parchment copy of the 1784 constitution; the earliest existing parchment copy was created following the incorporation of the amendments of 1792. That copy contains several nonsubstantive, minor changes in punctuation and wording that have become an accepted part of the constitution.

# TABLE AND APPENDICES

TABLE 1 **Constitutional Conventions in New Hampshire**

| Year of Convention | Dates of Convention |
|---|---|
| Convention of 1778[1] | Convened June 10, 1778, Oct. 13, 1778; draft constitution completed June 5, 1779; met to count returns, Sept. 21, 1779 |
| Convention of 1781 | Convened June 5 or 12, 1781,[2] draft constitution completed Sept. 14, 1781; met Jan. 23, 1782 to count returns; met Aug. 1782 and completed second draft constitution Aug. 21, 1782; met Dec. 31, 1782 to count returns; met June 3, 1783 and completed third draft constitution; met Oct. 31, 1783 to count returns |
| Convention of 1791 | Sept. 7–16, 1791; Feb. 8–24, 1792 |
| Convention of 1850 | Nov. 6–22, 1850; Dec. 3, 1850–Jan. 3, 1851 |
| Convention of 1876 | Dec. 6–15, 1876 |
| Convention of 1889 | Jan. 2–12, 1889 |
| Convention of 1902 | Dec. 2–19, 1902 |
| Convention of 1912 | June 5–22, 1912 |
| Convention of 1918 | June 5–7, 1918; Jan. 13–29, 1920; Jan. 28, 1921; Feb. 16, 1923 |
| Convention of 1930 | June 4–13, 1930 |
| Convention of 1938 | May 11, 1938–June 1, 1938; Nov. 8, 1938; Sept. 23–26, 1941 |
| Convention of 1948 | May 12, 1948–June 4, 1948 |
| Convention of 1956 | May 15, 1956–June 13, 1956; Dec. 2–4, 1959 |
| Convention of 1964 | May 13, 1964–June 10, 1964; July 8, 1964 |
| Convention of 1974 | May 8, 1974–June 26, 1974 |
| Convention of 1984 | May 9, 1984–June 28, 1984 |

[1] There are no journals for the conventions of 1778 or 1781 and so no official record of the exact dates on which those conventions met. Lynn Turner, *The Ninth State: New Hampshire's Formative Years* (Chapel Hill: University of North Carolina Press, 1983), 18, 21.

[2] Though the convention was called to meet on the first Tuesday of June, there is some doubt as to whether it actually met on the first or the second Tuesday.

**TABLE 2 Constitutional Amendments Proposed for Ratification Grouped by Topic**
*(Note: This Chart Does Not Contain Every Topic)*

| Topic | Amendment Adopted* | Amendment Rejected* |
|---|---|---|
| *Taxation* | | |
| Inheritance tax (alone or in combination) | 1902 | 1912, 1920, 1921, 1938, 1948, 1964 |
| Tax reform (two or more tax topics in same question) | | 1912, 1923, 1938, 1948, 1964 |
| Income tax (alone or in combination) | | 1912, 1920, 1921, 1930, 1938, 1964, 2012 |
| Current use taxation | 1968 | |
| Taxation of franchises | 1902 | |
| Timber tax (alone or in combination) | 1942 | 1912, 1938 |
| Stock-in-trade tax (alone or in combination) | | 1948, 1964 |
| Estate tax | | 1930 |
| Public utilities tax | | 1948 |
| *Governor's Powers* | | |
| Governor, item veto | | 1912, 1920, 1930 |
| Governor, take away pocket veto power | | 1976 |
| Governor's executive powers | 1956, 1966, 1968 | |
| Four-year term for governor | | 1970, 1982, 1984 |
| Authority of governor (and council) to adjourn or prorogue (extend recess of) legislature | | 1792, 1976, 1984 |
| Gubernatorial succession | 1792, 1889, 1968, 1984 | 1976, 1980 |
| *Executive Council* | | |
| Councilor districts to be based on population | 1912 | |
| Substitute "lieutenant-governor" for "council" | | 1792, 1850 |
| Housekeeping amendment to reflect that councilors elected from councilor districts, not counties | | 1980 |
| Abolish executive council | | 1850 |
| *House and Senate* | | |
| Size and apportionment of house | 1876, 1889, 1942, 1960, 1964, 1978, 2006 | 1850, 1902, 1912, 1920, 1921, 1930, 1948, 1976, 1984 |
| Annual vs. biennial legislative sessions | 1876, 1966 (invalidated), 1984 | 1850, 1970, 1972, 1976, 1978 |
| Time of meeting of legislature | 1889 | 1976 |

| Topic | Amendment Adopted* | Amendment Rejected* |
|---|---|---|
| *House and Senate (Cont.)* | | |
| Calling of special legislative sessions by legislature | | 1976 |
| Legislative mileage and compensation | 1889, 1960, 1966 (invalidated), 1984 | 1964, 1968, 1970, 1972, 1974, 1976, 1978 |
| Limitations on adjournment of legislature | 1948, 1966 | |
| Legislative procedure (roll calls, journals, time of organizational meeting) | 1966, 1974 | 1850 |
| Increase size of senate | 1876 | 1792, 1850, 1912, 1964, 1974, 1984 |
| Basis of representation in senate | 1964 | 1850 |
| Senatorial districts, allowing division of towns, etc. | 1978 | |
| Residency requirements for senators | 1976 | 1966, 1978, 1980 |
| Age requirements for senators (alone or in combination with other offices) | | 1980, 1984, 1998 |
| Filling of vacancies in senate | 1889 | |
| New senate elections in case of plurality | 1968 | |
| *Judicial Branch* | | |
| Jurisdiction of police courts | 1912 | 1902 |
| Creation of court districts | | 1976 |
| Justices of the peace, jurisdiction, appeals | 1792, 1876 | 1850 |
| Election of judges | | 1850 |
| Judges to hold office during good behavior | 1792 | |
| Set age limitation for judges | 1792 | |
| Remove age limitation for judges | | 1850 |
| Judicial compensation | | 1978 |
| Supreme and superior courts made constitutional courts | 1966 | |
| Chief justice of supreme court administrative head of courts | 1978 | |
| Rights of commissioned officers in cases of impeachment (including judges) | 1966 | |
| Rules governing the judicial branch | 1978 | 2002, 2004, 2012 |
| *Bill of Rights Topics* | | |
| Bill of rights gender neutral | | 1980 |
| Prohibit discrimination | 1974 | |
| Right to bear arms | 1982 | 1978 |

| Topic | Amendment Adopted* | Amendment Rejected* |
|---|---|---|
| *Bill of Rights Topics (Cont.)* | | |
| Sectarian references in Art. 6 of bill of rights | 1968 | 1850 (twice), 1876, 1889, 1902, 1912, 1920 |
| Public's right-to-know | 1976 | |
| Voting rights; right to hold elective office | 1902, 1912, 1942, 1956, 1958, 1968, 1976, 1984 | 1902, 1921, 1930, 1938, 1968, 1972, 1980 |
| Conscientious objectors | 1964 | 1920, 1950 |
| Right to counsel at state expense if need is shown | 1966 | |
| Reduce legal burden of proof to commit a person acquitted of a crime by reason of insanity | 1984 | |
| Change of venue, criminal defendant | 1978 | |
| Jury trial amount in controversy | 1876, 1960, 1988 | 1956, 1976, 1984, 1986, 1992 |
| Right to free speech | 1968 | |
| Funding of state-mandated programs | 1984 | |
| Home rule | 1966, 1984 | 2000 |
| *Restrictions on Use of Public Money* | | |
| No use of public money or credit to benefit corporation | 1876 | 1850 |
| Restriction of motor vehicle revenues for highway purposes (highway fund) | 1938 | |
| No use of public money for religious schools | 1876 | |
| Retirement funds restricted | 1984 | |
| Lottery revenues used for education | 1990 | |
| *Miscellaneous* | | |
| Civil pensions, one-year restriction | | 1850, 1912, 1920, 1974, 1976 |
| Abolish property requirements for office | 1850 (2nd vote) | 1792, 1850 (1st vote) |
| Abolish religious test for office | 1876 | 1792, 1850 |
| State militia | 1976 | 1948 |
| Method of amending constitution | 1792, 1964, 1980 | 1850, 1948 |
| No footnotes in budget bills | 1984 | |
| Administrative rules veto | | 1988, 1992 |
| Eminent domain | 2006 | |
| Education funding | | 2008 |

* The year is the year the question appeared on the constitutional question referendum ballot.

# APPENDIX 1

## *Text of 1776 Constitution*

This text is transcribed from the Journal of the House of Representatives under the Constitution adopted January 5, 1776, in the handwriting of Noah Emery, Assistant Clerk of the House. The journal is located at the New Hampshire Department of State, Division of Records Management and Archives:

In Congress at Exeter Jan'y 5th 1776

Voted That this Congress Take up Civil Government for this Colony in the manner & Form Following Viz—

We the Members of the Congress of New Hampshire Chosen and Appointed by the Free Suffrages of the People of Said Colony,—and—Authorized and Impowered by them to meet together, and use Such means and Pursue Such Measures as we Should Judge best for the Public Good; And in Particular to Establish Some Form of Government, Provided that Measure Should be recommended by the Continental Congress: And a Recommendation to that Purpose having been Transmitted to us From the Said Congress: Have Taken into our Serious Consideration the Unhappy Circumstances, into which this Colony is Involved by means of Many Grievous and Oppressive Acts of the British Parliament, Depriving us of our Natural & Constitutional rights & Priviledges; To Enforce Obedience to which Acts, A Powerfull Fleet and Army have been Sent into this Country, by the Ministry of Great Britain, who have Exercised a Wanton & Cruel Abuse of their Power, in Destroying the Lives & Properties of the Colonists in many Places with Fire & Sword: Taking the Ships & Lading from many of the Honest and Industrious Inhabitants of this Colony Employ'd in Commerce, Agreeable to the Laws & Customs a long time used here.—

The Sudden & Abrupt Departure of his Excellency John Wentworth Esq: our Late Governor, & Several of the Council, Leaving us Destitute of Legislation,—and no Executive Courts being open to Punish Criminal Offenders; whereby the Lives & Propertys of the Honest People of this Colony, are Liable to the Machinations & Evil Designs of wicked men; Therefore for the Preservation of Peace and good order, and for the Security of the Lives & Properties of the Inhabitants of this Colony, We Conceive ourselves Reduced to the Necessity of Establishing A Form of Government to Continue During the Present Unhappy and Unnatural Contest with Great Britain; Protesting & Declaring that we Never Sought to throw off our Dependance upon Great Britain, but felt ourselves happy under her Protection, while we Could Enjoy our Constitutional Rights & Priviledges.—And that we Shall Rejoice if Such a Reconciliation between us and our Parent State can be Effected as Shall be Approved by the Continental Congress in whose Prudence and Wisdom we Confide:

Accordingly Pursuant to the Trust reposed in us, We do Resolve That This Congress, Assume the Name, Power & Authority of a house of Representatives or Assembly for the Colony of New Hampshire. And that Said House then Proceed to Choose Twelve Persons, being Reputable Freeholders and Inhabitants within this Colony, in the Following manner viz, Five in the County of Rockingham, Two in the County of Strafford, Two in the County of Hillsborough, Two in the County of Cheshire, and one in the County of Grafton, To be a Distinct & Separate branch of the Legislature, by the Name of A Council for this Colony, to Continue as Such untill the Third Wednesday in December next; any Seven of whom to be a Quorum to do Business.

That Such Council Appoint their President; and in his Absence that the Senior Councellor Preside.

That a Secretary to Appointed by both Branches, who may be a Councellor, or otherwise as they Shall Choose.

That no Act or resolve Shall be Valid & put into Execution unless agreed to and passed by both Branches of the Legislature.

That all Publick Officers for the Said Colony, and Each County, for the Current Year, be Appointed by the Council & Assembly, Except the Several Clerks of the Executive Courts, who Shall be Appointed by the Justices of the respective Courts—

That All Bills, Resolves or Votes for Raising Levying & Collecting money Originate in the House of Representatives.

That at any Session of the Council and Assembly, Neither Branch Shall Adjourn for any Longer time than from Saturday till the Next Monday—without Consent of the other.

And it is further Resolved, That if the Present unhappy Dispute with Great Britain Should Continue longer than this present year, & the Continental Congress Give no Instruction or Direction to the Contrary, the Council be Chosen by the People of Each respective County in Such manner as the Council & house of Representatives shall order—

That General & field officers of the Militia, on any Vacancy, be Appointed by the Two houses & all Inferior Officers be Chosen by the Respective Companys.—

That all officers of the Army be Appointed by the Two houses, Except they Should Direct otherwise in Case of any Emergency—

That all Civil officers for the Colony & for Each County be Appointed, & the time of their Continuance in Office, be Determined by the Two houses, Except Clerks of Court, & County Treasurers & recorders of Deeds.—

That a Treasurer and a recorder of Deeds for Each County be Annually Chosen by the People of Each County Respectively: The Votes for Such officers to be returned to the respective Courts of General Sessions of the Peace in the County, there to be ascertained as the Council & Assembly Shall hereafter Direct.—

That Precepts in the name of the Council & Assembly, Signed by the President of the Council & Speaker of the House of Representatives, Shall Issue Annually at or before the first day of November, for the Choice of A Council and house of Representatives to be returned by the third Wednesday in December then next Ensuing, in Such manner as the Council & Assembly Shall hereafter Prescribe.—

# ■ APPENDIX 2

## *Text of 1784 Constitution*

This is the text of the 1784 constitution, as printed at Portsmouth, New Hampshire, in 1783. The version included in this appendix retains the use of capitalizations and spellings in the printing, except for the printer's convention of capitalizing all the letters of the first word of each paragraph:

**A CONSTITUTION CONTAINING A BILL OF RIGHTS, AND FORM OF GOVERNMENT,**

Agreed upon by the DELEGATES of the PEOPLE of the State of NEW-HAMPSHIRE, in CONVENTION, held at CONCORD, on the first Tuesday of *June*, 1783; submitted to, and approved of by the people of said State; and established by their Delegates in Convention, *October* 31, 1783.

**PART I.**
**THE BILL OF RIGHTS.**
**Article I.**

All Men are born equally free and independent; therefore, all government of right originates from the people, is founded in consent, and instituted for the general good.

**II.**

All men have certain natural, essential, and inherent rights; among which are—the enjoying and defending life and liberty—acquiring, possessing and protecting property—and in a word, of seeking and obtaining happiness.

**III.**

When men enter into a state of society, they surrender up some of their natural rights to that society, in order to insure the protection of others; and, without such an equivalent, the surrender is void.

**IV.**

Among the natural rights, some are in their very nature unalienable, because no equivalent can be given or received for them. Of this kind are the RIGHTS OF CONSCIENCE.

## V.

Every individual has a natural and unalienable right to worship GOD according to the dictates of his own conscience, and reason; and no subject shall be hurt, molested, or restrained in his person, liberty or estate for worshipping GOD in the manner and season most agreeable to the dictates of his own conscience, or for his religious profession, sentiments or persuasion; provided he doth not disturb the public peace, or disturb others in their religious worship.

## VI.

As morality and piety, rightly grounded on evangelical principles, will give the best and greatest security to government, and will lay in the hearts of men the strongest obligations to due subjection; and as the knowledge of these, is most likely to be propagated through a society by the institution of the public worship of the DEITY, and of public instruction in morality and religion; therefore, to promote those important purposes, the people of this State have a right to impower, and do hereby fully impower the Legislature to authorize from time to time, the several towns, parishes, bodies-corporate, or religious societies within this State, to make adequate provision at their own expense, for the support and maintenance of public protestant teachers of piety, religion and morality:

*Provided notwithstanding*, That the several towns, parishes, bodies-corporate, or religious societies, shall at all times have the exclusive right of electing their own public teachers, and of contracting with them for their support and maintenance. And no person of any one particular religious sect or denomination, shall ever be compelled to pay towards the support of the teacher or teachers of another persuasion, sect or denomination.

And every denomination of christians, demeaning themselves quietly, and as good subjects of the State, shall be equally under the protection of the law: And no subordination of any one sect or denomination to another, shall ever be established by law.

And nothing herein shall be understood to affect any former contracts made for the support of the ministry; but all such contracts shall remain, and be in the same state as if this Constitution had not been made.

## VII.

The people of this State, have the sole and exclusive right of governing themselves as a free, sovereign and independent State, and do, and forever hereafter shall, exercise, and enjoy every power, jurisdiction and right pertaining thereto, which is not, or may not hereafter be by them expressly delegated to the United States of America in Congress assembled.

### VIII.

All power residing originally in, and being derived from the people, all the magistrates and officers of government, are their substitutes and agents, and at all times accountable to them.

### IX.

No office or place whatsoever in government, shall be hereditary—the abilities and integrity requisite in all, not being transmissible to posterity or relations.

### X.

Government being instituted for the common benefit, protection, and security of the whole community, and not for the private interest or emolument of any one man, family, or class of men; therefore, whenever the ends of government are perverted, and public liberty manifestly endangered, and all other means of redress are ineffectual, the people may, and of right ought, to reform the old, or establish a new government. The doctrine of non-resistance against arbitrary power, and oppression, is absurd, slavish, and destructive of the good and happiness of mankind.

### XI.

All elections ought to be free, and every inhabitant of the State having the proper qualifications, has equal right to elect, and be elected into office.

### XII.

Every member of the community has a right to be protected by it in the enjoyment of his life, liberty and property; he is therefore bound to contribute his share in the expence [*sic*] of such protection, and to yield his personal service when necessary, or an equivalent. But no part of a man's property shall be taken from him, or applied to public uses, without his own consent, or that of the Representative body of the people. Nor are the inhabitants of this State controllable by any other laws than those to which they or their Representative Body have given their consent.

### XIII.

No person who is conscientiously scrupulous about the lawfulness of bearing arms, shall be compelled thereto, provided he will pay an equivalent.

### XIV.

Every subject of this State is entitled to a certain remedy, by having recourse to the laws, for all injuries he may receive in his person, property or character, to obtain right and justice freely, without being obliged to purchase it; completely, and without any denial; promptly, and without delay, conformably to the laws.

### XV.

No subject shall be held to answer for any crime, or offence [*sic*], until the same is fully and plainly, substantially and formally described to him; or be compelled to accuse or furnish evidence against himself. And every subject shall have a right to produce all proofs that may be favorable to himself; to meet the witnesses against him face to face, and to be fully heard in his defence [*sic*] by himself, and counsel. And no subject shall be arrested, imprisoned, despoiled, or deprived of this property, immunities, or privileges, put out of the protection of the law, exiled or deprived of his life, liberty, or estate, but by the judgment of his peers, or the law of the land.

### XVI.

No subject shall be liable to be tried, after an acquittal, for the same crime or offence [*sic*].—Nor shall the Legislature make any law that shall subject any person to a capital punishment, excepting for the government of the army and navy, and the militia in actual service, without trial by jury.

### XVII.

In criminal prosecutions, the trial of facts in the vicinity where they happen, is so essential to the security of the life, liberty and estate of the citizen, that no crime or offence [*sic*] ought to be tried in any other county than that in which it is committed; except in cases of general insurrection in any particular county, when it shall appear to the Judges of the Superior Court, that an impartial trial cannot be had in the county where the offence [*sic*] may be committed, and upon their report, the assembly shall think proper to direct the trial in the nearest county in which an impartial trial can be obtained.

### XVIII.

All penalties ought to be proportioned to the nature of the offence [*sic*]. No wise Legislature will affix the same punishment to the crimes of theft, forgery and the like, which they do to those of murder and treason; where the same undistinguishing severity is exerted against all offences [*sic*]; the people are led to forget the real distinction in the crimes themselves; and to commit the most flagrant with as little compunction as they do those of the lightest dye. For the same reason a multitude of sanguinary laws is both impolitic and unjust. The true design of all punishments being to reform, not to exterminate, mankind.

## XIX.

Every subject hath a right to be secure from all unreasonable searches and seizures of his person, his houses, his papers, and all his possessions. All warrants, therefore, are contrary to this right, if the cause or foundation of them be not previously supported by oath, or affirmation; and if the order in the warrant to a civil officer, to make search in suspected places, or to arrest one or more suspected persons, or to seize their property, be not accompanied with a special designation of the persons or objects of search, arrest, or seizure; and no warrant ought to be issued but in cases, and with the formalities prescribed by the laws.

## XX.

In all controversies concerning property, and in all suits between two or more persons, except in cases in which it has been heretofore otherwise used and practised [*sic*], the parties have a right to a trial by jury; and this method of procedure shall be held sacred, unless in causes arising on the high seas, and such as relate to mariners wages, the Legislature shall think it necessary hereafter to alter it.

## XXI.

In order to reap the fullest advantage of the inestimable priviledge [*sic*] of the trial by Jury, great care ought to be taken that none but qualified persons should be appointed to serve; and such ought to be fully compensated for their travel, time and attendance.

## XXII.

The Liberty of the Press is essential to the security of freedom in a State; it ought therefore to be inviolably preserved.

## XXIII.

Retrospective laws are highly injurious, oppressive and unjust. No such laws therefore should be made, either for the decision of civil causes, or the punishment of offences [*sic*].

## XXIV.

A well regulated militia is the proper, natural, and sure defence [*sic*] of a State.

## XXV.

Standing armies are dangerous to liberty, and ought not to be raised or kept up without the consent of the Legislature.

### XXVI.

In all cases, and at all times, the military ought to be under strict subordination to, and governed by the civil power.

### XXVII.

No soldier in time of peace shall be quartered in any house without the consent of the owner, and in time of war such quarters ought not to be made but by the civil magistrate, in a manner ordained by the Legislature.

### XXVIII.

No subsidy, charge, tax, impost or duty shall be established, fixed, laid, or levied, under any pretext whatsoever, without the consent of the people or their Representatives in the Legislature, or authority derived from that body.

### XXIX.

The power of suspending the laws, or the execution of them, ought never to be exercised but by the Legislature, or by authority derived therefrom, to be exercised in such particular cases only as the Legislature shall expressly provide for.

### XXX.

The freedom of deliberation, speech, and debate, in either House of the Legislature, is so essential to the rights of the people, that it cannot be the foundation of any action, complaint, or prosecution, in any other Court or place whatsoever.

### XXXI.

The Legislature ought frequently to assemble for the redress of grievances, for correcting, strengthening and confirming the laws, and for making new ones, as the common good may require.

### XXXII.

The people have a right in an orderly and peaceable manner, to assemble and consult upon the common good, give instructions to their Representatives; and to request of the Legislative-body, by way of petition or remonstrance, redress of the wrongs done them, and of the grievances they suffer.

### XXXIII.

No magistrate or court of law shall demand excessive bail or sureties, impose excessive fines, or inflict cruel or unusual punishments.

## XXXIV.

No person can in any case be subjected to law-martial, or to any pains, or penalties, by virtue of that law, except those employed in the army or navy, and except the militia in actual service, but by authority of the Legislature.

## XXXV.

It is essential to the preservation of the rights of every individual, his life, liberty, property and character, that there be an impartial interpretation of the laws, and administration of justice. It is the right of every citizen to be tried by judges as impartial as the lot of humanity will admit. It is therefore not only the best policy but for the security of the rights of the people, that the Judges of the Supreme (or Superior) Judicial Court should hold their offices so long as they behave well; and that they should have honorable salaries, ascertained and established by standing laws.

## XXXVI.

Oeconomy [*sic*] being a most essential virtue in all States, especially in a young one, no pension shall be granted, but in consideration of actual services, and such pensions ought to be granted with great caution, by the Legislature, and never for more than one year at a time.

## XXXVII.

In the government of this State, the three essential powers thereof, to wit, the Legislative, Executive and Judicial, ought to be kept as seperate [*sic*] from and independent of each other, as the nature of a free government will admit, or as is consistent with that chain of connection that binds the whole fabric of the constitution in one indissoluble bond of union and amity.

## XXXVIII.

A frequent recurrence to the fundamental principles of the Constitution, and constant adherence to justice, moderation, temperance, industry, frugality, and all the social virtues, are indispensably necessary to preserve the blessings of liberty and good government; the people ought therefore, to have a particular regard to all those principles in the choice of their Officers and Representatives: And they have a right to require of their law-givers and magistrates, an exact and constant observance of them in the formation and execution of the laws necessary for the good administration of government.

## PART II
## THE FORM OF GOVERNMENT

The People inhabiting the Territory formerly called the Province of New-Hampshire, do hereby solemnly and mutually agree with each other, to form themselves into a free, sovereign, and independent Body-Politic or State, by the name of the STATE of NEW-HAMPSHIRE.

### THE GENERAL COURT

The Supreme Legislative power within this State shall be vested in the Senate and House of Representatives, each of which shall have a negetive [*sic*] on the other.

The Senate and House shall assemble every year on the first Wednesday of June, and at such other times as they may judge necessary; and shall dissolve, and be dissolved, seven days next preceding the said first Wednesday of June; and shall be stiled [*sic*] THE GENERAL COURT OF NEW-HAMPSHIRE.

The General Court shall forever have full power and authority to erect and constitute judicatories and courts of record, or other courts, to be holden in the name of the State, for the hearing, trying, and determining all manner of crimes, offences [*sic*], pleas, processes, plaints, actions, causes, matters and things whatsoever, arising, or happening within this State, or between or concerning persons inhabiting, or residing, or brought within the same, whether the same be criminal or civil, or whether the crimes be capital, or not capital, and whether the said pleas be real, personal, or mixed; and for the awarding and issuing execution thereon. To which courts and judicatories are hereby given and granted full power and authority, from time to time to administer oaths or affirmations, for the better discovery of truth in any matter in controversy, or depending before them.

And, farther, full power and authority are hereby given and granted to the said General-Court, from time to time, to make, ordain, and establish, all manner of wholesome and reasonable orders, laws, statutes, ordinances, directions and instructions, either with penalties or without; so as the same be not repugnant, or contrary to this Constitution, as they may judge for the benefit and welfare of this State, and for the governing and ordering thereof, and of the subjects of the same, for the necessary support and defence [*sic*] of the government thereof; and to name and settle annually, or provide by fixed laws, for the naming and settling all civil officers within this State, such officers excepted, the election and appointment of whom, are hereafter in this Form of Government otherwise provided for; and to set forth the several duties, powers and limits, of the several civil and military officers of this State, and the forms of such oaths or affirmations, as shall be respectively administred [*sic*] unto them, for the execution of their several offices and places, so as the same be not repugnant or contrary to this Constitution; and also to impose fines, mulcts, imprisonments, and other punishments; and to impose and levy proportional and reasonable assessments, rates and taxes, upon all the inhabitants of, and residents within the said State; and upon all estates within the same; to be issued and disposed of by warrant under the hand of the President of this State for the time being, with the advice and consent of the Council, for the public service, in the necessary defence [*sic*] and support of the Government of this State, and the protection and preservation of the subjects thereof, according to such acts as are, or shall be in force within the same.

And while the public charges of government or any part thereof, shall be assessed on polls and estates in the manner that has heretofore been practised [*sic*]; in order that such assessments may be made with equality, there shall be a valuation of the estates within the State taken anew once in every five years at least, and as much oftener as the General Court shall order.

## SENATE

There shall be annually elected by the freeholders and other inhabitants of this State, qualified as in this Constitution is provided, twelve persons to be Senators for the year ensuing their election; to be chosen in and by the inhabitants of the districts, into which this State may from time to time be divided by the General Court, for that purpose: And the General-Court in assigning the number to be elected by the respective districts, shall govern themselves by the proportion of public taxes paid by the said districts; and timely make known to the inhabitants of the State, the limits of each district, and the number of Senators to be elected therein; provided the number of such districts shall never be more than ten, nor less than five.

And the several counties in this State, shall until the General Court shall order otherwise, be districts for the election of Senators, and shall elect the following number, viz.

*Rockingham*, five.
*Strafford*, two.
*Hillsborough*, two.
*Cheshire*, two.
*Grafton*, one.

The Senate shall be the first branch of the Legislature: And the Senators shall be chosen in the following manner, viz. Every male inhabitant of each town and parish with town privileges in the several counties in this State, of twenty-one years of age and upwards, paying for himself a poll tax, shall have a right at the annual or other meetings of the inhabitants of said towns and parishes, to be duly warned and holden annually forever in the month of March; to vote in the town or parish wherein he dwells, for the Senators in the county or district whereof he is a member.

And every person qualified as the Constitution provides, shall be considered an inhabitant for the purpose of electing and being elected into any office or place within this State, in that town, parish and plantation where he dwelleth and hath his home.

The Selectmen of the several towns and parishes aforesaid, shall, during the choice of Senators, preside at such meetings impartially, and shall receive the votes of all the inhabitants of such towns and parishes present and qualified to vote for Senators, and shall sort and count the same in the meeting, and in presence of the Town-Clerk, who shall make a fair record in presence of the Selectmen, and in open meeting, of the name of every person voted for, and the number of votes against his name; and a fair copy of this record shall be attested by the Selectmen and Town-Clerk, and shall be sealed up and directed to the Secretary of the State, with a superscription expressing the purport thereof, and delivered by said Clerk to the Sheriff of the county in which such town or parish lies, thirty days at least, before the first Wednesday of June; and the sheriff of each county, or his deputy, shall deliver all such certificates by him received, into the Secretary's office, seventeen days at least, before the first Wednesday of June.

And the inhabitants of plantations and places unincorporated, qualified as this Constitution provides, who are or shall be required to assess taxes upon themselves towards the support of government, or shall be taxed therefor, shall have the same privilege of voting for Senators in the plantations and places wherein they reside, as the inhabitants of the respective towns and parishes aforesaid have. And the meetings of such plantations and places for that purpose, shall be holden annually in the month of March, at such places respectively therein, as the assessors thereof shall direct; which assessors shall have like authority for notifying the electors, collecting and returning the votes, as the Selectmen and Town Clerks have in their several towns by this Constitution.

And, that there may be a due meeting of Senators on the first Wednesday of June, annually, the President and three of the Council for the time being, shall as soon as may, examine the returned copies of such records; and fourteen days before the said first Wednesday of June, he shall issue his summons to such persons as appear to be chosen Senators by a majority of votes, to attend and take their seats on that day: Provided, nevertheless, that for the first year the said returned copies shall be examined by the President and five of the Council of the former Constitution of Government; and the said President shall in like manner notify the persons elected, to attend and take their seats accordingly.

The Senate shall be final judges of the elections, returns, and qualifications of their own members, as pointed out in this Constitution, and shall on the said first Wednesday of June annually, determine and declare, who are elected by each district to be Senators by a majority of votes: And in case there shall not appear to be the full number returned elected by a majority of votes for any district, the deficiency shall be supplied in the following manner, viz. The members of the House of Representatives and such Senators as shall be declared elected, shall take the names of such persons as shall be found to have the highest number of votes in each district, and not elected, amounting to twice the number of Senators wanting, if there be so many voted for; and out of these shall elect by joint ballot the number of Senators wanted for such district: And in this manner all such vacancies shall be filled up in every district of the State, and in like manner all vacancies in the Senate, arising by death, removal out of the State, or otherwise, shall be supplied as soon as may be after such vacancies happen.

*Provided nevertheless,* That no person shall be capable of being elected a Senator, who is not of the Protestant Religion, and seized of a freehold estate in his own right of the value of *two hundred pounds,* lying within this State, who is not of the age of thirty years, and who shall not have been an inhabitant of this State for seven years immediately preceding his election; and at the time thereof he shall be an inhabitant of the district for which he shall be chosen.

The Senate shall have power to adjourn themselves, provided such adjournment do [*sic*] not exceed two days at a time.

The Senate shall appoint their own officers, and determine their own rules of proceedings. And not less than seven members of the Senate shall make a quorum for doing business; and when less than eight Senators shall be present, the assent of five at least shall be necessary to render their acts and proceedings valid.

The Senate shall be a Court with full power and authority to hear and determine all impeachments made by the House of Representatives, against any officer or officers of the State, for misconduct or mal-administration in their offices. But previous to the trial of any such impeachment, the members of the Senate shall respectively be sworn, truly and impartially to try and determine the charge in question according to evidence. Their judgment, however, shall not extend farther than removal from office, disqualification to hold or enjoy any place of honor, trust or profit under this State; but the party so convicted, shall nevertheless be liable to indictment, trial, judgment, and punishment, according to laws of the land.

## HOUSE OF REPRESENTATIVES

There shall be in the Legislature of this State a representation of the people annually elected and founded upon principles of equality: And in order that such representation may be as equal as circumstances will admit, every town, parish, or place intitled [*sic*] to town privileges, having one hundred and fifty rateable male polls, of twenty-one years of age, and upwards, may elect one Representative; if four hundred and fifty rateable polls, may elect two Representatives; and so proceeding in that proportion, making three hundred such rateable polls the mean increasing number, for every additional Representative.

Such towns, parishes or places as have less than one hundred and fifty rateable polls shall be classed by the General Assembly for the purpose of chusing [*sic*] a Representative, and seasonably notified thereof. And in every class formed for the above-mentioned purpose, the first annual meeting shall be held in the town, parish, or place wherein most of the rateable polls reside; and afterwards in that which has the next highest number, and so on annually by rotation, through the several towns, parishes or places, forming the district.

Whenever any town, parish, or place intitled [*sic*] to town privileges as aforesaid, shall not have one hundred and fifty rateable polls, and be so situated as to render the classing thereof with any other town, parish, or place very inconvenient, the General Assembly may upon application of a majority of the voters in such town, parish, or place, issue a writ for their electing and sending a Representative to the General-Court.

The members of the House of Representatives shall be chosen annually in the month of March, and shall be the second branch of the Legislature.

All persons qualified to vote in the election of Senators shall be intitled [*sic*] to vote within the town, district, parish, or place where they dwell, in the choice of Representatives. Every member of the House of Representatives shall be chosen by ballot; and for two years at least next preceding his election, shall have been an inhabitant of this State, shall have an estate within the town, parish, or place which he may be chosen to represent, of the value of *one hundred pounds*, one half of which to be a freehold, at the time of his election, an inhabitant of the town, parish, or place he may be chosen to represent; shall be of the Protestant Religion, and shall cease to represent such town, parish, or place immediately on his ceasing to be qualified as aforesaid.

The travel of each Representative to the General-Assembly, and returning home, once in every session, and no more, shall be at the expence [*sic*] of the State, and the wages for his attendance, at the expence [*sic*] of the town, parish, or places he represents; such members attending seasonably, and not departing without licence [*sic*]. All intermediate vacancies in the House of Representatives, may be filled up from time to time, in the same manner as annual elections are made.

The House of Representatives shall be the grand inquest of the state, and all impeachments made by them, shall be heard and tried by the Senate.

All money bills shall originate in the House of Representatives, but the Senate may propose or concur with amendments as on other bills.

A majority of the members of the House of Representatives shall be a quorum for doing business: but when less than two thirds of the Representatives elected shall be present, the assent of two thirds of those members shall be necessary to render their acts and proceedings valid.

No member of the House of Representatives or Senate, shall be arrested, or held to bail on mean process, during his going to, returning from, or attendance upon the court.

The House of Representatives shall choose their own speaker, appoint their own officers, and settle the rules of proceedings in their own house. They shall have authority to punish by imprisonment, every person who shall be guilty of disrespect to the house in its presence, by any disorderly and contemptuous behavior, or by threatening, or ill treating any of its members; or by obstructing its deliberations; every person guilty of a breach of its privileges in making arrests for debt, or by assaulting any member during his attendance at any session; in assaulting or disturbing any one of its officers in the execution of any order or procedure of the house, in assaulting any witness, or other person, ordered to attend by and during his attendance of the house, or in rescuing any person arrested by order of the house, knowing them to be such. The Senate, President and Council, shall have the same powers in like cases; provided that no imprisonment by either, for any offence [*sic*], exceed ten days.

The journals of the proceedings of both houses of the General-Court, shall be printed and published, immediately after every adjournment, or prorogation; and upon motion made by any one member, the yeas and nays upon any question, shall be taken and entered in the journals.

## EXECUTIVE POWER.
## PRESIDENT.

There shall be a Supreme Executive Magistate [*sic*], who shall be stiled [*sic*], The PRESIDENT of the STATE of NEW-HAMPSHIRE; and whose TITLE shall be his EXCELLENCY.

The PRESIDENT shall be chosen annually; and no person shall be eligible to this office, unless at the time of his election, he shall have been an inhabitant of this State for seven years next preceding, and unless he shall be of the age of thirty years; and unless he shall, at the same time, have an estate of the value of *five hundred pounds*, one half of which shall consist of a freehold, in his own right, within the State; and unless he shall be of the protestant religion.

Those persons qualified to vote for Senators and Representatives, shall within the several towns, parishes or places, where they dwell, at a meeting to be called for that purpose, some day in the month of March annually, give in their votes for a President to the Selectmen, who shall preside at such meeting, and the Clerk in the presence and with the assistance of the Selectmen, shall in open meeting sort and count the votes, and form a list of the persons voted for, with the number of votes for each person against his name, and shall make a fair record of the same in the town books, and a public declaration thereof in the said meeting; and shall in the presence of said inhabitants, seal up a copy of said list attested by him and the Selectmen, and transmit the same to the Sheriff of the county, thirty days at least before the first Wednesday of June, or shall cause returns of the same to be made to the office of the Secretary of the State, seventeen days at least before said day, who shall lay the same before the Senate and House of Representatives on the first Wednesday of June, to be by them examined: And in case of an election by a majority of votes through the State, the choice shall be by them declared, and published; but if no person shall have a majority of votes, the House of Representatives shall by ballot elect two out of four persons who had the highest number of votes, if so many shall have been voted for; but if otherwise, out of the number voted for; and make return to the Senate of the two persons so elected, on which the Senate shall proceed by ballot to elect one of them who shall be declared President.

The President of the state shall preside in the Senate, shall have a vote equal with any other member; and shall also have a casting vote in case of a tie.

The President with advice of Council, shall have full power and authority in the recess of the General-Court, to prorogue the same from time to time, not exceeding ninety days in any one recess of said Court; and during the session of said Court, to adjourn or prorogue it to any time the two houses may desire, and to call it together sooner than the time to which it may be adjourned, or prorogued, if the welfare of the State should require the same.

In cases of disagreement between the two Houses, with regard to the time of adjournment, or prorogation, the President, with advice of Council, shall have a right to adjourn or prorogue the General-Court, not exceeding ninety days, at any one time, as he may determine the public good may require. And he shall dissolve the same seven days before the said first Wednesday of June. And in case of any infectious distemper prevailing in the place where the said Court at any time is to convene, or any other cause whereby dangers may arise to the healths or lives, of the members from their attendance, the President may direct the session to be holden at some other the most convenient place within the State.

The President of this State for the time being, shall be commander in chief of the army and navy, and all the military forces of the State, by sea and land; and shall have full power by himself, or by any chief commander, or other officer, or officers, from time to time, to train, instruct, exercise and govern the militia and navy; and for the special defence [*sic*] and safety of this State, to assemble in martial array, and put in warlike posture, the inhabitants thereof, and to lead and conduct them, and with them to encounter, expulse, repel, resist and pursue by force of arms, as well by sea as by land, within and without the limits of the State; and also to kill, slay, destroy, if necessary, and conquer by all fitting ways, enterprize [*sic*] and means, all and every such person and persons as shall, at any time hereafter, in a hostile manner, attempt or enterprize [*sic*] the destruction, invasion, detriment, or annoyance of this State; and to use and exercise over the army and navy, and over the militia in actual service, the law-martial in time of war, invasion, and also in rebellion, declared by the Legislature to exist, as occasion shall necessarily require: And surprize [*sic*] by all ways and means whatsoever, all and every such person or persons, with their ships, arms, ammuition [*sic*], and other goods, as shall in a hostile manner invade, or attempt the invading, conquering, or annoying this State: And in fine, the President hereby is entrusted with all other powers incident to the office of Captain-General and Commander in Chief, and Admiral, to be exercised agreeably to the rules and regulations of the Constitution, and the laws of the land: provided that the President shall not at any time hereafter, by virtue of any power by this Constitution granted, or hereafter to be granted to him by the Legislature, transport any of the inhabitants of this State, or oblige them to march out of the limits of the same, without their free and voluntary consent, or the consent of the General-Court, nor grant commissions for exercising the law-martial in any case, without the advice and consent of the Council.

The power of pardoning offences [*sic*], except such as persons may be convicted of before the Senate by impeachment of the house, shall be in the President by and with the advice of the Council: But no charter of pardon granted by the President with advice of council, before conviction, shall avail the party pleading the same, notwithstanding any general or particular expressions contained therein, descriptive of the offence or offences [*sic*] intended to be pardoned.

All Judicial officers, the Attorney-General[,] Solicitor-General, all Sheriffs, Coroners, Registers of Probate, and all officers of the navy, and General and field-officers of the militia, shall be nominated and appointed by the President and Council; and every such nomination shall be made at least seven days prior to such appointment, and no appointment shall take place, unless three of the Council agree thereto. The captains and subalterns in the respective regiments shall be nominated and recommended by the field officers to the President, who is to issue their commissions immediately on receipt of such recommendation.

No officer, duly commissioned to command in the militia, shall be removed from his office, but by the address of both houses to the President, or by fair trial in court martial, pursuant to the laws of the State for the time being.

The commanding officers of the regiments shall appoint their adjutants and quarter-masters; the brigadiers their brigade-majors; the major-generals their aids [*sic*]; the captains and subalterns their non-commissioned officers.

The President and Council, shall appoint all officers of the Continental army, whom by the confederation of the United States it is provided that this State shall appoint, as also all officers of forts and garrisons.

The division of the militia into brigades, regiments and companies, made in pursuance of the militia laws now in force, shall be considered as the proper division of the militia of this state, until the same shall be altered by some future law.

No monies shall be issued out of the treasury of this state, and disposed of (except such sums as may be appropriated for the redemption of bills of credit or treasurers notes, or for the payment of interest arising thereon) but by warrant under the hand of the President for the time being, by and with the advice and consent of the Council, for the necessary support and defence [*sic*] of this

State, and for the necessary protection and preservation of the inhabitants thereof, agreeably to the acts and resolves of the General-Court.

All public boards, the commissary-general, all superintending officers of public magazines and stores, belonging to this State, and all commanding officers of forts and garrisons within the same, shall once in every three months, officially, and without requisition, and at other times, when required by the President, deliver to him an account of all goods, stores, provisions, ammunition, cannon, with their appendages, and small arms with their accoutrements, and of all other public property under their care respectively; distinguishing the quantity, and kind of each, as particularly as may be; together with the condition of such forts and garrisons: And the commanding officer shall exhibit to the President, when required by him, true and exact plans of such forts, and of the land and sea or harbor or harbors adjacent.

The President and Council shall be compensated for their services from time to time by such grants as the General-Court shall think reasonable.

Permanent and honorable salaries shall be established by law for the Justices of the Superior Court.

Whenever the chair of the President shall be vacant, by reason of his death, absence from the State, or otherwise, the senior Senator for the time being shall, during such vacancy, have and exercise all the powers and authorities which by this Constitution the President is vested with when personally present.

## COUNCIL

Annually on the first meeting of the General-Court, two members of the Senate and three from the House of Representatives, shall be chosen by joint ballot of both Houses as a Council, for advising the President in the Executive part of government, whom the President for the time being, shall have full power and authority to convene from time to time, at his discretion, and the President with the Counsellors, or three of them at least, shall and may from time to time hold and keep a Council, for ordering and directing the affairs of the State, according to the laws of the land.

The qualifications for Counsellors, shall be the same as those required for Senators. The members of the Council shall not intermeddle with the making or trying impeachments, but shall themselves be impeachable by the House and triable by the Senate for mal-conduct.

The resolutions and advice of the Council shall be recorded in a register, and signed by the members present, and this record may be called for at any time, by either house of the Legislature, and any member of the Council may enter his opinion contrary to the resolution of the majority.

And whereas the elections appointed to be made by this Constitution on the first Wednesday of June annually, by the two houses of the Legislature, may not be completed on that day, the said elections may be adjourned from day to day until the same shall be completed. And the order of the elections shall be as follows; the vacancies in the Senate, if any, shall be first filled up; the President shall then be elected, provided there should be no choice of him by the people: And afterwards the two houses, shall proceed to the election of the Council.

## SECRETARY, TREASURER, COMMISSARY-GENERAL, & TC.

The Secretary, Treasurer, and Commissary-General, shall be chosen by joint ballot of the Senators and Representatives assembled in one room.

The records of the State shall be kept in the office of the Secretary, who may appoint his deputies, for whose conduct he shall be answerable, and he shall attend the President and Council, the Senate and Representatives, in person, or by deputy, as they may require.

## COUNTY-TREASURER, & TC.

The Country-Treasurers, and Registers of deeds shall be elected by the inhabitants of the several towns, in the several counties in the State, according to the method now practised [*sic*], and the present laws of the State: And before they enter upon the business of their offices, shall be respectively sworn faithfully to discharge the duties thereof and shall severally give bond with sufficient sureties, in a reasonable sum for the use of the county, for the punctual performance of their respective trusts.

## JUDICIARY POWER

The tenure, that all commission [*sic*] officers shall have by law in their offices, shall be expressed in their respective commissions. All judical [*sic*] officers, duly appointed, commissioned and sworn, shall hold their offices during good behaviour, excepting those concerning whom there is a different provision made in this Constitution: *Provided nevertheless*, the President with consent of Council, may remove them upon the address of both houses of the Legislature.

Each branch of the Legislature, as well as the President and Council, shall have authority to require the opinions of the justices of the Superior court upon important questions of law and upon solemn occasions.

In order that the people may not suffer from the long continuance in place of any justice of the peace, who shall fail in discharging the important duties of his office with ability and fidelity, all commissions of justices of the peace shall become void, at the expiration of five years from their respective dates; and upon the expiration of any commission, the same may if necessary, be renewed, or another person appointed, as shall most conduce to the well-being of the State.

The judges of probate of wills, and for granting letters of administration, shall hold their courts at such place or places, on such fixed days, as the convenience of the people may require. And the Legislature shall from time to time, hereafter appoint such times and places, until which appointments, the said Courts shall be holden at the times and places which the respective judges shall direct.

All causes of marriage, divorce and alimony, and all appeals from the respective judges of probate, shall be heard and tried by the Superior-Court, until the Legislature shall, by law make other provision.

## CLERKS OF COURT

The Clerks of the Superior Court of Judicature, Inferior Courts of Common Pleas, and General Sessions of the Peace, shall be appointed by the respective courts during pleasure. And to prevent any fraud or unfairness in the entries and records of said Courts, no such Clerk shall be of counsel in any cause in the Court of which he is Clerk, nor shall he fill [*sic*] any writ in any civil action whatsoever.

## DELEGATES TO CONGRESS

The Delegates of this State to the Congress of the United States, shall some time between the first Wednesday of June, and the first Wednesday of September annually, be elected by the Senate and House of Representatives in their seperate [*sic*] branches; to serve in Congress for one year, to commence on the first Monday in November then next ensuing. They shall have commissions under the hand of the President, and the great seal of the State; but may be recalled at any time within the year, and others chosen and commissioned, in the same manner, in their stead: And they shall have the same qualifications, in all respects, as by this Constitution are required for the President.

No person shall be capable of being a delegate to Congress, for more than three years in any term of six years; nor shall any person being a delegate, be capable of holding any office under the United-States, for which he, or any other for his benefit, receives any salary, or emolument of any kind.

## ENCOURAGEMENT OF LITERATURE, & TC.

Knowledge, and Learning, generally diffused through a community, being essential to the preservation of a free government, and spreading the opportunities and advantages of education through the various parts of the country, being highly conducive to promote this end; it shall be the duty of the Legislators and magistrates, in all future periods of this government to cherish the interest of literature and the sciences, and all seminaries and public schools, to encourage private and public institutions, rewards and immunities for the promotion of agriculture, arts, sciences, commerce, trades, manufactures and natural history of the country; to countenance and inculcate the principles of humanity and general benevolence, public and private charity, industry and economy, honesty and punctuality, sincerity, sobriety, and all social affections, and generous sentiments, among the people.

*OATH and Subscriptions; Exclusion from Offices; Commissions; Writs; Confirmation of Laws; Habeas Corpus; the Enacting Stile; Continuance of Officers; Provision for a future Revision of the Constitution, &tc.*

Any person chosen President, Counsellor, Senator, or Representative, military or civil officer, (town officers excepted) accepting the trust, shall before he proceeds to execute the duties of his office, make and subscribe the following declaration, viz.

*I, A.B. do truly and sincerely acknowledge, profess, testify and declare, that the State of New-Hampshire is, and of right ought to be, a Free, sovereign and Independent State; and do swear that I will bear faith and true allegiance to the same, and that I will endeavor to defend it against all treacherous conspiracies and hostile attempts whatever: And I do further testify and declare, that no man or body of men, hath or can have, a right to absolve me from the obligation of this oath, declaration or affirmation; and that I do make this acknowledegment [sic], profession, testimony, and declaration, honestly and truly, according to the common acceptation of the foregoing words, without any equivocation, mental evasion, or secret reservation whatever. So help me GOD.*

I, A.B. do solemnly and sincerely swear and affirm, that I will faithfully and impartially discharge and perform all the duties incumbent on me as according to the best of my abilities, agreeably to the rules and regulations of this Constitution, and the laws of the State of New-Hampshire. So help me GOD.

*Provided always,* When any person chosen or appointed as aforesaid, shall be of the denomination called Quakers, or shall be scrupulous of swearing, and shall decline taking the said oaths, such shall take and subscribe them, omitting the word *"swear,"* and likewise the words *"So help me God,"* subjoining instead thereof, *This I do under the pains and penalties of perjury.*

And the oaths or affirmations shall be taken and subscribed by the President before the senior Senator present, in the presence of the two Houses of Assembly; and by the Senate and Representatives first elected under this Constitution, before the President and three of the Council of the former Constitution, and forever afterwards, before the President and Council for the time being; and by the residue of the officers aforesaid, before such persons, and in such manner as from time to time shall be prescribed by the Legislature.

All commissions shall be in the name of the State of New-Hampshire, signed by the President, and attested by the Secretary, or his deputy, and shall have the great seal of the State affixed thereto.

All writs issuing out of the Clerks' office in any of the Courts of law, shall be in the name of the State of New-Hampshire; shall be under the seal of the Court whence they issue, and bear test of the chief, first, or senior Justice of the Court; but when such Justice shall be interested, then the writ shall bear test of some other Justice of the court, to which the same shall be returnable; and be signed by the Clerk of such Court.

All indictments, presentments and informations shall conclude against the peace and dignity of the State.

The estates of such persons as may destroy their own lives, shall not for that offence [*sic*] be forfeited, but descend or ascend in the same manner, as if such persons had died in a natural way. Nor shall any article, which shall accidentally occasion the death of any person, be henceforth deemed a deodand, or in any wise forfeited on account of such misfortune.

All the laws which have heretofore been adopted, used and approved, in the Province, Colony, or State of New-Hampshire, and usually practised [*sic*] on in the courts of law, shall remain and be in full force, until altered and repealed by the Legislature; such parts thereof only excepted, as are repugnant to the rights and liberties contained in this Constitution: Provided that nothing herein contained; when compared with the twenty-third article in the bill of rights, shall be construed to affect the laws already made respecting the persons, or estates of absentees.

The privilege and benefit of the Habeas-Corpus, shall be enjoyed in this State, in the most free, easy, cheap, expeditious, and ample manner, and shall not be suspended by the Legislature, except upon the most urgent and pressing occasions, and for a time not exceeding three months.

The enacting stile [*sic*] in making and passing acts, statutes and laws, shall be—*Be it enacted by the Senate and House of Representatives in General-Court convened.*

No President or Judge of the Superior-Court, shall hold any office or place under the authority of this State, except such as by this Constitution they are admitted to hold, saving that the Judges of the said Court may hold the offices of Justice of the Peace throughout the State; nor shall they hold any place or office, or receive any pension or salary, from any other State, Government, or Power whatever.

No person shall be capable of exercising at the same time, more than one of the following offices within this State, viz. Judge of Probate, Sheriff, Register of Deeds; and never more than two offices of profit, which may be held by appointment of the President, or President and Council, or Senate and House of Representatives, or Superior or Inferior courts; Military offices, and offices of Justices of the Peace, excepted.

No person holding the office of Judge of the Superior-Court, Secretary, Treasurer of the State, Judge of Probate, Attorney-General, Commissary-General, Judge of the Maritime-Court, or Judge of the Court of Admiralty, Military officers receiving pay from the Continent or this State, excepting officers of the militia occasionally called forth on an emergency; Judge of the Inferior-Court of Common-Pleas, Register of Deeds, President, Professor or Instructor of any College, Sheriff, or Officer of the Customs, including Naval-Officers, shall at the same time have a seat in the Senate or House of Representatives, or Council; but their being chosen or appointed to, and accepting the same, shall operate as a resignation of their seat in the Senate, or House of Representatives, or Council; and the place so vacated shall be filled up.

No person shall ever be admitted to hold a seat in the Legislature, or any office of trust or importance under this government, who in the due course of law, has been convicted of bribery or corruption, in obtaining an election or appointment.

In all cases where sums of money are mentioned in this Constitution, the value thereof shall be computed in silver at *six shillings and eight pence* per ounce.

To the end that there may be no failure of justice or danger arise [*sic*] to this State from a change of the form of Government, all civil and military officers, holding commissions under the Government and People of New-Hampshire, and other officers of the said Government and People, at the time this Constitution shall take effect, shall hold, exercise and enjoy all the powers and authorities to them granted and committed, until other persons shall be appointed in their stead. All Courts of law in the business of their respective departments, and the Executive, and Legislative bodies and persons, shall continue in full force, enjoyment and exercise of all their trusts and employments, until the General-Court, and the Supreme and other Executive officers under this Constitution, are designated, and invested with their respective trusts, powers and authority.

This form of Government shall be enrolled on parchment, and deposited in the Secretary's office, and be a part of the laws of the land, and printed copies thereof shall be prefixed to the books containing the laws of this State, in all future editions thereof.

To preserve an effectual adherence to the principles of the Constitution, and to correct any violations thereof, as well as to make such alterations therein, as from experience may be found necessary, the General-Court shall at the expiration of seven years from the time this Constitution shall take effect, issue precepts, or direct them to be issued from the Secretary's office, to the several towns and incorporated places, to elect delegates to meet in Convention for the purposes aforesaid: The said delegates to be chosen in the same manner, and proportioned as the Representatives to the General-Assembly; provided that no alteration shall be made in this Constitution before the same shall be laid before the towns and unincorporated places, and approved by two thirds of the qualified voters present, and voting upon the question.

# BIBLIOGRAPHICAL ESSAY

## TEXTS OF THE CONSTITUTIONS

The texts of the 1776 and 1784 constitutions appear in Appendix 1 and Appendix 2, respectively. The text of the 1776 constitution is a transcription of the manuscript of the 1776 constitution in the Journal of the House of Representatives from January 5, 1776, located at the New Hampshire Department of State, Division of Records Management and Archives in Concord, New Hampshire. The printed text of the 1776 constitution found in the *New Hampshire State Papers,* Vol. VIII, pp. 2–4 varies in only minor respects, primarily punctuation and capitalization. A broadside of the 1776 constitution from the New Hampshire Historical Society Broadside Collection is reproduced in *The First State Constitution: Three Addresses Given at the Commemoration of the Adoption of New Hampshire's First State Constitution, January 5, 1776, Held at the New Hampshire State House, January 5, 1976* (Concord, NH: New Hampshire American Revolution Bicentennial Commission, 1977), 4–5.

The 1784 constitution in Appendix 2 is based on the earliest known printed version, produced in Portsmouth, New Hampshire, in 1783. Unfortunately, there is no known manuscript version of that constitution as it went into effect in 1784. The earliest known manuscript version has incorporated into it the amendments ratified in 1792 and is located at the New Hampshire Department of State, Division of Records Management and Archives in Concord. Other printed versions of the 1784 constitution, which contain minor variations from the Portsmouth edition, may be found in *New Hampshire State Papers,* Vol. IX, pp. 896–918 and Colby's *Manual* of 1912, pp. 101–123. The text of the 1784 constitution, after the revision of 1792, is printed in *New Hampshire State Papers,* Vol. X, pp. 169–196.

## JOURNALS OF FIFTH PROVINCIAL CONGRESS AND CONSTITUTIONAL CONVENTIONS

The journal of the so-called fifth provincial congress is printed in the *New Hampshire State Papers,* Vol. VII, pp. 690–710. The congress resolved itself into the state's first house of representatives and drafted the first constitution in 1776.

Journals for the conventions that first assembled in 1778 and 1781 have never been located, but the constitutions proposed by these conventions are printed in Vol. IX of the *New Hampshire State Papers* as follows: the proposed constitution of 1779, pp. 837–842; the proposed constitution of 1781, pp. 852–877; and the proposed constitution of 1782, pp. 882–895. The journal of the 1791 convention is printed in *New Hampshire State Papers*, Vol. X, pp. 23–168.

There is no published journal for the 1850 convention, though the original manuscript of the journal is available at the New Hampshire Department of State, Division of Records Management and Archives in Concord. The handwritten journal gives basic information regarding the acts of the convention, but goes into little detail. A contemporary record of the 1850 convention appears in the *New Hampshire Patriot and State Gazette*; the newspaper employed "phonographic reporters" who were to give "verbatim reports" to be published in the edition of the next day. Beginning November 7, 1850, the newspaper faithfully recorded the actions of the 1850 convention, identifying each speaker and summarizing his remarks.

The journal of each convention, beginning in 1876, was published after the convention under the title *Journal of the Convention to Revise the Constitution.*

## ■ SELECTED SOURCES: NEW HAMPSHIRE HISTORY

George Barstow. *The History of New Hampshire, From Its Discovery, in 1614, to the Passage of the Toleration Act, in 1819* (Boston: Little & Brown, 1853) (2d ed.).

Jeremy Belknap. *History of New Hampshire* (Philadelphia: T. Aitken, 1784; Boston: I. Thomas and E.T. Andrews, 1791; and Boston: Belknap and Young, 1792) (New York: Johnson Reprint Corp., 1970).

Charles E. Clark. *The Eastern Frontier: The Settlement of Northern New England 1610–1763* (New York: Alfred A. Knopf, 1970).

Donald B. Cole. *Jacksonian Democracy in New Hampshire, 1800–1851* (Cambridge, MA: Harvard University Press, 1970).

Jere R. Daniell. *Colonial New Hampshire: A History* (Millwood, NY: KTO Press, 1981).

——. *Experiment in Republicanism: New Hampshire Politics and the American Revolution, 1741–1794* (Cambridge, MA: Harvard University Press, 1970).

Elizabeth Forbes Morison & Elting E. Morison. *New Hampshire: A Bicentennial History* (New York: W.W. Norton & Co., 1976).

Fletcher Haulley. *A Primary Source History of the Colony of New Hampshire* (New York: The Rosen Publishing Group, Inc., 2006).

Nancy Coffey Heffernan and Ann Page Stecker. *New Hampshire: Crosscurrents in its Development* (Hanover, NH: University Press of New England, 1996).

John Phillip Reid. *Legitimating the Law: The Struggle for Judicial Competency in Early National New Hampshire* (DeKalb, IL: Northern Illinois University Press, 2012).

——. *Legislating the Courts: Judicial Dependence in Early National New Hampshire* (DeKalb, IL: Northern Illinois University Press, 2008).

——. *Controlling the Law: Legal Politics in Early National New Hampshire* (DeKalb, IL: Northern Illinois University Press, 2008).

Edwin D. Sanborn. *History of New Hampshire, from Its First Discovery to the Year 1830* (Manchester, NH: J. B. Clarke, 1875).
James Duane Squires. *The Granite State of the United States: A History of New Hampshire from 1623 to the Present* (New York: American Historical Association, 1956).
Everett S. Stackpole. *History of New Hampshire* (New York: The American Historical Society, 1916).
Lynn W. Turner. *The Ninth State: New Hampshire's Formative Years* (Chapel Hill: University of North Carolina Press, 1983).
Richard Francis Upton. *Revolutionary New Hampshire: An Account of the Social and Political Forces Underlying the Transition from Royal Province to American Commonwealth* (Hanover, NH: Dartmouth College Publications, 1936; reprinted with a new introduction, New York: Octagon Books, 1971).

The best printed compilation of primary sources for the early history of New Hampshire is a 40-volume compilation, Nathaniel Bouton, et al., eds. *Documents and Records Relating to New Hampshire, 1623–1800* (Concord and Manchester, NH: NH State Printer, 1867–1943), often referred to as the *State Papers* or *Provincial Papers*. The collection includes the Provincial Papers in Vols. I–VII (1623–1776), XVIII (1725–1800) (including both Provincial and State materials), and XIX; the State Papers (1776–1793) in Vols. VIII, IX (appendix contains documents relating to state constitutional conventions held during the Revolutionary War), X, and XX–XXIII; and the Revolutionary Papers in Vols. XIV–XVII (Revolutionary Rolls), and XXX (Revolutionary Rolls and miscellaneous documents). R. Stuart Wallace has written a guide to the papers. See R. Stuart Wallace, "The State Papers: A Descriptive Guide," *Historical New Hampshire*, XXXI (1976): 119.

## SELECTED SOURCES: NEW HAMPSHIRE CONSTITUTIONAL CONVENTIONS

Willis G. Buxton. *Four Constitutional Conventions and Congress* (Concord, NH: W. B. Ranney, 1928).
Allan Chester Clark. "The Constitutional Convention," *The Granite Monthly* (January 1903): 3.
James F. Colby. *Manual of the Constitution of the State of New Hampshire, Compiled from Official Sources and Edited, with Sketch of the Constitutions of the State, the Basis of Representation, and Appendix* (Concord, NH: Evans Printing Co., 1902 and Manchester: J. B. Clarke, 1912).
John J. Dinan. *The American State Constitutional Tradition* (Lawrence, KS: University Press of Kansas, 2009).
Ruth Jeffries and Philip A. Hazelton. *New Hampshire Constitutional Conventions* (Concord, NH: New Hampshire State Library Legislative Service, 1956).
Joseph A. Millimet. "Thoughts on the 1964 Constitutional Convention," *New Hampshire Bar Journal* 6 (April 1964): 212.

*Report to the Fifteenth Constitutional Convention by the Commission to Study the State Constitution* (Concord, NH, 1964). This report is summarized in "A Modern Constitution for New Hampshire," *New Hampshire Bar Journal* 6 (April 1964): 208.

*Report to the Sixteenth Constitutional Convention by the Commission to Study the State Constitution* (Concord, NH, 1974).

*Report to the Seventeenth Constitutional Convention by the Task Force to Study the State Constitution* (Concord, NH, 1984).

Constance T. Rinden and Jane Lyman. *New Hampshire Constitutional Amendment Proposals* (Concord, NH: New Hampshire State Library, Law Division, 1984) (revising and updating the Jeffries/Hazelton 1956 publication up to the amendments proposed in 1984).

Richard Francis Upton. "The Proposals to Amend the Constitution with Respect to the Judicial Department and the Power of Taxation," *New Hampshire Bar Journal* 6 (April 1964): 215.

Robert William Upton. "Remarks to the New Hampshire House," *Journal of the New Hampshire House of Representatives* (July 14, 1955), 1152 (providing background on the 1956 convention and describing major concerns of previous New Hampshire constitutional conventions).

Eugene M. Van Loan, III. "Amending the Constitution by Convention," *New Hampshire Bar Journal* 42 (June 2001): 55.

## ■ SELECTED SOURCES: NEW HAMPSHIRE CONSTITUTIONAL HISTORY AND JURISPRUDENCE

Karen E. Andréson. "A Return to Legitimacy: New Hampshire's Constitution of 1776," *Historical New Hampshire* XXXI (Winter 1976): 155.

Lorence L. Bravenec. "The New Hampshire Bill of Rights in the Constitution of 1784 and the Treatment of Dissenters During the American Revolution," *New Hampshire Bar Journal* 8 (Summer 1966): 244.

William Martin Chase. "A Review of Organic Law Development," *Journal of the Convention to Revise the Constitution* (Concord, 1903), 208.

Walter F. Dodd. "The Constitutional History of New Hampshire, 1775–1792," *Proceedings of the Bar Association of the State of New Hampshire* 2 (1904–1908), 379–400.

Charles G. Douglas, III. "The Unique Role of State Constitutions: Raising State Issues in New Hampshire," *New Hampshire Bar Journal* 28 (Summer 1987): 309.

——. "Judicial Review and the Separation of Powers under the New Hampshire Constitutions of 1776 and 1784," *Historical New Hampshire* XXXI (Winter 1976): 176.

——. "The Gubernatorial Veto Power in New Hampshire," *New Hampshire Bar Journal* 15 (October 1973): 9.

Deborah Downs. "The New Hampshire Constitution of 1776: Weathervane of Conservatism," *Historical New Hampshire* XXXI (Winter 1976): 164.

Jonathan M. Flagg. "The Role of the Primacy Doctrine in New Hampshire Criminal Procedure: An Expansion of Individual Constitutional Rights," *New Hampshire Bar Journal* 28 (Summer 1987): 357.

Lawrence Friedman. "The Endurance of State Constitutions: Preliminary Thoughts and Notes on the New Hampshire Constitution," *Wayne Law Review* 60 (2014): 203.

——. "Common Law Decisionmaking, Constitutional Shadows, and the Value of Consistency: the Jurisprudence of William F. Batchelder," *University of New Hampshire Law Review* 12 (2013): 1.

——. "Path Dependence and the External Constraints on Independent State Constitutionalism," *Penn State Law Review* 115 (2011): 783.

——. "Reactive and Incompletely Theorized State Constitutional Decision-making," *Mississippi Law Journal* 77 (2007): 265.

William C. Gardner et al. *New Hampshire, the State That Made Us a Nation: A Celebration of the Bicentennial of the United States Constitution* (Concord, NH: P.E. Randall 1989).

Scott Douglas Gerber. *A Distinct Judicial Power: The Origins of an Independent Judiciary, 1606–1787* (New York: Oxford University Press, 2011).

Nancy L. Girard. "Sustainable Development and Transportation Choices: Why Article 6-a of the New Hampshire Constitution Should Be Repealed," *New Hampshire Bar Journal* 42 (December 2001): 14.

Philip Hamburger. *Law and Judicial Duty* (Cambridge, MA: Harvard University Press, 2008).

Richard Hesse. "The Legislature, the Court and the Constitution," *New Hampshire Bar Journal* 41 (March 2000): 38.

Marcus Hurn. "State Constitutional Limits on New Hampshire's Taxing Power: Historical Developments and Modern State," *Pierce Law Review* 7 (2009): 251.

Martin R. Jenkins. "Property Rights under Constitutional Law," *New Hampshire Bar Journal* 28 (Summer 1987): 373.

Frank R. Kenison. "The Judiciary under the New Hampshire Constitution, 1776–1976," *The First State Constitution: Three Addresses Given at the Commemoration of the Adoption of New Hampshire's First State Constitution, January 5, 1776, Held at the New Hampshire State House, January 5, 1976* (Concord, NH: New Hampshire American Revolution Bicentennial Commission, 1977), 12.

Charles B. Kinney, Jr. *Church and State: The Struggle for Separation in New Hampshire* (New York: Columbia University Press, 1955).

Richard M. Lambert. "The 'Ten Pound Act' Cases and the Origins of Judicial Review in New Hampshire," *New Hampshire Bar Journal* 43 (March 2002): 37.

Timothy A. Lawrie. "Interpretation and Authority: Separation of Powers and the Judiciary's Battle for Independence in New Hampshire, 1786–1818," *American Journal of Legal History* 39 (1995): 322.

Richard B. McNamara. "The Separation of Powers Principle and the Role of the Courts in New Hampshire," *New Hampshire Bar Journal* 42 (June 2001): 66.

Edward C. Mosca. "The Original Understanding of the New Hampshire Constitution's Education Clause," *Pierce Law Review* 6 (2007): 209.

——. "New Hampshire's *Claremont* Case and the Separation of Powers," *Pierce Law Review* 4 (2006): 409.

Walter L. Murphy and Martha Van Oot. "Please Be Careful with the Constitution: A Call for the Preservation of Judicial Independence," *New Hampshire Bar Journal* 42 (June 2001): 11.

Richard Noyes. "Time Frame as a Variable in the Fifth Provincial Congress," *Historical New Hampshire* XXXI (Winter 1976): 192.

William Plumer. "The Constitution of New Hampshire," *Proceedings of the Bar Association of the State of New Hampshire*, n.s. 2 (1904–1908): 207.

Lorenca C. Rosal. *Eternal Vigilance: The Story of the New Hampshire Constitution* (Orford, NH: Equity Publishing Corp., 1986).

Arpiar G. Saunders, Jr. "The New Hampshire Constitution and Individual Rights: 'Developed Advocacy' Required," *New Hampshire Bar Journal* 28 (Summer 1987): 327.

Richard Francis Upton. "The Constitution of 1776 from the Viewpoint of the Legislative Branch," *The First State Constitution: Three Addresses Given at the Commemoration of the Adoption of New Hampshire's First State Constitution, January 5, 1776, Held at the New Hampshire State House, January 5, 1976* (Concord, NH: New Hampshire American Revolution Bicentennial Commission, 1977), 23.

——. "The Independence of the Judiciary in New Hampshire," *New Hampshire Bar Journal* 1 (July 1959): 28.

Eugene M. Van Loan, III. "Ten Pound Act: An Introduction to Original Research on the Origins of Judicial Review," *New Hampshire Bar Journal* 43 (March 2002): 34.

# TABLE OF CASES

## A



## B

## C

## D

## E



## F

## G



## H

# I



# J



# K

## N



## O

## P

## Q



## R



## S

## T

## U



## V



## W



## Z

# INDEX

## About the Author

Lawrence Friedman is a professor of law at New England Law | Boston in Massachusetts, where he teaches courses in constitutional law, state constitutional law, and national security law. He has written numerous articles on these and other subjects and is the author, with Lynnea Thody, of *The Massachusetts State Constitution* (Oxford, 2011) and, with Victor Hansen, of *The Case for Congress: Separation of Powers and the War on Terror* (Ashgate, 2009).

www.ingramcontent.com/pod-product-compliance
Ingram Content Group UK Ltd.
Pitfield, Milton Keynes, MK11 3LW, UK
UKHW021135160926
475595UK00020B/64

9 780199 965021